THE TRIPLE CROWN

THE CLOSED DOOR
From 'Conclavi de' Pontifici Romani, 1668

THE
TRIPLE CROWN

AN ACCOUNT OF
THE PAPAL CONCLAVES
FROM THE FIFTEENTH CENTURY
TO MODERN TIMES

BY

VALÉRIE PIRIE

SPRING BOOKS · LONDON

J'aime un ouvrage sérieux qui ne
soit point écrit trop sérieusement
Voltaire

Originally published 1935 by
Sidgwick & Jackson, Ltd. Copyright.
This edition published 1965 by Spring Books,
Westbook House · Fulham Broadway · London

Printed in England by
Richard Clay (The Chaucer Press) Ltd., Bungay, Suffolk

FOR RIO

WHEN HE HAS REACHED
YEARS OF DISCRETION

PREFACE

AN Eastern origin can undoubtedly be ascribed to the papal tiara, but it is not known under what circumstances or by which of Peter's early successors it was first adopted. Not till after the IVth century are the Popes represented wearing a circle round the base of the conical-shaped cap which formerly had been quite plain. Boniface VIII, presumably with the object of making it more impressive, added a second diadem to the pontifical head-dress, and later Benedict XII superimposed yet a third above the other two. Several Popes of the Middle Ages disapproved of these innovations and reverted to the diadem with the single crown; but by the XVth century, the period at which this book opens, the Triple Crown or Triregnum had been definitely adopted as the Pope's official head-dress for all ceremonial occasions.

A symbolical significance was now ascribed to the three circlets which were described as the emblems of the Roman Pontiff's spiritual supremacy, of his temporal dominion and of his suzerainty over all other monarchs.

As the Holy See's power and riches increased, so did the Triple Crown gain in splendour and costliness. The more magnificent-minded Popes lavished fortunes on their tiaras, and by the end of the XVIIIth century the papal treasury contained at least a dozen examples of inestimable value.

When the French Revolutionary army occupied Rome in 1798 its leaders appropriated several of these gorgeous jewels, and the remainder were handed over to the French Government after the Treaty of Tolentino, the unfortunate Pius VI being reduced to the humiliating necessity of wearing a gilt cardboard substitute. Symbolism has its pitfalls!

After the signing of the Concordat, Napoleon presented Pius VII with a splendid Triregnum which, fifty years later, Pius IX, in view of the unsettled condition of his Kingdom, deemed it advisable to have copied in imitation gems, while the original was deposited in a place of safety.

By its very vicissitudes, the Triple Crown seems to represent most fittingly that which each successive conclave was empowered to bestow: Julius II's great blazing tiara, Pius VI's pathetic cardboard crown, or Pius IX's tawdry replica of a safely guarded treasure.

The reader who is interested in the election would naturally want to know something of its outcome. I have therefore appended to the account of the conclave itself a brief sketch of the man chosen by each of these strange assemblies to occupy the highest office in Christendom.

As frequent references are made to sums of money quoted in obsolete currencies, it may assist the reader to form some estimate of their value by knowing that:

The crown was worth approximately   5s.
The ducat   ,,   ,,   9s. 4d.
The doubloon   ,,   ,,   £3 : 12s.

The value of these coins was naturally subject to a certain amount of fluctuation through the ages, and would be four or five times as great in present-day currency.

I have to thank the authorities of the London Library for kindly allowing me to reproduce the illustrations of my preliminary chapter from their copies of *Conclavi de' Pontifici Romani* and *Histoire des Conclaves depuis Clement V jusqu'à 1703.*

A list of all sources of information will be found at the end of the volume.

V. P.

CONTENTS

LIST OF PLATES

THE TRIPLE CROWN

PRELIMINARY CHAPTER

PERHAPS the greatest blessing that was ever bestowed upon the Church of Rome was the loss of her temporal power. It eliminated automatically all those unprincipled, ambitious candidates who coveted the triple crown merely for the immense riches and power it conferred on its wearer. It seems incredible that anyone acquainted with the scandalous intrigues, the simony, the unbridled display of human passions seething behind the closed doors of papal conclaves, should still uphold or wish to see restored a state of things which caused, by the discredit it brought on the Roman Church, such a religious upheaval as the Reformation with its ensuing trail of bloodshed and persecutions. To vest in one frail mortal, who has not even been trained to govern, complete autocratic power over his subjects in this world, and over all Christendom in the next, is to exalt him abruptly to Olympian heights from which only a deity inured to such altitudes could look down with a steady head.

Before entering upon the subject of this book it seems advisable to give a brief outline of the mechanism upon which papal elections are based, the sequence of events which influenced their formation, and the ceremonial with which they were attended.

In all probability the early bishops of Rome, who had inherited Peter's Apostolic pre-eminence, themselves named their successors; but after the third century the Senate, the clergy and the people of Rome participated in their bishop's election.

It is not till the end of the IVth century that the title of Pope appears to have been used, and it was not a recognised appellation reserved exclusively to the bishops of Rome till after the Roman Council of 1076.

The riots and disorder caused by the popular elections having called for the intervention of the Emperor, the Church then entered upon a period of most humiliating subjection to the Empire. Besides paying a heavy tribute, popes were constrained to wait for a ratification of their election from Constantinople before occupying the Apostolic See; the interminable delays, caused either by circumstances or ill-will, resulted in vacancies of many months' duration, entailing anarchy in Christendom. Nor was the situation improved when Byzantine rule in Italy was replaced by that of the Lombards. By the middle of the VIIIth century they were threatening Rome itself and the Pope was constrained to appeal for help to the ruler of the Franks. This led eventually to the revival of the Empire in the West and also to that of secular intervention in papal affairs. The Papacy was drawn into the whirlpool of international politics and there followed a long period during the Middle Ages when the history of the Papacy offers a confused impression of popes and antipopes, popes who had abdicated, popes who had been deposed, popes in captivity, popes in exile, all hurling futile excommunications and anathemas at one another; mock thunderbolts whose only effect, one imagines, would be to cause the utmost perplexity within the fold where the bewildered sheep were hard put to it to distinguish between the shepherd and the wolf.

The collective instinct of self-preservation was sufficiently powerful, however, to evolve out of all that chaos a scheme which, maturing through the centuries, reached a settled and definite form after the Council of Constance in 1417. The right to elect the Pope was then recognised as the special prerogative of cardinals and has remained so ever since. As the Pope in turn creates the cardinals there results an autonomous system resembling a circle everlastingly revolving upon itself.

There are four classes of cardinals: cardinal-bishops, cardinal-priests, cardinal-deacons and lay cardinals. Their number has varied from 6 or 7 to 76. In 1585 Sixtus V fixed it definitely at 70 in memory of the 70 aged men who assisted Moses. All but the lay cardinals have a right to vote at the conclave even if they are under a ban of excommunication or ecclesiastical censure. Nowadays the Pope can no longer suspend that right, but up to the end of the XVIIIth century pontiffs occasionally did so. Julius II, for instance, pronounced the exclusion of all pro-French cardinals, who were thus debarred from attending his successor's election, and Pius VI in 1786 temporarily suspended the Cardinal de Rohan, who had been compromised in the famous "Affaire du Collier". Lay cardinals could vote if they had obtained a special permit to that effect, or they could be ordained deacons within the conclave itself. The cardinalate being merely a dignity could be resigned with the Pope's consent. In former times it was even possible in the case of cardinal-deacons to return to lay life and marry. It happened in several cases, as with Césare Borgia and the last of the Medici who had been a cardinal for twenty-five years. Cardinals have occasionally been deposed but few popes have resorted to such an extreme punishment. Restrictions were promulgated periodically concerning the age at which the hat could be bestowed, but were never adhered to. There have been cardinals of nine and ten and many of seventeen. The cardinals created by a pope are known as his "creatures". The word is used in its literal sense and is meant in no way as a term of opprobrium. The statute making priesthood compulsory for cardinals only dates from 1917. Cardinal Antonelli, a great diplomatic figure of the XIXth century, was never ordained.

A conclave consists of a congregation of cardinals forming the Sacred College, assembled within enclosed premises with the object of electing a Pope. Two-thirds of the total number of votes forms the required majority. On principle the cardinals may elect any man they think fit to occupy the papal throne. If the new pope has not received Holy Orders they are at once conferred on him by the Bishop of Ostia, who is by traditional right Doyen of the Sacred College. Such cases were common in the early days of the Church and still occurred during the XVIth century, after which period it became a general practice to elect bishops. There were still a few exceptions to this rule during the XVIIIth and as late as the XIXth century, Gregory XVI, who was only a priest, being elected in 1831.

There are many strange stories connected with early papal elections; none was so strange; none obtained such a hold on popular imagination in the Middle Ages as the one concerning the elevation of a woman to the Papal See. All orthodox historians, of course, treat the legend with the utmost contempt. They make varied suggestions as to its origin; the most generally accepted being that Pope John VIII, a weak and vacillating Pontiff reigning at the end of the IXth century, was given the nickname of Pope Joan by the Roman populace, who taunted him with behaving like a woman. To take this appellation literally, the above authors contend, was too tempting a slip for chroniclers to resist. It lent itself so readily to salacious flights of fancy that its appeal was immediate, widespread and persistent. It did not, however, appear incredible to many serious and devout writers living in the Middle Ages and even later, for in the XVIth century we find a fervent Catholic and a man of the highest repute like Etienne Pasquier to have been a firm believer in the existence of a female Pope. The post-Reformation German writers naturally made great capital out of the tale, adducing the famous porphyry throne as a proof of its authenticity. This chair is shaped in all respects like the now obsolete piece of furniture commonly known as a commode. It was undoubtedly used during the ceremony of the pope's enthronement and is alleged to have been introduced to enable the electors to verify the sex of the successful candidate, and thus obviate the recurrence of such an awkward accident. Whatever the reason which may have inspired the adoption of this singular throne for such a solemn occasion (and the one laying it at the psalmist's door is scarcely less indelicate), it can in no way have been connected with Pope Joan, as the porphyry chair is mentioned in much earlier accounts of papal investitures than the period (IXth century) ascribed to the incident. It continued to figure in these ceremonies up to 1513, date of Leo X's enthronement, after which it was relegated to a gallery in the Lateran where several travellers of the XVIIth and XVIIIth centuries report having seen it. Pius VI placed it in the Vatican museum and it was numbered among the eighty pieces of sculpture sent to Paris after the Treaty of Tolentino. In 1815 Pius VII presented it as a personal gift to Louis XVIII and it is still to be seen in the Musée du Louvre in Paris. This curious relic is supposed to have come originally from the baths of Caracalla. All Roman *sudatoriums* appear to have been equipped with chairs of this model, mostly in marble, the orifice being provided to allow the sweat to run off the bather's body.

The general consensus of modern opinion amongst writers of all parties is that Pope Joan is a mythical personage. She is as out-of-date as the cards upon which she figured in the Italian game of "Tarot" so popular in olden days, and which no doubt helped considerably to spread her fame.

Le Card. Camērlinoue, avant que d'entrer au Conclave, va par la Ville avec les Gardes du Pape.

La Maniere de porter publiquement le Pape Mort de Monte-Car

CONVEYING THE DEAD POPE'S REMAI

...rgé de S. Pierre transporte le Pape dans la Chapelle de la S. Trinité.

...tican.

Discours pag. 23.

ROUGH THE STREETS OF ROME

The first conclave, properly so-called, was held at Viterbo. In the spring of 1271 seventeen cardinals having been assembled for over two years without reaching an agreement, the irritated townspeople prevailed on their magistrates to confine the dilatory prelates within the episcopal palace and to wall up all the outlets. Some weeks having gone by and no Pope having yet been elected, the now exasperated citizens removed the roof of the building, to afford an easier access to the Holy Ghost, and only allowed the cardinals a small ration of bread and water for all nourishment. These drastic measures produced the desired effect and resulted in the election of Gregory X, after the longest vacancy the Pontifical See has ever known. The Savellis who happened to have been in charge of the punitive operations conferred upon themselves the hereditary office of "Custodians of the Conclaves", which title was officially ratified by Gregory X. They held it for several centuries and it has now passed into the Chigi family.

So favourably impressed was the new Pontiff with the advantages of a system to which he owed his elevation that he gave it his solemn sanction, laying down the most stringent regulations to be observed at future conclaves. To those new statutes were no doubt due the speed with which his successor was elected, the Sacred College coming to an understanding in less than twenty-four hours.

The preliminaries of the conclave are subject to regulations as meticulous as those of the conclave itself. As soon as the Pontiff has breathed his last they can be said to begin. The Cardinal Camerlengo now assumes control. He approaches the bed upon which the dead man lies and strikes his forehead three times with a silver hammer, calling him each time by his Christian name in clear, loud tones. He then turns to those present and says: "The Pope is dead". The Master of Ceremonies thereupon slips the "fisherman's" ring off the dead Pontiff's finger and hands it to the Camerlengo to be destroyed by him later together with the die of the great leaden seals used during the late pontificate. The body is then embalmed; it used to be carried in great pomp in an open litter through the streets of Rome and deposited in St. Peter's, where it was exposed for three days. President de Brosses, describing Clement XII's obsequies, says that the deceased Pontiff's face was so skilfully rouged and made up that he looked far healthier in death than he had ever looked in life.

Nine days are allowed for the funeral ceremonies and the preparations of the conclave. During the vacancy of the Holy See the Camerlengo is virtually the ruler of the Church, though the entire Sacred College representing the Papacy receive the honours due to Sovereigns.

On the morning of the tenth day, after the Mass of the Holy Ghost has been sung, all the cardinals present form into a procession to enter the conclave. They sing the "Veni Creator", probably with as loud a voice as they can manage, so as to drown the threats, gibes, imprecations and advice which the people drawn up on either side of the cortège do not fail to shout at them. Gregory X had ruled that the conclave should take place wherever the Pope had died, but the observance of this clause often proved impossible or inexpedient and was not then complied with. The crowd of diplomats, friends and relations who have accompanied the cardinals having been at last induced to depart, the doors are locked and sealed and all other outlets walled up. Boards are placed over the lower parts of the windows allowing only enough uncovered space at the top to admit a dim beam of light. Two wooden cubicles have been contrived for each cardinal. As some of these cells are larger or more commodious than others, the cardinals draw lots for them. They are hung with purple serge for the cardinals created by the last Pope, with green for the others, and the occupant's coat-of-arms is placed on the door.

Every cardinal is allowed to bring into the precincts of the conclave a secretary or conclavist, and a servant. In the days when the Sacred College was an aristocratic body cardinal princes or cardinals belonging to reigning houses were entitled to the services of three conclavists and later this favour was extended to cardinals *pairs-de-France*, grandees of Spain, Roman princes, all foreign prelates, etc., so that few indeed could not claim this privilege. It was a more important one than might appear to the uninitiated, for the conclavist if he were clever, tactful and sufficiently unscrupulous could render the greatest assistance to his master. He could creep stealthily about in the dark, in stockinged feet, listening through the ill-fitting joists of the cubicles for scraps of conversation; or spy on the comings and goings between the cardinals' cells. He could spread rumours, lie, flatter and conciliate, and many a candidate has been made or marred by his conclavists. It was a much sought-after office. The emolu-

Au bout de la premiere loge il y a dans
une cloifon de bois deux tours qu'on ap-
pelle *Ruote* pour recevoir les viandes, que
les domeftiques des Cardinaux apportent
tous les jours avec ceremonie & avec quel-
que cortege d'étrangers au Conclave.

ARRIVAL OF THE CARDINALS' MEALS

ments were considerable—and it conferred a patent of nobility, not to mention the privilege of looting the Pope's cell as soon as he was elected.

Besides these personal attendants many others also entered the conclave. They were: a sacristan with his clerk, two masters of ceremonies, a confessor, two doctors, a surgeon, a chemist with his attendants, a carpenter, a mason, a barber with his apprentices and a number of general servants. It is easy to imagine the hardships and discomforts inflicted on the inmates by cooping up such a large crowd of people in premises intended for other purposes—devoid of ventilation, scarcely lighted, and provided with only the most rudimentary attempts at sanitation. In the sweltering summer heat fever was rampant, and the stench of so much confined humanity made the oppressive atmosphere unbreathable. In the cold winter months when the icy Tramontana found its way through the tiniest crevices, the older cardinals huddled round the inadequate *braseros* vainly trying to warm their creaky joints. The doctors must have had a busy time, for many are the cases of illness and death reported in the history of conclaves; and considering the conditions under which they were held it is surprising that they did not claim more victims.

Gregory X had limited the cardinals' meals to one dish only if a pope had not been elected within three days, reducing them to bread and water after a lapse of three weeks. But this rule soon fell into disuse, and one of the most curious sights of Rome used to be the procession of gala coaches carrying their Eminences' meals in large tin boxes painted with their coats-of-arms and attended by their major-domos, butlers and servants in gorgeous liveries, driving in state from their palaces to the conclave. These boxes were handed in with great ceremony to each cardinal's servant by the officers of his household through the opening provided to that effect at the entrance of the conclave. Supervisors within were supposed to examine all packages to ascertain that they contained no letters or messages of any kind, but this needless to say was done in a most perfunctory manner and interfered in no way with the communication the cardinals held with the outer world. In these more utilitarian and less opulent times kitchens have been installed within the precincts of the conclave and the frugal *pastas* have probably superseded the epicurean fare which filled those heraldic boxes.

There were four different manners of electing a pope: by acclamation, adoration, compromise and scrutiny.

The first kind only took place in the early days when the people and the clergy voiced their selection. Election by adoration occurred when a powerful group of cardinals, certain of the following of at least the necessary majority, prostrated themselves before one of the members of the Sacred College; the others of course immediately joining them. Gregory XV was thus elected in 1621, but he himself subsequently laid such stringent restrictions on this mode of election that it was definitely abandoned. Election by compromise consists in an understanding by which the cardinals who have failed to agree about the choice of a candidate delegate their powers to one or several of their colleagues who nominate the pope. This mode of election is very rarely resorted to. The last and most usual form is by scrutiny.

Twice a day the cardinals assemble in a chapel reserved for the purpose and record their votes on a specially prepared form. It is divided into three spaces. In the top one the cardinal signs his own name, in the centre he writes the name of the candidate to whom he gives his vote and in the lower space he inscribes a number and motto of his own choosing. He folds over and seals the two extremities leaving the candidate's name exposed. He then doubles it over, approaches the altar holding his paper at arm's-length and deposits it on a paten with which he slips it into the gold chalice. Voting is compulsory on all cardinals present within the conclave, those who are ill in bed place their papers through a slit into a sealed box which is carried round to them by special officials nominated to collect them. When all the votes have been recorded it is the duty of three cardinals, called scrutators, to read, announce and check the names inscribed on the forms, breaking the lower seals only, to see that no cardinal has voted twice. The upper seal is never broken except in the case of a candidate having obtained *exactly* the number of votes required, this being done to ascertain that he has not voted for himself, which would make his election void.

After each scrutiny the voting papers are immediately burnt in a stove placed for that purpose within the chapel itself. The extremity of the stove-pipe protruding through a window-pane is the accepted medium of information given to the outer world. If there has been

THE SCRUTINY

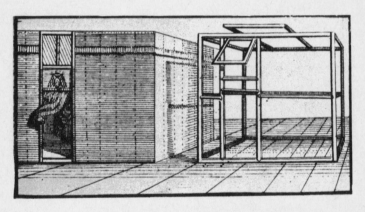

THE CARDINALS' CELLS

no election a handful of damp straw is added to the papers producing the famous "Sfumata" which can be seen by the anxious watchers outside. If a pope has been elected the forms are also burnt, but without the straw, and occasion a quick blaze of which the smoke is practically invisible.

Many qualifications and, generally speaking, not too many virtues were necessary for a candidate to be considered "papabile", that is, acceptable to a reasonable amount of voters. Such qualities of course varied with the ages, being their natural resultant. Roman society of the Renaissance would intrigue for a cardinal likely to make an indulgent, luxurious, pleasure-loving pope, who would allow the women to wear low dresses and enjoy life. But certain conditions never varied. The perfect candidate must be over sixty, older if possible. Mere delicate health had proved a snare, as sickly cardinals had been known to turn most unaccountably into robust and long-lived popes. It was an excellent thing of course that the candidate should have never given offence to any of his colleagues, but it was far more important that he should have received none; the sweets of revenge being deemed irresistible. He must be broad-minded, acceptable to the great European Powers, and above all *generous*. His family also had to be considered, adding to or detracting from his chances of success, for his relations would rise to power with him, and his nephew would wield enormous influence.

The office of cardinal-nephew or *padrone* was a recognised institution. Tradition ordained that immediately after his accession the Pope should bestow the hat on his nephew and make him prime minister; therefore his personality was scarcely less important than that of his uncle. Having no nephew was a tremendous asset for a would-be pope, as in that case one of the cardinals of his party would be given the coveted post. Many promising candidatures were wrecked by the arrogant or rash behaviour of a nephew. In truth it was a most desirable post. Captain-general of the pontifical army and confidential adviser to the head of the State, the Cardinal Padrone was the channel through which flowed benefices one way and gold the other. All-powerful during his uncle's lifetime, he would still after his death be the recognised leader of his "creatures" at the next conclave, and therefore have yet to be reckoned with. A far-reaching and redoubtable influence indeed! Treated as the heir-apparent of a ruling monarch, the cardinal-nephew was entitled on reception of the hat to a royal salute from the guns of S. Angelo, an honour which he alone shared with princes of the blood. The scandalous riches amassed by these personages, their crimes and exactions, the terror they inspired to the population of Rome, raised such a universal outcry that at last in 1692 Innocent XII officially and finally abolished nepotism. The cardinal-nephew was then replaced by a secretary of state chosen by each new pope from among the members of the Sacred College.

To all the currents and cross-currents of intrigue swaying the electors this way and that, must be added the interference of the Powers. At first they were content with pronouncing an *exclusion*, which merely meant that, acting on the instructions of their sovereigns, cardinals would under no circumstances give their voice to some particular candidate. By degrees, however, certain Powers quietly assumed the right of *veto*, by which they became enabled to annul a perfectly valid election. Mildly contested at first, this privilege was fully recognised and accepted by the Sacred College during the second half of the XVIIth century, thereby allowing the Sovereigns of France, Spain and Austria direct precedence over the Holy Ghost.

To give it a legal value, it was agreed between Rome and the above-mentioned Powers that the *veto* could only be pronounced *once* by each government against a single candidate and had to be notified officially to the Doyen of the Sacred College before the scrutiny took place, by a cardinal accredited for this special purpose. "The veto is a weapon which, once drawn, can only wound one adversary, but while still sheathed can disable many", wrote Count Brunati, an Austrian diplomat of the XVIIIth century; and the wily cardinal who wished to exclude several candidates would be an adept at rattling the sword in the scabbard. He would not scruple to hint that he held a veto against one or another aspirant, thereby considerably reducing their chances of success, while he would give unlimited rope to his real victim, knowing that if he proved dangerous he could even at the last minute be pulled up with a jerk. No doubt it must have been a fascinating game for Machiavellian minds. The immense power wielded by Charles V during the XVIth century and the vast extent of his Empire was in a great measure responsible for the inception of this political interference, as almost all the cardinals were his subjects and dared not disregard his wishes. When France claimed a like prerogative during the reign of the Emperor Maximilian II it was difficult to deny her, as she occupied part of Italy, too potent an argument to be ignored. France's interests being in direct opposition to those of the Empire, she adopted the simple policy of reserving her *exclusion* for the Emperor's candidate, who naturally retaliated in kind. The outcome of this mutual checkmating was apt to prove disastrous to both parties, occasionally resulting in the election of a pope inimical to *all* foreigners. Many cardinals were also in receipt of allowances and benefices from foreign Powers and therefore bound to act on their instructions without, of course, showing their hand. So entangled were all the cardinals in the webs of these tortuous intrigues that they were powerless to prevent the original negative *exclusion* from being transmuted into the imperative *veto*. If the intricate manœuvres brought about by this innovation often resulted in protracted conclaves, it also caused some very rapid ones; for if the Sacred College could manage to elect a pope before the prohibitive instructions had time to arrive, the veto would be null and void. To this stratagem Pius IX owed his elevation in 1846, as the bearer of Austria's veto against him arrived just in time to receive, no doubt with feelings of due reverence and piety, the Apostolic blessing which the Holy father was bestowing on the faithful.

No sooner has the newly elected pope accepted the great dignity bestowed upon him and chosen the name he wishes to bear, with, we will presume, a becoming show of unpreparedness and hesitation, than all the cardinals who, only a moment before, were still his equals, fall on their knees in adoration. The canopies over their stalls are all lowered, his alone remains aloft. The great moment has arrived. After years of subservience he has suddenly become the embodiment of absolutism, combining in his person a dual autocracy both theocratic and monarchical. He is allowed a few moments in which to compose himself and is then conducted behind the altar and clothed in one of the sets of white robes which have been provided in three different sizes. In the meantime workmen have demolished the masonry and contrived an opening through which the senior Cardinal-Deacon announces the great news to the expectant crowd below.

The pontiff then appears and blesses the people and all Christendom. In the days when the pope was king he was greeted by a blast from the silver trumpets of his guards, the guns of S. Angelo immediately fired a salute and the bells of every church in Rome broke into a deafening peal of jubilation. Meanwhile the conclavists ransacked the new pope's cubicle, stripping it bare, while the mob rushed helter-skelter to loot his palace.

The details of the enthronement ceremony would fill a volume and have scarcely altered to this day. Varied influences can be traced in their archaic symbolism and Oriental splendour, not omitting a reminder of those sinister days when poison was used so freely. The precautions so essential then are still in practice, for during the Pontifical Mass a portion of the wine and water to be consecrated is poured into a cup and drunk by an acolyte. For the same reason three wafers are presented to the cardinal-deacon, who places one only on the paten while an attendant swallows the others. To make assurance doubly sure, the pope breaks off two particles of the remaining wafer which he himself places on the tongues of the deacon and sub-deacon. All the punctilious formalities of the great ceremonial are meticulously observed, though the loss of the temporal power necessarily put an end to its festive manifestations. A picturesque custom connected with the pope's accession but now long obsolete was the *cavalcata*.

A few days after his enthronement the pontiff went in state to take possession of the Lateran. This pageant, known as the *cavalcata*, is described by many travellers to Rome. It varied in pomp and magnificence with the centuries, being naturally influenced by the trend of the times. Nicholas V, for instance, in 1447, preceded by the Host, rode a white jennet, holding in his left hand a golden rose while he blessed the crowd with his right. At an earlier date the popes had been carried in a litter surrounded by cardinals, senators, princes and patriarchs; while heading the procession was an auditor of the *rota* riding a white mule and carrying the papal cross. During the XVIth century the pageant showed a decidedly military influence, which soon became a regular triumphal march. The Renaissance displayed all its splendour on the passage of the cavalcade. Triumphal arches draped with cloth of gold and garlands of flowers, platforms hung with costly tapestries on which *tableaux vivants* were enacted, streets strewn with rushes, showers of alms and indulgences, but no more

Host. The mob considered it a day of unbridled licence and followed in the wake of the procession pillaging and looting unchecked. The principal sufferers of course were the Jews. To them had been allotted the decoration of the most expensive and vulnerable erections. A deputation of rabbis holding huge waxen candles awaited the passage of the pontiff to do him homage. They presented their Holy Book to him, which he would accept, returning it over his left shoulder, saying: "We neither confirm nor infirm". Early in the XVth century the Jewish community having had the unfortunate idea of tendering the Pentateuch wrapped in a rich covering, the Pope sent to claim it after the ceremony, and so the custom became established for the Jews to make a gift of a finely bound specimen of their Holy Book to every new pontiff. Leo X, however, the haughty and fastidious Medicean prince, to whom the rabbis offered a specially beautiful and costly volume, having received it and pronounced the ritual formula, examined it with great deliberation and dropped it contemptuously in the dust.

Evening came; as the gates of the ghetto closed on the Jews, bonfires blazed up in all open spaces, every house was illuminated, be it palace or hovel, and all Rome echoed with the sound of carousal and revelry. From the heights could be seen a flaming serpent creeping through the city—being a torchlight procession of nobles mounted on milk-white steeds and proceeding towards the Vatican, in front of which they held a mock tourney "to the great content of His Holiness and the delight of the people".

In the XVth and XVIth centuries the vacancy of the Holy See was a recognised time of lawlessness and licence in Rome. The criminals who had been liberated at the late Pope's death, when it was customary to proclaim a general amnesty, roamed the streets in gangs, breaking into unprotected houses, plundering, raping and murdering as they went. Unchecked by fear of punishment, the princely houses renewed their feuds, drew chains across the streets to defend their palaces, armed all available retainers and hastened to pay off old scores. The mob attacked the cardinals' palaces, but all precautions had usually been taken by those prelates, their most valuable possessions removed to a place of safety and armed guards stationed within their mansions. It was the traditional privilege of the populace to loot the new pope's residence, being the reason which prompted them always to clamour for a Roman Pope. The slightest rumour of any cardinal resident in the city having been elected was deemed a sufficient excuse and acted upon at once. To add to the confusion, the cardinal-nephew still in command of the Castle of S. Angelo and of the papal troops might make sorties to settle a few outstanding quarrels while he was still in a position to do so; or the nobles whose possessions had been confiscated by the late pope might attempt to regain them by armed force, so that open fighting in the city was the order of the day.

Meanwhile the numberless non-combatant hangers-on of the mighty were faced with the unpleasant necessity of providing for their own needs. Pawn-shops thrived on this state of things. From an average of 800 or 900 crowns business rose to 90,000 or 100,000 a month. Trade otherwise was at a standstill, all sittings of the law-courts suspended, great houses closed—in fact socially Rome was a dead city. Great animation, however, prevailed in the gambling-dens, where the odds on the candidates to the papal throne ran sometimes very high. The punters would stick at nothing to ruin the chances of their favourites' competitors. Calumny and ridicule, all weapons were useful. Scurrilous pamphlets, lampoons and pasquinades flooded the town, always anonymous of course, as backing the wrong horse openly might result in one's losing a good deal more than one's money. Much of this edifying literature was smuggled into the conclave with the object of influencing the cardinals' votes, and no doubt afforded their Eminences and their conclavists a few moments of hilarity at one another's expense.

With the pope's proclamation some semblance of order was restored in the city, but the perpetual change of ruler, each one introducing new political and personal tendencies, to be grafted on to the traditional policy of the Holy See, caused a feeling of instability, a want of equilibrium, most prejudicial to law and order. The Romans learned to disregard laws that might be so short-lived as to be evaded by procrastination, and to make light of penal sentences and incarceration in prisons of which the doors were continually being thrown open. It is on record that debtors petitioned to be excluded from these unwelcome amnesties, as only in gaol did they feel sufficiently protected from the vengeance of their blood-thirsty creditors.

XVTH CENTURY

Calixtus III · Pius II · Paul II · Sixtus IV
Innocent VIII · Alexander VI

THE death of Nicholas V in 1455 found the Papacy definitely settled in Rome. Both the great schism and the titanic struggle with the Germanic Empire were at an end. No longer would the emperors have to journey to Rome to be crowned, for Nicholas V had bestowed the imperial dignity on Frederick III and his descendants as a hereditary right, and whatever claim the Emperor may have had to be represented at the Pope's coronation was now a thing of the past. But the Holy See was not yet to enter on an era of peace. For another sixty years or so it would be at war with the other Italian States either in the field of battle or of diplomacy, in a grim contest to secure its own establishment and to maintain an equilibrium between all the small States that fractioned Italy. By the mere force of circumstances, having dominions the pope must protect them, and even add to them if possible, thus laying aside the crook for the sword. Consequently the conclaves, during the period of papal history covering the second half of the XVth century, are mostly swayed by local ambitions and intrigues and are of less general interest than they became later on. It has seemed advisable therefore to give a very summary account of them. The stage set against the same invariable background, and the identical protagonists reappearing so often under similar circumstances, of too restricted an appeal, would make monotonous and wearisome reading.

CALIXTUS III (Alfonso Borgia)

1455–1458

❧

At the conclave which assembled in 1455 to elect a successor to Nicholas V only fifteen cardinals were present, six of whom were lay cardinals and anything but serious-minded or God-fearing. The Sacred College was divided into two camps. One headed by Colonna favoured Florence; the other under the leadership of Orsini stood for the interests of the *League* formed by Milan, Venice and Naples. The Colonna and Orsini were hereditary foes, whom we shall find invariably opposing one another. Out of these fifteen cardinals, nine were set on being themselves elected and therefore would not vote consistently. To add to the complexity of the situation, the lay cardinals formed an independent faction voting against any candidate irrespective of parties who showed signs of being a disciplinarian. Thus they defeated Bessarion, who was gaining ground on both sides, as they could not risk having a Pope who had only recently been converted from the Greek schismatic Church, and was therefore zealous as all neophytes are. Besides he wore a long flowing beard which the worldly prelates considered an outrage. Matters seemed at a standstill, and the lay cardinals were growing desperate. The claustration, the barbarous discomforts were making them restive, and only the scented notes which their fair friends smuggled into the conclave relieved the tedium of their existence.

At last from one of them came a welcome inspiration! Instead of merely defeating any candidate behind whom they saw looming the shadow of a monastery or a prison, why not adopt one of their own who would ensure a continuance of the life they were used to leading? Cardinal Alfonso Borgia seemed the very man. A Spaniard: pleasantly cynical and making no mystery of his licentiousness or of his illegitimate children, in fact a pope after their own hearts. The success of this suggestion was immediate. The enthusiastic prelates would brook no delay. They selected a spokesman who dashed off hot-foot to request an interview with

Orsini. To that startled dignitary he declared without any circumlocutions that the lay cardinals were determined to break the seals and abandon the conclave unless Borgia became Pope. His manner must have carried conviction for the horrified leader called a hasty meeting of his followers, who agreed that *anything* must be done to avert such an unheard-of scandal. Calixtus III was therefore elected, and the Borgias descended upon the Church of Rome, across whose history they were to leave such a sinister trail of blood-stained magnificence.

PIVS . II . PAPA . SENENSIS .

PIUS II
From a print in the British Museum

PIUS II (Piccolomini)
1458–1464

❧

BESIDE the political pawns of the rival Italian States, two formidable candidates were on the ranks at the conclave which assembled at the death of Calixtus III. They were Sylvius Piccolomini and Guillaume d'Estouteville, Cardinal of Rouen. The first had played an important part at the Council of Bâle, where he had most eloquently upheld the supremacy of the council over the pope. He stood out among his colleagues as the foremost personality. He was widely travelled, cultivated, clever, resourceful, had a vast experience of the world and was flexible and deadly as well-tempered steel.

The Cardinal of Rouen, his rival, had none of these qualities and knew it. So he did not waste his time or his energies on an unequal struggle of wits, but put all his trust in the cupidity of his colleagues. To the Cardinal of Avignon he promised his Roman palace and the coveted post of Chancellor. To Bessarion and the other Greeks he paid large sums of money. With the Italian cardinals he made various bargains which were all committed to writing and discussed and settled near the latrines, which spot offered the only semblance of privacy or seclusion to be found within the precincts of the conclave. But even that malodorous sanctuary was evidently not proof against the prying eyes of the conclavists, for Piccolomini got wind of the transactions just as everything seemed most satisfactorily settled, and turned the tables by a daring and masterly stroke. As the cardinals assembled in the morning to hear Mass and proceed to the scrutiny which would certainly have made Rouen Pope, they found Piccolomini standing across the threshold of the chapel, barring the entrance. With stirring eloquence he adjured them not to elect a French pope. He drew a vivid picture of the Holy See transferred once more to Avignon; of Rome deserted, of the trials and expenditure incurred by the cardinals perpetually on the roads and in perpetual danger. He hinted delicately at the bargains that had been concluded but might so easily be repudiated; and when he considered his audience sufficiently

impressed by his persuasive fluency he led the way into the chapel
confident of success. As soon as Mass was over the scrutiny took
place and the chalice containing the votes was deposited before the
scrutators. As chance would have it, both Rouen and his supporter
Colonna were scrutators that day. Colonna examined each paper
and handed it to Rouen, who read it aloud. Every cardinal bending
anxiously over his list of candidates marked the number of votes
each one obtained. Then Rouen announced the total results, giving
Piccolomini eight votes only. Immediately there was a hubbub—
Piccolomini leaping to his feet accused the scrutators of dishonesty;
he appealed to the Sacred College to witness that he had been robbed
of a vote. The Cardinal Doyen thereupon called for a second tally,
and Rouen, half fainting and speechless with emotion, did not even
attempt a protest. Piccolomini's name registered nine votes, and his
partisans, wishing to follow up this advantage, suggested the
"accessus", which consists of a second ballot, the first votes being
transferable orally to another candidate.

Two cardinals immediately gave Piccolomini their voices; only
one more was needed now for him to reach the necessary
majority. A couple of Rouen's demoralised supporters hurriedly
left the chapel under the only admissible pretext, but Bessarion,
the bearded bugbear of the lay cardinals in the last conclave, stood
firm by his deserted patron. He had sufficiently deteriorated in the
Roman atmosphere of corruption to accept a large bribe from
Rouen, but at any rate did not turn traitor. A moment of tense
silence and expectancy now ensued. It is said that Piccolomini's
gaze travelled slowly round the assembled prelates and came
to rest on Colonna with such a power of concentrated authority
and promise that he rose like an automaton to obey the unspoken
command. But before he could utter a word Rouen and Bessarion
had flung themselves upon him in an attempt to silence him by main
force. There was a violent scuffle, during which Colonna managed to
free himself sufficiently to pronounce the necessary formula. In a
moment, the panting, dishevelled cardinals fell apart and were prostrated in adoration. Piccolomini was Pope. Needless to say that
Pius II utterly condemned Cardinal Piccolomini's findings in favour
of the supremacy of the council over the pope, and with equal
eloquence decreed the supremacy of the pope over the council.

Once having recanted his former indiscretions, Pius II pursued a consistent and virile policy. He was an able man, of dignified bearing, not overburdened with scruples. He suffered martyrdom from the stone but bore pain with the most admirable stoicism, never letting it interfere with his duties. A greater contrast to his successor could scarcely have been found.

PAUL II (Pietro Barbo)
1464–1471

⚜

Only a trifling incident seems worth recording in connection with the conclave which elected Pietro Barbo to the Holy See in 1464. He was a Venetian, probably the handsomest man who ever wore the triple crown. There was a not unnatural murmur of disapprobation therefore when he announced to the Sacred College that he wished to be known as Formoso (beautiful). The scandalised cardinals persuaded him that in his case such a name would lead to misinterpretation, and Marco, his second choice, having been ruled out as too reminiscent of the Venetian war-cry (*Marco! Marco!*), he decided on Paul, against which no objection could possibly be raised. The name which would really have suited him was Narcissus, as he was infatuated with his own regular features, fine presence and patrician hands. He was a voluptuary, revelling in sumptuous clothes, perfumes and jewelry, and intensely susceptible to beauty in all its forms. His court was crowded with lovely women and graceful youths. He would play with precious stones as though their contact gave him a sensuous delight, and watch with a fascinated gaze their prismatic sparkles as he let them trickle through his shapely fingers. He could not rest unless the gems lay under his pillow. He hoarded them secretly, and many years after his death *caches* would be accidentally discovered in the Vatican brimful of gorgeous jewels.

Paul II's idea of government was to give the people a perpetual round of amusements which, he said, kept them far more contented than any amount of improvements and good works. He introduced the carnival to the Romans, and considering the zest with which they adopted and clung to it through the ages, it was evidently a most judicious innovation exactly suited to their temperament. This Pope's death is shrouded in mystery. Some historians tell us that the weight of a jewelled tiara entirely encrusted with precious stones and for which he had paid a king's ransom, gave him an apoplectic fit the

23

first time he wore it. Others say that he was strangled in the dead of night under most sordid circumstances. What the real mode of his end may have been it has never been definitely ascertained, which is perhaps just as well.

SIXTUS IV
1471–1484

❧

PAUL II, in spite of the immense sums he squandered, had left the treasury well filled, and Cardinal della Rovere having promised to divide the proceeds equally among the cardinals, was elected without demur. He was the first Pope of humble birth to found a great and powerful house. Under his reign nepotism developed with such alarming rapidity that it had soon reached the proportions of a giant octopus, whose suckers were so firmly fastened into the institution on which it fed that it took centuries to hack away the last of its tentacles. The money with which Sixtus supplied his insatiable family, or which he himself needed for his debauches and the perpetual warfare waged against his neighbours, was raised by the most cruel extortions on his subjects, the sale of all ecclesiastical dignities and benefices, taxes on houses of prostitution and a tariff for the absolution of all crimes with plenary indulgence to anyone who killed a Venetian. His hatred of the powerful Republic was maniacal. He had of course anathematised and excommunicated its citizens time and again. So much for the spiritual side. But not content with consigning them to the everlasting furnace, he threatened to seize any Venetian ecclesiastics found outside the dominions of the Republic and to sell them as slaves to the Turks.

We are told, no doubt quite rightly, that a man should be judged by the standards of the epoch in which he lived, but this precept is difficult to put into practice. To get the exact focus across such a wide space of time calls for a keenness of vision granted to few. At whatever angle one places oneself, Sixtus IV still appears as a singularly unattractive specimen of humanity. If one turns to his contemporaries for a verdict one finds little mercy shown him. The indictment of his crimes compiled by Infessura is a revelation of all that human turpitude can devise; but then Infessura hated him, so cannot be trusted. The most moderate, however, seemed to consider that he would be in need of some of his own most potent indulgences when the reckoning came, for the cautious envoy of the Medici in Rome announces the news of the Pontiff's death to his master in these words: "To-day at 5 o'clock His Holiness Sixtus IV departed this life—may God forgive him!"

INNOCENT VIII
1484-1492

❦

SIXTUS IV is said to have died of rage on hearing that the Italian States had signed a peace treaty without his knowledge. There is no doubt that common hatred of his person had brought them together. He had been the most pitiless of enemies and the most treacherous of allies. The moment the breath was out of his body the looting commenced in his apartments, and as the sacristan fancied the papal bed, the corpse was lifted out and placed on a table. No cloth, no towels, no basins were to be found with which to perform his last toilet, and no underclothes were forthcoming into which he could be changed. A cope was at last produced which was wrapped round the body to conceal the soiled linen and the old red felt slippers which the scavengers had not considered worth carrying away, and which constituted the only footwear available.

In the meantime Rome was in a ferment. Jerome and Peter Riario, the dead Pope's nephews, held S. Angelo with their troops and made constant sallies on the city, exciting the mob against the cardinals, who dared not leave their palaces. This situation might have lasted a considerable time if the Neapolitan army who were advancing upon Rome had not appeared most opportunely, and from attackers turned into rescuers; for the bellicose Riarios, seeing the game was up, surrendered the fortress, and so the Sacred College was at last enabled to enter into conclave. Besides the usual elements of internal and external intrigues, a new influence, that of the cardinal-nephews, was to make itself felt most potently in this conclave. There were two of these prelates present—Rodrigo Borgia, nephew of Calixtus III, and della Rovere, nephew of Sixtus IV. They both meant to be Pope some day, but knew that their time had not yet come; and thought that in the meanwhile it would be expedient to secure a pontiff of their own choice. They met secretly during the night, disguised in their servants' clothes—at the usual trysting place—and settled on the election of Cardinal Cibo, an intimate friend of della Rovere's.

He was rather young, of course, only fifty-four, and as strong as a bull, but licentious, easy-going, with no apparent will of his own, and as tractable as a child. The next step was to purchase the votes of which they were not already assured. They immediately went round from cell to cell, waking up the cardinals with the news that the Pope was made and giving them each signed promises of lavish grants and benefices. Not one of the prelates demurred. So fearful were they of being outstripped by their colleagues in the race for favour, that aged cardinals could be seen rushing half clothed from their cubicles pursued by their conclavists, who dressed them as they ran. They found Cibo kneeling by a bench upon which he was signing all petitions without even reading them. A few hours later he became Pope Innocent VIII.

As might have been expected from such an irresponsible nature, he repudiated all his promises and left his signatures unhonoured, slyly revelling in his immunity. He abandoned the conduct of affairs entirely to della Rovere, and settled down to enjoy life in his own slothful way. He was a despicable creature; ungrateful, avaricious and cowardly. His only interest seems to have been the establishment of his numerous illegitimate progeny. The Vatican became a patriarchal abode overrun by his sons and daughters, their children and grandchildren. The marriage festivities which took place when his daughters and granddaughters contracted brilliant alliances were conducted on a scale of regal magnificence. For the first time in the history of Papacy women sat at the Pontiff's table, openly and unashamed, to the intense indignation of even the most unrighteous. Innocent dropped even the thinnest veil of decorum which might protect the Holy See from the vulgar gaze, and enable the world at large to ignore what it was undesirable to discern.

His brood was as supine as he was himself and therefore comparatively harmless. They desired no special honours and certainly no dangerous conquests. They were perfectly content to while away the leisurely hours in Decameronic domesticity. Innocent VIII slept almost continuously. When awake his favourite occupation consisted in persecuting the Jews. He squeezed every shekel he could out of them, and reduced the ghetto to a state of sordid misery and terror. Such gross self-indulgence would naturally undermine the strongest constitution. The Pontiff grew immensely fat, which is scarcely surprising, and his health gradually declined. By the summer of 1492 he had become an inert mass of flesh, "incapable", writes Valori, "of assimilating any nourishment but a few drops of milk from a young woman's breast". A Jewish doctor offered to attempt a blood transfusion to save his life; which shows how far above petty vindictiveness devotion to science will raise a man. He only needed, he said, the blood of three healthy young men—Christians presumably. The victims were procured at one ducat per head, a reasonable price even for those days one imagines, and the operation resulted in the three healthy young men escorting their flaccid Pontiff to a better world. The Jew, adds the chronicler, was never seen again.

ALEXANDER VI
From a fresco in the Vatican

ALEXANDER VI (RODRIGO BORGIA)
1492–1503

🌸

TWENTY-THREE cardinals entered the conclave to elect a successor to Innocent VIII on August 6th, 1492. There were four recognised candidates of whom only two survived the first few scrutinies. These two were Rodrigo Borgia and Sforza. Almost forty years had elapsed since Borgia had been summoned from Spain by his uncle Calixtus III to become Cardinal-Nephew. His morals were in all respects those of his times, but he had been born and bred in Spain, where a decorous bearing was *de rigueur* and an outward show of devotion most advisable. So although he sent for his mistress and their children as soon as he was settled in the Vatican, he did not give himself away by installing them in Rome. Venice was the nearest he dared risk. He led a life dissolute enough, but still concealed under the cloak of piety. It is said that after nights of wildest orgy he would creep into a church at dawn, staggering out, drawn and haggard, as the first worshippers assembled, much impressed, poor simple souls, by this ascetic apparition! But as he got more familiar with the language and customs of Rome, Borgia discovered that Spanish methods were of no practical use in Italy. Determined as he was to occupy the Holy See some day, he now realised that it was not through a reputation for piety that his object was to be attained, but through the possession of sufficient riches. He therefore threw off the mask. He made no more mystery of his illegitimate offspring—quite the contrary! By Vanozza Catanei, a Roman, he had several children, the famous Cesare and Lucretia among them, and he provided for his family on a magnificent scale. Being naturally arrogant, superb and handsome, they soon occupied the position to which they considered themselves entitled and to which their father had destined them. During the pontificates of Sixtus IV and Innocent VIII Rodrigo Borgia had grown less lavish in his mode of life, hoarding the money he would soon be needing for the purchase of his ultimate goal. Even his extravagant sons had agreed to reduce their expenditure, knowing full well that it would be made up to them a hundredfold when their father became Pope.

Borgia had sold his influence and accumulated immense riches during his uncle's lifetime, and managed under the following pontificates to add considerably to his store. He used to boast that he could fill the Sixtine Chapel with sacks of gold. He was the first cardinal with sufficient foresight to build defensive towers at the entrance to his palace to safeguard it against the attacks of the mob. He was a man who left nothing to chance. He possessed an irresistible charm of manner with which he enslaved women and duped men. A formidable opponent was Rodrigo Borgia, an opponent who was not going to allow Sforza, clever as he might be, to stand between him and the prize he had systematically worked for all these years. He sent a message to his rival proposing a nocturnal interview in a cell occupied by Cardinal Savelli, one of his supporters, and which happened to be fairly secluded. Savelli meanwhile was to create a diversion in some other quarter and thus ensure their privacy. No sooner were the two prelates face to face than Borgia laid his cards on the table. They both wanted to be elected, he said, and they both had a chance of success. The question was who could buy the most votes. The cardinals would be very exacting; the way Innocent VIII had cheated them would make them wary of mere promises; it would be necessary to pay heavily and in hard cash. The whole question in a nutshell was: could Sforza outbid him? He then went on to enumerate his possessions. The vaults of his palace were full of money. He held three archbishoprics, the richest prebends in Italy, a dozen opulent abbeys; palaces, jewels and silver plate galore. His adversary could have his pick of the lot. Sforza was staggered by the munificence of the offer. He was beaten; but on such terms capitulation was scarcely a defeat. He promised to meet Borgia the next night, under similar circumstances, with a signed document accepting the transaction. Borgia did not allow the grass to grow under his feet; he immediately sent a note to his son Francis, and as day broke four mules in magnificent trappings could be seen leaving the Borgia stronghold, wending their way slowly through the streets of Rome, bearing their weighty burden of gold to Sforza's palace.

During the day Borgia settled accounts with the cardinals, nor did he neglect the conclavists, who also shared in the distribution of largesse. While the father was buying up the conclave at a price that would have made Croesus himself look thoughtful, the sons were busy canvassing the outer world. Valori, writing to the Council of Ten, says that he could not confide to paper what were the means they employed! On August 11th the cardinals, all up at cock-crow, flocked to the chapel to implore Pentecostal guidance. Cardinal Sforza, whose nerves, after two sleepless nights of intense excitement, were probably a bit out of control, forgot himself so far as to rail against the delay caused by such mummery, saying that at all the conclaves at which he had been present the Pope had been made without the Holy Ghost's assistance, and that the sooner they got to business the better. Rodrigo Borgia was unanimously elected and took the name of Alexander VI.

This Pontiff's mode of life is familiar to all. As to his death, if it is true as alleged that it was brought about by his drinking, in error, of the poisoned wine prepared for his guests, it is the most perfect *dénouement* ever devised by fate. At his obsequies the Papal Guards who were escorting the funeral litter picked a quarrel with the clergy, who started to belabour them with their lighted candles. The soldiers drew their swords and the fighting then became serious. The churchmen fled; the guards pursued them while the dead Pope's body was abandoned by the wayside. Some mendicant friars dragged the litter into St. Peter's, but the corpse soon became so black and swollen that it lost all semblance of humanity and was horrible to behold. It emitted such a stench that no one could bear to approach it. At nightfall six scavengers inured against all unpleasant sights and odours were induced to carry the body into a side chapel and deposit it in a coffin. By the light of guttering torches they stripped the late Pontiff of all ornaments and vestments, rolled the remains in a piece of tattered carpet, and as the coffin was too small, stamped and leapt upon the bundle to force it in.

With this macabre scene the curtain falls on one of the most outstanding figures of papal history. He merged the Pontiff entirely in the Sovereign. A man of indomitable energy, a born diplomat, a doting parent, he set himself with an iron determination to the task of making his house the greatest and most powerful in Italy. Unhampered by scruples of any kind, the means by which he accomplished his ends, whether poison or indulgences, mattered to him not at all. He never oppressed the people, preferring to tax the rich by selling, as his predecessors had done, all ecclesiastical benefices and dignities. When he needed money he either created a cardinal or murdered one, appropriating the dead man's possessions. He strove continuously to break and ruin the unruly nobles and made praiseworthy efforts to establish some form of justice for the poor.

Like all popes who ruled during the heyday of nepotism, it seems impossible to dissociate him from his family. The cardinal-nephew, or the son who passed as such, seems invariably to be a projection of the older man's personality. There could be no stronger argument in favour of the laws of heredity than its manifestations in papal history. Whether it is the ostentation and brutality of the upstart della Roveres, the indolence of the pleasure-loving Cibos, or the ruthlessness of the ambitious Borgias, the younger men seem to mirror the tastes and characteristics of their elders with the blatancy resulting from stronger vitality and lack of experience; as though Dr Faustus, instead of being rejuvenated in his own person, found, standing at his side, the reincarnation of his youth, buoyant with all his own aspirations. Bound together as closely by the ties of interest as by those of blood, these two beings complete and complement one another. And so the inseparable figures of Alexander VI and Cesare Borgia form an epitome on a grand scale of the vices and qualities of their epoch; a colossal effigy of Might such as it was understood at the close of the XVth century.

XVIth CENTURY

Pius III · Julius II · Leo X · Adrian VI
Clement VII · Paul III · Julius III · Marcellus II
Paul IV · Pius IV · Pius V · Gregory XIII
Sixtus V · Urban VII · Gregory XIV
Innocent IX · Clement VIII

PIUS III

1503

❦

CESARE BORGIA was prepared for every eventuality which might occur at the time of his father's death, he said, except that of being himself helpless on a bed of sickness. He had also partaken of the poisoned beverage which killed Alexander, but his youth and iron constitution saved him from a similar fate. Living as he did in the Vatican itself, he was the first to hear the tragic news so fatal to all his hopes and ambitions; for Alexander VI was striving to create a hereditary principality for him carved out of his neighbour's lands and a portion of the Romagnas, and it was even rumoured that the Holy See itself might form part of his apanage. Cesare's ambition was overweening. His principality, which should be the most powerful of all Italy, was only to be a stepping-stone to far greater things. He was utterly heartless. He had not hesitated to murder his brother because his father loved him, for Cesare would admit of no sharing of benefits. He had slaughtered Pierotto, a favourite of the Pope's, under His Holiness's very mantle, where the cowering wretch had sought sanctuary; the blood had spurted all over the Pontiff's face. Cesare did not fear his father; he knew how weak his parental fondness made him. He himself suffered from no filial inhibitions. His utter callousness for his father's feelings must have been a terrible and condign punishment for the crimes that his love for Cesare made that Pontiff commit or condone.

The shattering blow which would have prostrated most men in Borgia's enfeebled condition acted on his adamantine nature as a stimulant. He was determined to live and be revenged on others for this cruel trick of fate. He gave orders that all the doors of the palace should be closed at once, before the cardinals could assemble. He sent Michelotto, the captain of his guards and his *âme damnée*, to secure the person of the Cardinal Treasurer. At the point of the dagger that official was compelled to give up his keys, and 400,000 crowns thus passed into Borgia's possession, with all the valuables which could be collected in so short a time. Then only were the clamouring cardinals admitted. To their great relief they found that a plain-looking case containing the late Pope's rarest gems had been over-looked by Michelotto in the scramble; having shared the contents they then appropriated the furniture and ornaments. Their servants carried off the remnants, and the great empty rooms now stood silent and deserted, strewn with litter and wreckage.

A strong guard was posted at all the approaches to Cesare Borgia's apartments, where the Spanish cardinals, creatures of the late Pope, had fled for protection, and where the sick man lay, near to death, but concentrating all his energies on living. Their prayers for his recovery must indeed have been fervent, for they were unlikely to survive him if he died at this juncture. As the hours passed and nothing happened, they recovered some degree of equanimity. There were no signs of an attack; the only sound audible to their straining ears was the steady tramp of their guards echoing through the great empty palace. They remained unmolested. So great was the terror the Borgia inspired, so cowed were his enemies, that no attempt was made to rush what must have been a very precarious stronghold, wherein the hated tyrant lay helpless at their mercy. They probably hoped he would die; but things were not to be made so easy for them as that—such creatures are notoriously hard to kill. Borgia struggled back to life, and the sixteen trembling cardinals who had barricaded themselves in the Convent of the Minerva heard with consternation that the ogre was about once more.

By rights, the Sacred College, representing the Government, should have been in possession of the Vatican, so Borgia had to be asked on what terms he would be willing to evacuate the palace. He brutally refused even to discuss the matter. The non-plussed electors then decided to hold the conclave in the castle of S. Angelo, but the governor, who was friendly with Borgia, refused to give up the keys, saying that what he held from the Pope he would only surrender to the Pope. The Sacred College were in a nice quandary. Orsini and his bandits were hovering on the outskirts of Rome; Colonna had joined forces with Borgia and a civil war seemed far more imminent than a conclave. Furthermore, the leaders of the French army, marching southwards to Naples, had thought the moment opportune to come out of their way as far as Isola to see how things were progressing in the Holy City. The Sacred College in desperation appealed to the foreign ambassadors for help, and their intervention resulted in an offer from Borgia to leave the Vatican on condition that S. Angelo was handed over to him and his troops. This proposal was mere mockery, as the castle was in the immediate vicinity of the Vatican, which it commanded. Negotiations were therefore at a standstill, when unexpectedly Borgia himself offered to renew them. He sent hostages to the Sacred College to prove his good faith and asked for Cardinal Sanseverino to be empowered to treat with him. The upshot of this interview was that Borgia left Rome at the head of his men, and the safety of the Spanish cardinals was guaranteed by the Sacred College. This sudden move on Borgia's part was due to French influence. France was most anxious that the Cardinal d'Amboise should be made Pope and had struck a bargain with Cesare to that effect, paying him 20,000 ducats down and 20,000 when he was outside the city.

The Vatican was now open to the cardinals, but it seemed a terribly inauspicious moment for them to immure themselves in conclave. The French army was encamped under the walls of Rome, Borgia only just out of sight, their own unruly and discontented mercenaries causing perpetual brawls and bloodshed in the town; in fact the poor cardinals had every cause to be uneasy. So encompassed by dangers did they feel both within and without the conclave that several of them extorted a promise from the custodians to throw open the doors at a given signal and so enable them to escape if necessary. The first consideration under such critical circumstances was undoubtedly celerity, but as usual every candidate seemed to be cursed with some insuperable drawback—Della Rovere was too much of a firebrand, Colonna too unbending an aristocrat; this one was too mean, and that one too healthy. As to the French candidate d'Amboise, although he was blissfully unaware of the fact, his nationality alone made his election impossible. His career, so far, had been one of easy success. Bishop at fourteen, Archbishop of Rouen a few years later, he had been created cardinal and Papal Legate to France by Alexander VI. Louis XII had appointed him prime minister on his accession, and now encouraged him in his ambition to occupy the Holy See. D'Amboise considered his election a foregone conclusion. Had not France bought for him from Borgia the voices of the eleven Spanish Cardinals? In addition to these and to his French supporters, he counted also on the Venetians, which would make his majority more than secure. Borgia's instructions to the Spanish electors, of which the French Ambassador held a copy, were refreshingly clear and pithy. "I order you", he wrote, "to vote for the Cardinal d'Amboise. In case of disobedience you will be cut to pieces as others have been before you." This document had, as we have seen, cost Louis XII 40,000 ducats, and the Frenchmen never doubted its efficacy. So certain were they of victory, that d'Amboise, rather prematurely, announced his elevation to the King. His amazement and disappointment were therefore boundless when at the first scrutiny he only got an insignificant number of votes.

For twenty-four hours he strove with all the energy of despair to avert a defeat which would be such a bitter humiliation, and cover him with ridicule; but all his efforts proved fruitless. From those who had accepted his bribes he met with nothing but polite apathy. Whatever their inner dissentions might be, the Italian cardinals all joined issue when it came to fooling a Frenchman. It now became evident that Borgia also had played him false and that the Spanish element had been less impressed by those drastic and expensive orders than the French Ambassador and his party. The Cardinal d'Amboise met his first defeat gallantly. With commendable philosophy he resigned himself to the inevitable and bore up bravely under his mortifying failure.

Meanwhile Sforza, the erstwhile rival of Alexander VI whose experience of human nature was rich and varied, and who could appraise to a nicety all the moods and tempers of a conclave, took the situation in hand. He considered that the circumstances called for a postponement of personal authority, in fact for a disguised interregnum. As luck would have it, the very man to fulfil his purpose lay to hand in the next cubicle to his own. A gentle and timid soul, bedridden, decrepit, childish and practically moribund, Cardinal Piccolomini had all the qualities required by Sforza, if not by the Holy Ghost, to make the perfect candidate. Cautiously, after dark, Sforza crept round to his neighbour and, dismissing the weary conclavist who acted as his nurse, offered to sit with the invalid for a while. As soon as they were alone, in feverish whispers, he conveyed to the palsied prelate what was expected of him. The result of his words was surprising. The old man was instantly galvanised into a semblance of vigour. The clouded brain cleared, his response to the call was immediate. Probably well concealed, but tenacious as it is in the hearts of most cardinals, had lain dormant for years the ambition which was to be fulfilled at last, on the brink of the grave.

Sforza was too astute to have any illusions as to his own chances. He had known many vicissitudes since that night eleven years before when Rodrigo Borgia had laid such riches at his feet. His brother had now lost Milan, his family was banished and ruined, he himself had been incarcerated. He was without money or influence, except that of his own personality. He was quick to see the opportunity fate had given him to retrieve something of his fallen fortunes and was not likely to let it slip through his fingers. He had prepared a contract the nature of which made his candidate's election a certainty, and he read it to Piccolomini, who appended his shaky signature to it without a murmur. Sforza, in possession of the precious document, immediately sent messages to his most influential colleagues convening them to a secret meeting. The news leaked out as perhaps it was intended to do. The whole Sacred College, demoralised and irresolute, was thrown into a flutter of expectation. What had that wily Sforza got up his sleeve? When the appointed hour struck, a seething mass of cardinals, d'Amboise among them, were pushing, pressing, panting in their efforts to squeeze into Sforza's cell, all eagerness to know what was afoot. It took Sforza but a few moments to enlighten them. Having made the difficulties of the situation clear, he calmly proposed Piccolomini as "temporary Pope". This was indeed a bombshell. A few cardinals demurred, uncertain of what benefit the arrangement would be to them—but when Sforza exhibited his impressive document duly signed and sealed there was a hush of suspense.

It was indeed a gratifying contract. Not only were they all richly provided for, but their spiritual as well as their temporal welfare had been generously dealt with. By a special clause, marking a welcome innovation, they were all to receive a plenary absolution, without need of confession, for all crimes of any nature whatsoever which they might have committed up to date. A murmur of delighted approbation soon grew into a pæan of jubilation; not only was the devil cheated, which was a shrewd and pleasing stroke of ecclesiastical diplomacy, but the recipients of this favour were also whitewashed in the eyes of the law, a consideration which certainly had its merits. As a compensation for the scurvy way in which the Cardinal d'Amboise had been treated, the hat was bestowed on his nephew; let us hope he thought it an adequate return for his expenditure. The success of the transaction was so overwhelming that Sforza had the greatest difficulty in preventing the Sacred College from electing Piccolomini then and there by "adoration". Only the danger, which he pointed out, of the frail old man dying of excitement on the spot, could restrain their eagerness. The scrutiny took place the next morning and Piccolomini was given every voice but his own. The cardinals rushed to his cell to adore him. He kissed them all on the mouth and chose the name of Pius III. He was carried to St. Peter's and propped against the altar, as he could neither kneel nor stand. When the cortège entered the papal apartments at the Vatican not a bed could be found to lay him on and he had to buy back from the conclavists the furniture of the cell he had just vacated.

The fatigue of the coronation ceremonies proved too great for the aged Pontiff, and he slowly sank and died after a pontificate of twenty-five days.

JULIUS II
From the painting by Raphael in the Uffizi Gallery, Florence

JULIUS II (Della Rovere)
1503-1513

🏵

SEVERAL of the cardinals, amongst them d'Amboise, had thought it
advisable to remain in the Vatican while awaiting the Pontiff's death,
and so had enjoyed every facility and ample leisure to discuss terms
with one another and lay their plans for the coming election. Cesare
Borgia having obtained a safe-conduct from Pius III, had returned
to his apartments in the papal palace and did not fail to make his
presence felt. Although actually less powerful he was scarcely less
feared in Rome, and had also to be reckoned with in the Sacred
College, as no election could be made without the support of the
Spanish cardinals whom he commanded. He was universally detested
and his avowed enemy Orsini clamoured for his head; but his position
was a strong one as Colonna was his ally and as he could also count
on the Commandant of S. Angelo. Rome was now a seething mass
of men-at-arms—retainers of the Colonna or of the Orsini, French
troops, Spanish troops and independent bandits. Before entering into
conclave the Sacred College insisted on all the soldiery evacuating
the city. The various factions obeyed the injunction, all but Borgia,
who ensconced himself in the Castle of S. Angelo certain of impunity.

The cardinals knew for a fact what the result of the election would
be—so much so that they entered the Vatican with no personal effects
but their ceremonial robes. France and Spain had each had their
candidate, but by mutual "exclusion" had reached a stalemate. The
small Italian States were by now reduced to insignificance; Venice
alone retained an influence worth taking into account. Various in-
centives had brought all these conflicting interests to a common
issue resulting in the elevation of Cardinal della Rovere to the Holy
See as Pope Julius II. He was a nephew of Sixtus IV and had been in
his youth an intimate friend of Alexander VI, though he later became
his bitterest enemy. As Cardinal-Nephew he had amassed a large
fortune, and being no spendthrift and a good business man he was
now exceedingly rich. He had bided his time till he considered the

43

moment opportune to come forward, and results proved the accuracy of his judgment. In manner and personality he was a striking contrast to his colleagues. His low birth and early training had left an indelible mark on him. His utterance was rough and coarse, his temper uncontrolled. In an age and country where dissimulation was universal and deception the order of the day, he affected utter directness of speech and had never been known to go back on his word. Alexander VI used to say of him: "Della Rovere has all the vices except duplicity". This original attitude stood him in good stead. It saved him all the time and trouble usually expended on canvassing. To the Cardinal d'Amboise he made it perfectly clear why he could never be elected, and he gained the Frenchman's support by promising to befriend his country, and by conferring on him the legations of France and Avignon. To Sforza he swore to restore his brother to the Duchy of Milan—Borgia's bribes were important. He was to retain the command of the papal troops and be allowed to reconquer the Romagnas; he was also to become Great Penitentiary, to reside in the Vatican, and della Rovere proposed a matrimonial alliance between his own nephew and Borgia's daughter. Colonna was to have a palace in Rome, an abbey, an archbishopric, etc. Spaniards, Venetians, all had their share of gifts and benefices.

Promises had long been at a discount in Rome, but Julian della Rovere's word was as good as his bond, and to this eccentric peculiarity he owed the papal throne. The fisherman's ring duly engraved with his coat of arms was ready when the conclave assembled, so certain was the Sacred College of their unanimity.

There was nothing of the churchman about Julius II. He was completely militant. He faithfully kept his promises as to grants and favours, but was certainly not incapable of deception, for he tricked Cesare Borgia, leading on that dangerous and cunning fiend from pitfall to pitfall until he was finally exiled to die miserably in Spain. Towards France he proved friendly enough so long as he needed her help; but when she had served her purpose he made her expulsion from Italy the aim and object of his life. He was sixty-five at the time of his election and, according to Domenico Travasani, the Venetian envoy, he was gouty and suffered from the effects of the French disease contracted in his youth, but was still vigorous and a hard worker. He was not easily influenced, mostly keeping his own counsel and going his own way. He was abstemious and parsimonious, grudging all expenditure but that devoted to warfare. Although he appreciated Michelangelo's genius he bullied and browbeat him, making the great artist work like a slave and withholding from him even the necessary funds to provide for colours and scaffolding.

He traded on his privileged position to paralyse his foes, who naturally hesitated to lay hands on their Pontiff even when wearing a coat of mail. He sent peremptory orders to Venice to refrain from assisting Bologna when he set out to attack that city, and the Republic obeyed. He commanded assistance from France and Louis XII reluctantly complied. Under the circumstances the fall of Bologna can scarcely be accounted a great military triumph for the papal forces. It was lost to them later by the incapacity of Julius' nephew Urbino and the treachery of his favourite, Cardinal Alidosi. In his infatuation for that worthless creature the Pope completely exonerated him and laid all the blame for the disaster on his nephew. Urbino, enraged at such injustice and meeting Alidosi outside his uncle's residence in Ravenna, dragged him off his horse and ran him through with his sword. Julius II gave way to the most extravagant demonstrations of grief over the death of this contemptible knave, and it seems difficult to attribute such an excess of sorrow to mere friendship. On the journey which he hurriedly undertook to Rimini he could be heard lamenting wildly behind the closely drawn curtains of his litter, while his escort of cardinals rejoiced whole-heartedly at the disappearance of the man they all abhorred.

Julius II inaugurated the fashion for beards. He had let his own grow for the sake of convenience during his campaigns, and Francis I having followed his example, the vogue soon spread all over Europe. It was difficult to discern the Pope in this hirsute, armoured *condottiere*, the self-styled "liberator of Italy" who ruined Venice, imposed the tyrannical Sforzas on Milan, threw the French army on to the Bolognese and never rested until he had destroyed any power in Italy that could rival his own. But where Julius II differed from most popes was in the fact that he loved conquest for conquest's sake, that his ambition was disinterested and independent of personal advantages. His military successes established the security and power of the Holy See, they were not intended for the aggrandisement of his house. He had a daughter and nephews, but having suitably provided for them, he did not strive to exalt them unduly. His was a turbulent, ardent, impetuous nature; not ungenerous to a fallen foe; intensely virile—too impatient to be far-sighted yet not devoid of shrewdness. In his latter years he became obsessed by his hatred of France. As he lay on his deathbed he would continually call out in his delirium: "Out with the French!"

The Romans mourned him. He had been a rough but not an unkind ruler, and compared very favourably in their eyes with his immediate predecessors.

LEO X
From the painting by Raphael in the National Museum, Naples

꧁

WHATEVER the people may have felt about the late Pope's death, to the cardinals at any rate it came as an immense relief. They were weary beyond endurance of the clash of arms, the savage outbursts and the primitive conditions of life to which they had been subjected for so many years. They had strongly resented the inconsiderate manner in which Julius II had burdened them with his own apostolical *corvées*. When he started out on his first campaign for instance, he had expected them to follow the Host, at a foot's pace, along the dusty high-roads of Italy, while he, in whose honour the stately array was devised, took short cuts across the woods mounted on an excellent charger. Another of their grievances against the dead Pontiff was the persistent way in which he had thundered against simony, and considering the manner in which his own election had been conducted his indictment certainly seemed out of place, especially as he continued to sell the cardinalate exactly as his predecessors had done. One can easily understand the prelates' feeling of exasperation, therefore, when on his deathbed he issued a bull making simoniacal elections invalid and attaching every sort of penalty to this crime. They had paid heavily for their hats and were now to be deprived of the benefit of their outlay. They hastily disinterred another bull, one by which Paul II had made it incumbent on every Pope to allow 200 ducats a month to all cardinals whose revenues were below 4000 ducats. As Julius II had failed to observe this regulation they proposed to help themselves to the balance due to them out of the papal treasury, and with arrears it made a goodly sum for each claimant. Julius II had left a large amount of money and magnificent jewels, as valuable as any possessed by his predecessors, and the cardinals expected a rich booty. But the cautious Pontiff had deposited the treasure in the castle of S. Angelo and given strict injunctions to the commandant to hand it over to his successor only. These orders were firmly adhered to by the officer in charge, so the frustrated but helpless cardinals turned their attention to selecting a pope who would compensate them for their disappointment. They longed for a life of ease and culture and material well-being; a life conforming to the ideals of the Renaissance with which they were imbued.

No store was set by anything but wealth and learning in the Italy of the Renaissance. Leisure for intellectual pursuit and the quiet enjoyment of beauty were prized above all things. The invention of printing had helped immensely to disseminate these doctrines, for unlike those of other European countries, all classes in Italy, even the lowest, knew how to read and write. Greek poets were as familiar to men of refinement as were their own native bards. In Florence, where the Medici had originated the movement, and in other small States as well, the people seemed drugged with idealism, dealing more savagely with their would-be liberators than the tyrants themselves could have done. Religious festivals flavoured strongly of pagan rites, and Greek statuary found its way into the holiest precincts. Many deplored this tendency, but Savonarola's attempt to stem the tide of sensualism had cost him his life, and in Italy at least none was bold enough to follow in his footsteps.

The late Pontiff had put an interdict on the Francophile cardinals who had attended the Council of Pisa, so that they were debarred from taking part in the conclave which assembled after his death, and Louis XII feared that their absence might result in the election of another Julius II; but he need have had no anxiety on that score. Italy wanted a Maecenas and the Sacred College intended to find one. In fact the younger cardinals had already done so.

The Emperor Maximilian ingenuously confessed to a desire to become Pope himself. He had written to his daughter Margaret that he intended to refrain from contracting another marriage or even from having carnal intercourse with any woman in the future as he had well-founded hopes of wearing the papal as well as the imperial crown before long. But the Emperor's edifying self-denial availed him not at all. Chastity was at a discount in Rome, the electors valuing in the candidates qualifications of a very different order. Henry VIII and Wolsey favoured the Cardinal of S. Giorgio. England was now taking an active interest in papal affairs, for Henry VIII needed allies in his endeavour to check the growing power of France, and Wolsey coveted the hat, which was a difficult prize for an Englishman to secure.

Twenty-five cardinals entered the conclave. The absence of the French element left practically only two contending parties—the young and the old. The former had secretly settled on Giovanni de Medici; the second openly supported S. Giorgio, England's candidate. The first few days were spent by the Sacred College on the usual preliminaries, regulations and capitulations, mere pretexts for gaining time and throwing out cautious feelers. On the first Sunday following their entrance into conclave, while the cardinals attended High Mass Medici was under the surgeon's knife. He had brought his own medical attendants with him as he was suffering from a fistula "in a part of his person", says Varillas, "that decency forbids one to mention". Had it not been for his youth, it is likely that Medici would have been unanimously elected at once as he had all the qualifications required by circumstances, but the aged cardinals objected to his elevation. They considered that it would be an indignity for them to be ruled by a Pope of thirty-seven, and they would, besides, be signing away for ever any chances they might have of wearing the crown themselves, and that was too bitter a pill to swallow voluntarily. In the city the betting on the candidates was feverish. The odds were posted up at the Banchi as they are at a race-meeting, Medici rising to 25 while his competitor remained steadily at 15. The Sacred College had been assembled almost a week before the first serious scrutiny took place. Many of the cardinals, wishing to temporise and conceal their real intentions, had voted for the man they considered least likely to have any supporters. As luck would have it thirteen prelates had selected the same outsider, with the result that they all but elected Arborense, the most worthless nonentity present. This narrow shave gave the Sacred College such a shock that its members determined to come to some agreement which would put matters on a more satisfactory basis for both parties. In consequence Medici and S. Giorgio had a prolonged interview. As neither of them could manage to throw his adversary they agreed to fight it out between them, allowing their supporters no stray voting.

Meanwhile the custodians of the conclave were exercising most unwonted vigilance, amounting almost to sharp practice. Had they not, without a word of warning, cut a bell-rope communicating with the lower floor of the palace and along which a cord was slipped, continually carrying notes backwards and forwards between the inmates of the conclave and the outer world? Following on this first outrage they gave orders that the cardinals' meals were to be sent in earthenware containers and allowed no plate whatever to enter the conclave, as they had found a silver dish belonging to the English cardinal Bainbridge with the words "S. Giorgio or Medici" scratched upon it with a knife. The young party grew restive; the confinement and the impossibility of attending to their personal cleanliness exasperated them.   Still the two rivals struggled grimly on.   Slowly but surely Medici was gaining ground.

His doctors and his conclavists looked daily more troubled and dejected. It was evident that they took a very serious view of their patron's state of health. They confided to their colleagues under the strictest injunctions of secrecy that his scar would not heal and might at any moment become gangrenous. The trouble anyhow was incurable and might lead to fatal complications. The older cardinals nibbled at the bait. They watched with growing interest the frequent visits Medici's physicians paid to his cell; the patient's air of languor and fatigue. They were tamer, but still shy, and the proceedings might have dragged on for many a weary day had not Soderini, one of their leaders, suddenly resolved to clinch the matter. He was a Florentine like Medici, but of an enemy faction and had so far shown himself an obstinate opponent of the younger man's. His official visit to Medici's cell therefore caused intense excitement. The reason for Soderini's unexpected move was much discussed. Some said that the abrupt cutting of the bell-rope had interfered with the progress of an amorous intrigue and left him in a state of uncertainty which was driving him frantic: others thought that he simply saw more personal advantage in befriending his compatriot than in fighting S. Giorgio's losing battles. Whatever the cause, the result of his alliance with Medici completely turned the scales in that prince's favour.

Medici, realising how much he had to gain by Soderini's support, had received him with the greatest show of affability. He undertook to see the Soderinis reinstated in Florence, from which they had been exiled, and proposed a matrimonial alliance between one of his nephews and Soderini's niece. The satisfaction was mutual. Soderini's influence over the elder party ended the struggle. The next day Medici was elected and took the name of Leo X. The change of régime the cardinals had so much thirsted for had at last come to pass.

Leo X did not trouble to wear pontifical robes any more than Julius II had done, but his was not a martial accoutrement. Dressed in the richest silks and velvets as were the princes of his day, ablaze with jewels, delicately perfumed, he held his court in true Medicean style. Surrounded by the most beautiful women, by all the great artists and poets who have made his pontificate so famous, he would while away the hot summer days in the gardens of one or another of the papal villas. Under the shade of the ilex groves, or beside the splashing fountains, his courtiers grouped around him, he would discourse on philosophical subjects or dream through the hours to the sound of exquisite music. In other seasons the Pontiff would repair to his country estates to hunt or fish or go hawking, all princely pursuits to which he had been brought up. He led the life of a sybarite on whom fortune has showered all her choicest gifts.

His court was the most splendid and polished in Italy. He moved in a perpetual pageant of magnificence, a succession of masquerades, carnivals, plays and dancing. He was utterly disarmed by a timely jest, and would forgive any crime redeemed by a witty sally. He delighted in his jesters, of whom he had several, and loved comedies and buffooneries even of the crudest kinds. Being immune from retaliation the Pontiff had, like so many other princes, a great weakness for practical jokes. He would laugh uproariously when he had induced his guests to eat the flesh of a monkey or of a carrion crow cunningly disguised by exquisite sauces. He derived much amusement from their discomfiture when they were informed of the true nature of these dishes, and from their evident reluctance to partake of any further dainties. Leo made no pretence of piety or even of reverence. He encouraged the most unorthodox discussions on religious subjects, such as the immortality of the soul, which was the favourite theme of the classicists. He publicly embraced Aretino and Ariosto, the most licentious poets Italy has ever known, so carried away was he by his admiration for their genius.

He was charming, plausible and open-handed. But munificence is costly. The treasure left by Julius II had been entirely squandered on the spectacular display of Leo's coronation, the most lavish and sumptuous ever witnessed in Rome. As a son of Lorenzo the Magnificent and a Florentine, he wished to show the Romans what splendour really was, and no doubt he succeeded. They were soon indeed to learn that this amiable smiling prince was first and foremost a Medici and a Florentine. As a Medici he determined to make as many States of Italy as could be seized, bought or conquered, subservient to Florence. His internal and external policies were consistently directed to that end, he really knew no other. As a Florentine he concealed behind a gentle manner and a winning smile a surprising fund of Machiavellian duplicity. England, France, Germany, he betrayed them all as fast as he treated with them. The Italian rulers fared no better at his hands; even those who had befriended his house in its hour of need were tricked and despoiled by him to add to the might of the Medici. He needed money of course, masses of it. Besides the traditional sources of papal revenue such as the sale of hats and other ecclesiastical dignities he farmed out indulgences, so that they were openly staked for in gambling hells in Germany and elsewhere.

But other measures had to be devised to supply means for his stupendous prodigality, and he conceived a novel and most lucrative method of replenishing his ever-leaking coffers. Amongst other nobles dispossessed by him in favour of Florence was Borghese, Lord of Sienna, a brother of Cardinal Petrucci, one of his most ardent supporters at the conclave. Naturally indignant at such ingratitude and treachery, the cardinal had left Rome to assist his brother and had probably in his resentment spoken too openly of his feelings towards the Pope. It is not impossible, considering the mentality of the times, that he seriously considered being revenged on Leo by poison. Be that as it may, the Pontiff sent him honeyed words of forgiveness and a safe-conduct with orders to return to Rome. Petrucci rashly complied, and having left his armed escort outside the Vatican, presented himself in the Pope's audience chamber. He was immediately seized and imprisoned in S. Angelo, where he underwent most terrible tortures. His attendants were also submitted to the question and confessed to being privy to a plot of their master's to poison the Pontiff.

A reign of terror then began for the Sacred College. Daily the name of some prelate was wrung from the lips of the agonised wretches and a new victim was added to the list. One after the other, these alleged confederates were called before Leo X and, terrified at the idea of the fate that awaited them, would throw themselves on his mercy, offering him their entire fortunes in exchange for their freedom. Some he exiled after despoiling them, like Soderini to whom he owed the crown, others fled in a panic abandoning all their possessions and led a miserable existence in foreign lands, where a few died in abject poverty. There is no reason to think that any of them had ever conspired against the Pope, or that Leo X can have seriously believed in their guilt. Petrucci was strangled in his prison. His unfortunate servants had an even less merciful fate. They were dragged through the streets of Rome and their flesh was torn from their bones with red-hot pincers before they were hung on the bridge of S. Angelo. What remained of the Sacred College was far too scared to offer even the most timid remonstrance when Leo X announced his intention of creating thirty-one new cardinals entirely devoted to the Medicean interests. They humbly acquiesced.

Leo X's unexpected death naturally gave rise to suspicions of poison. It was always a popular verdict, pleasantly exciting to the public, and where the medical profession was concerned served much the same purpose as the familiar heart-failure of modern days. This Pope showed no inclination to receive the sacraments during the few hours of his last illness. Some historians accuse him of having been an unbeliever and he certainly died like one, to the great scandal of the Roman people, who escorted his body with curses and forcible expressions of contempt. The glamour of the Renaissance at its apogee so envelops the figure of this Pontiff that he has been endowed with all its glory, just as that of Alexander VI has been charged with all the odium of his own times. But the veneer of civilisation was only superficial. Under the exquisite culture and flowery garlands the essentials had not altered. Live and let live, which appeared to be the motto of the cultured, only applied with Leo X, as with all his contemporaries, to strictly impersonal matters. The cardinals, who had felt so aggrieved at the life of turmoil which Julius II had imposed on them, must have thought with regret of the coarse and rugged soldier, when they fled from the clutches of the refined and suave Pontiff to whom they had looked so confidently for riches and content. Henry VIII, Francis I and Charles V all knew him for what he was worth, and this knowledge perhaps explains why the Emperor, good Catholic as he was, treated Luther with so much leniency.

Leo X's death caused widespread ruin in Rome. He had borrowed from all those he could not bleed, and his debts amounted to 800,000 ducats. His sister who lived in the Vatican got away with whatever jewels she could lay hands on, and stark bankruptcy confronted the Holy See.

ADRIAN VI (Florent)

1522–1523

NEVER had the Sacred College been faced with a situation of such utter penury. The Vatican furniture was pawned and a few thousand ducats borrowed from the banker Chigi to pay the soldiery, as Medici, the nephew of the late Pope, was in residence at the Vatican with a bodyguard 500 strong and the cardinals scarcely considered that force a protection to themselves. No money whatever was available for the expenses of Leo X's obsequies and so none was spent. The candles, even, were the remnants of those used at Cardinal S. Giorgio's funeral, which had taken place the previous day. Had that prelate survived a few weeks longer he would certainly have worn the crown which Leo X had wrested from him. He was immensely wealthy and far too cunning to have allowed himself to be caught in the Medicean nets as so many of his colleagues had been. He never left his palace without an armed escort of 400 men and several less powerful cardinals lived entirely under his protection. His influence at the conclave would naturally have been preponderating and he was an irreparable loss to the older party.

A reasonable delay had to be allowed for those cardinals who were abroad to reach Rome, so that the conclave assembled a few days later than it should have done. It was anything but a friendly gathering. "There cannot be so much hatred and so many devils in hell as among these cardinals", the imperial envoy informed his master, and indeed the enmity of the factions seemed unusually bitter. Although the finances of the Holy See were in such a parlous state, candidates for the Papacy were not lacking. Out of the thirty-nine cardinals who entered the conclave on December 28th fifteen were partisans of Medici and twenty-three opposed him. But amongst the latter, eighteen coveted the papal crown themselves, a state of things which would probably lead to a protracted conclave the result of which was hard to foretell. At first Medici's chances seemed to increase, but he lacked the necessary funds to rally a sufficient number

55

of adherents and he had also to reckon with Soderini. During his exile Leo X's victim had had ample time to brood over his wrongs, and he had returned with such a store of hatred and such a thirst for revenge, that nothing could be more delectable to him than to thwart a Medici. His influence was great on the opposing faction and soon destroyed any chance Medici might have had of rallying any supporters from among their ranks. England had great hopes that Cardinal Wolsey's candidature would be successful. Cardinal Campeggio, who was in charge of his interests at the conclave, wrote him the most encouraging and optimistic letters, while in reality he was furthering no cause but his own, and knew perfectly well that a foreigner of Wolsey's overbearing disposition would never be even considered as "papabile" by the Sacred College. Much against his will Leo X had given him the hat. It had been a duel of wits between the two men and Wolsey had won, but Cardinal Bainbridge had made the English very unpopular in Rome and Wolsey's reputation was not calculated to improve matters.

The Emperor Charles favoured Adrian Florent, his former tutor; he was not attending the conclave and the cardinals knew nothing about him except that he was Flemish by birth and Charles' viceroy and Grand Inquisitor in Spain. Among the numerous names put forward tentatively were: Grimani, a typical Venetian of the old school—a profound politician, a scientist, a man of unblemished reputation, but too stern and unbending; Flisco, archbishop of Ravenna, whose greatest ambition in life was to coin money bearing his own effigy; Farnese, a convicted forger, known as "the petticoat cardinal", who had been liberated from prison and given the hat by Alexander VI on the instance of his beautiful sister Julia Farnese, with whom the Pope was infatuated; the Cardinal of Mantova, the most obese member of the Sacred College, whose passion in life was food in general and oysters in particular; Colonna, a regular *condottiere* who divided his time between fighting and love-making and who was later to sack the Vatican and occupy by force of arms the palace he had wished to reign over as Pontiff; Egidio, a rigid disciplinarian whose *idée fixe* was a crusade against the Turks. There were other competitors also, too numerous and uninteresting to be worth mentioning; but all, whether important or insignificant, were inacceptable to the majority—many of them also had large families to provide for, which was always a handicap, though the encumbrance was so general that it was almost looked upon as an inevitable evil.

The voting was so scattered at the first scrutinies that Medici soon realised the hopelessness of his own cause and declared himself openly for Farnese. The opposition appeared undecided and their votes fluctuated wildly. Grimani sought and obtained a permit to leave the conclave on the grounds of ill-health. Many thought this move a silent protest against the probable election of the infamous "petticoat cardinal". Several days went by without any headway being made and the provisions of wood and candles had to be renewed. It was bitterly cold in the Vatican and the faint grey daylight failed to penetrate the gloom of the great apartments, so small were the apertures allowed above the boarded window-panes, and the immured crowd of cardinals and conclavists lived in perpetual darkness.

At the Banchi, Farnese was favourite, and considering the state of bewilderment and irresolution of the Sacred College his election might very well have been carried by some bold stroke; but his partisans had not sufficient tactical experience to rush the defences, and his exceptionally shady past added to their difficulties. He gained ground very slowly therefore, but sufficiently to incite Cardinal Cesarini to send a message to the Banchi with an order to back Farnese for 1000 ducats. The news soon spread and a few more electors rallied to his support. Seeing that the situation was really perilous, Egidio then stepped forward and openly harangued the Sacred College on the outrage it would be to Christendom if they elected a man of Farnese's antecedents to occupy the Apostolic See. He reminded them of his shameful and felonious past, and to the list of his crimes, with which they were already acquainted, he added other and more secret ones of which they had been ignorant. He asked them what trust they could put in a forger to fulfil his engagements, and this argument had probably far greater weight with them than the knowledge of his villainy. As Egidio was highly respected and had been Farnese's confessor at one time, they never doubted the truth of his assertions and the wisdom of his advice. Farnese's supporters dwindled immediately to an insignificant minority, and the voting became as erratic and aimless as it had been at first.

The old cardinals were determined not to be duped by the younger ones this time and steadily opposed whatever candidate they brought forward. The situation seemed to have reached a deadlock. The aged prelates suffered terribly from the cold; the younger ones, many of whom were attending their first conclave, were driven desperate by the gloom and uncleanliness. This was the auspicious moment chosen by Cardinal S. Sisto to come forward with a letter from the Emperor expressing his wishes for the election of Adrian Florent. Amongst all the names, likely and unlikely, read out at the scrutinies his had never once been heard. He was quite unknown in Rome, therefore he had at least no enemies. The older cardinals were all anxious to be in Charles' good graces, and much impressed with what S. Sisto had to tell them of Adrian's virtues and ability. S. Sisto being an influential member of their own party they readily accepted his advice, slyly rejoicing at the idea of giving the younger cardinals a Pope they would probably detest. To win over Medici and his followers was a harder task, but S. Sisto accomplished it by hinting that the new reign would in all probability be a short one, and by informing Medici that he was empowered by the Emperor to offer him a pension of 10,000 ducats and a promise of his support at the next conclave. Without enthusiasm, but seeing no better solution, Medici accepted the bargain and Adrian Florent was proclaimed Pope.

The people received this surprising announcement with hoots and hisses. The cardinals themselves seemed troubled and perplexed by what they had done, and slunk home escorted by the curses of the mob. Placards were hung on the Vatican bearing the words "Palace to let", and Rome was flooded with indecent caricatures and lampoons directed against the Sacred College. Three delegates were sent to notify Adrian of his elevation, and in due course letters arrived from Spain informing the cardinals that His Holiness had chosen to keep his own name, which was a breach of papal etiquette and met with general disapproval.

During the interregnum three cardinals ruled the State in rotation for the period of a month, so they found some compensation for the odium they had incurred, and no doubt made full use of their opportunities. It was not till the end of August 1522 that Adrian VI, escorted by a fleet of fourteen galleys supplied by the Emperor, sailed into the port of Civita Vecchia. He was accompanied by a thousand Spanish and Flemish attendants, besides the cardinals who had joined him at Livorno a couple of days before. The plague then raging in

Rome had seemed an excellent excuse to the Sacred College for omitting all the usual costly reception festivities, and Adrian VI entered the Vatican with as little pomp and ostentation as he could well have wished. His unobtrusive modesty did not extend, however, to his dealings with the cardinals, as he allowed them to kiss his feet three times while wearing their hats and stoles at his first reception, and to repeat the same performance in St. Peter's. It was customary for the Pontiff to raise the prelates after the first osculation and offer his hand and cheek in succession. This Adrian did not do and his unbending attitude was much resented.

A régime was now inaugurated in the Vatican the like of which had not been seen or even dreamed of since the earliest days of the Papacy. Adrian was the son of a Flemish ship's-carpenter and had risen to eminence entirely through his own merit and learning. He had been chosen for his great qualities and blameless life to be tutor to Charles V, who had always held him in great veneration and later entrusted him with an office of the highest responsibility in Spain. The Pontiff had always led the rigid life of a devout monk and saw no reason to alter his habits. He rose at dawn to say his Mass after only a few hours of sleep, broken by attendance at Matins. He was as temperate and frugal as an anchorite, and had imported an old Flemish housekeeper who cooked his simple meals, cleaned out his room, and did his washing; while two Spanish page-boys waited on him at table. Every evening the Pope carefully extracted one crown from his purse which he handed to the disgusted major-domo for the next day's catering, and under no pretext was he permitted to exceed this allowance. While the papal laundry was spread out to dry in the august apartments of the Vatican, the Pope himself was ensconced in a small bare study where no one dared disturb him. Although he seemed to set great store by Cardinal Medici's opinions, he never admitted him to any sort of intimacy, and all the other cardinals were kept distinctly at arm's-length.

Adrian VI was of a silent, retiring disposition, fond of study and solitude. He was slow in his movements and still slower in his speech. He invariably spoke Latin, but with such a "barbarous" pronunciation that it was practically unintelligible to Italians. His own familiars were all Flemish and his advisers quite unused to secular business and out of touch with their new surroundings. He himself was completely lacking in worldly wisdom and sympathy. His hard, morose countenance, his taciturnity, repelled and alarmed the Romans. He was stiff without being dignified. There was too much of the Grand Inquisitor and too little of the Sovereign about him. He was no statesman—besides, prayer and study left him little leisure to attend to affairs of the State. He lacked confidence in his own judgment and his invariable answer to all questions was "We will see". His circumspection was such that *any* decision seemed to him fraught with danger and all matters were allowed to drift.

One would imagine that such an upright, virtuous Pope would have restored dignity to the Holy See, and by suppressing abuses and scandal have gained universal admiration and respect. Yet it was not so. The simple mode of life adopted by Adrian VI was utterly out of keeping with his environment and called forth nothing but derision and abuse. He was intensely shocked by the profanity of Renaissance art, and threatened to whitewash the Sixtine Chapel and throw the Laocoon into the Tiber. All the superfluous officials, with whose services he had dispensed, added to the ever-increasing throng of his dissatisfied and recriminating subjects. As to dealing with the corruption in the Sacred College he simply did not know where to begin. He could not in justice prevent the cardinals from reaping the benefits of their position without refunding them the money they had spent on the purchase of their hats, which he was far too poor to do —nor could he drastically renounce the revenues from the sale of indulgences without making it impossible for the Holy See to face its obligations. On every side he was beset with difficulties he was quite unable to cope with. He fell back on details, ordering the young cardinals to shave their beards and lead a better life; but all his efforts at raising the moral standard of the Sacred College met with a concerted resistance, a power of hostile inertia which completely defeated him. His own example carried no weight whatever. He was considered a miser in Rome and a meddlesome fool abroad.

He knew nothing of European politics. His mission, he thought, consisted in preaching peace to the Christian princes, and he antagonised all the Sovereigns, even his patron Charles V, by his perpetual efforts to induce them to kiss and be friends and run off together and fight the Turks; quite oblivious of the fact that they were fully occupied wrestling with their private difficulties and national rivalries, and wanted help, not advice.

He never grasped the Italian mentality nor the intricacies of internal politics. He longed for a state of things that would allow him to indulge his theological pursuits in the quiet retreat of his study; but the cold, contemptuous tone adopted by his former pupil at last made him understand that such a dream was impossible, and he reluctantly allowed himself to be dragged into the league against France. Adrian VI is a pathetic figure floundering helplessly in an entanglement of misunderstandings. He was not even given credit for his austerity. Creighton tells us that when the Pope was dying the cardinals hastened to his deathbed, not to receive his last blessing, but to demand where he had hidden his treasure. They were convinced that the simplicity of Adrian's habits was due to avarice, and urged him to reveal where he had hidden his hoard. Vainly did he assure them that his entire possessions consisted of one thousand ducats; with growing anger they returned to their cross-questioning, and treated the Pope as though he were a criminal on the rack. The Duke of Sessa had to interfere to put an end to this hideous scene, and the cardinals at last withdrew, defeated but still incredulous. When a few hours later the Pontiff passed away, the news was greeted with a universal sigh of relief. The most disappointing and disappointed of popes was mourned by no one but his Flemish attendants, and a statue was erected in due course to his doctor, Maserata, inscribed with the words "Liberatori Patriae!"

CLEMENT VII
From the painting by del Piombo in the National Museum, Naples

CLEMENT VII (Medici)

1523–1534

❧

THE crowd that gathered about the cardinals as they entered the conclave after Adrian's death voiced its feelings without a shade of reticence. The people would not put up with another foreign pope.

The Romans announced their intention, if the Sacred College proved dilatory, of battering in the Vatican doors and assisting them forcibly to make up their minds. The cardinals bolted into the conclave like frightened rabbits into a warren. The menacing attitude of the mob lent their unattractive cubicles a welcome air of safety, and the electors showed no reluctance whatever at being immured. Thirty-four cardinals entered the conclave on October 1st; on the 3rd, news was brought that the Duke of Ferrara had seized Reggio, a Papal town, and was preparing to occupy Modena. Bankers were hastily summoned, and through the wicket terms were agreed upon for money to be sent at once to the menaced city to prepare it for defence. On October 6th three French cardinals arrived, so anxious to be in time to lend support to their party, that they did not even wait to change their clothes, but rode straight to the Vatican and demanded admittance. These travel-stained, booted and spurred prelates were received with disapproving glances by the custodians, who, however, had no choice but to usher them in. The Cardinal of Lorraine was wearing a crane-coloured velvet suit and a feathered hat which he discarded before entering. The French faction was jubilant at a reinforcement which they had not hoped for so early in the proceedings. Their party now numbered twenty-two, as Soderini had been liberated from S. Angelo to join the ranks of Medici's enemies. He had foolishly allowed himself to be caught red-handed in a plot to deliver Naples to the French, and Adrian VI had, on the advice of Medici, incarcerated him and deprived him of his right to vote at the conclave; but the majority of cardinals had insisted on his release, and so the late Pope's decree had been simply ignored.

The French party was subdivided into groups and lacked cohesion.

Most of their Italian adherents had merely joined forces with them through hatred for Medici. Colonna was their leader and was well supported by Soderini. At a meeting in Colonna's cell his followers had bound themselves by a solemn oath not to elect Medici under any circumstances whatsoever. England still believed in the possibility of Wolsey's elevation and was distributing large sums of money among the electors. France was backing Monti or Farnese, and being quite ignorant of all the complexities of the situation, considered that the one or the other of her candidates was certain of success. The Emperor Charles had been as good as his word and was supporting Medici. The Spanish party, though only commanding seventeen votes, was really the strongest of the two, because it was united by a single purpose and could be absolutely trusted to remain staunch. As by October 8th the Sacred College had not even begun to vote seriously, the Romans prepared to put their threats into execution, and clamoured loudly for the enforcement of the regulations concerning the cardinals' meals. By October 25th Monti had collected nineteen votes and the French party was exultant. But Medici damped their spirits by declaring that a pope could not be made without him, and that he and his seventeen followers would sooner die in the Vatican than abandon their aim. In a few hours all Rome was informed how matters stood, and the Banchi were now offering odds on the length of the conclave instead of on the candidates.

The city magistrates again approached the custodians and insisted on the application of all the most rigorous measures obsolete or otherwise. On October 28th a great sensation was caused in the Vatican by the four chief French cardinals appearing at the turnstile and protesting against the excessive severity of their seclusion. They appealed to the officers for freedom to take exercise in the Belvedere gardens for two hours every morning and two hours every afternoon; and indeed their request was not unreasonable, as the conclavists, who considered that money was not free enough at this conclave, neglected their duties disgracefully. Most of the cells were in a repulsive state of filth and the general atmosphere more unbearably fetid than usual. The custodians called a meeting of the ambassadors, clergy, barons and Roman gentry, and the conclave was officially suspended for twenty-four hours, during which a deputation visited the premises. The result of this sanitary inspection was not only a refusal to grant the four hours' outing requested, but a general tightening-up of all restrictions. This of course was disappointing, but if they failed to obtain the fresh air they craved for, the cardinals got something else in exchange. With the deputation news of the greatest moment had penetrated into the conclave. In Northern Italy, where the armies of Charles V and Francis I were fighting, the French appeared to be losing ground and were retreating from Monza. It seemed infinitely preferable to be on the winning side and there were several immediate defections among Monti's half-hearted supporters.

The leaders of the French party then proposed Farnese, but without much success, and the middle of November still found the situation of the two parties apparently unchanged. The mob had several times made hostile demonstrations outside the Vatican, but the Medici partisans, who were well organised in Rome, had held the rioters in check. Meanwhile Colonna, who hated Farnese, was manœuvring to bring forward a third candidate who he hoped would be acceptable to both parties, Cardinal Jacobacci. The French faction feigned acquiescence to his proposal, and he then decided to get into touch with Medici. He argued that an election of sorts must be made and that an outsider was the only solution. Medici, seemingly convinced, made no objection, only laying down one condition. He would give Jacobacci the votes he needed, if Colonna would guarantee that in the event of Jacobacci's failure his party would support Medici's. Colonna gave a written promise to that effect and the enemies parted on the best of terms. Medici had every reason to be satisfied, as he knew, by one of the French cardinals' conclavists who was in his pay, that the Cardinal de Lorraine though appearing to approve of Jacobacci had secretly given orders to his subordinates to vote against him; and so now the old fox Colonna was trapped at last!

When at the next scrutiny Jacobacci's name failed to reach the necessary majority Colonna's fury knew no bounds. He turned on the French cardinals in a paroxysm of rage, reproaching them for their treachery and deceit, and became so violent that he was with difficulty restrained from assaulting them. Medici looked on quietly with a smile of satisfaction. Certainly Colonna's situation was unenviable. He had incited his party to take a solemn oath not to vote for Medici under any circumstances on the one hand, and he had signed an undertaking to support his election on the other.

For three whole days Colonna debated and deliberated, wondering which of the two pledges to break; then on the evening of November 18th news reached the conclave that the Imperialists had inflicted a crushing defeat on the French, which produced an immediate reaction in Medici's favour. Colonna and his followers hesitated no longer: they repaired to the chapel and released one another from their vow by mutual absolution. The next day, after a conclave lasting seven weeks, Medici was elected Pope and adopted the name of Clement VII. Each cardinal received one thousand ducats; Colonna was given the vice-chancellorship and the Riario palace, and Soderini was restored to all his possessions.

By rights Clement VII should never have received the hat, as he was of illegitimate birth, which made him non-eligible; but Leo X considered that half a Medici was any man's equal. Documents had been forthcoming which somehow or other satisfied the Sacred College, and this minor accident had not been allowed to stand in his nephew's way. The Roman people were jubilant over Clement's election; they hailed with acclamations the restorer of familiar pageants and festivities, little knowing the horrors and desolation which were awaiting them under this promising pontificate.

It was soon apparent that if the new Pope had ever deserved the reputation for wisdom and political sagacity which he had earned during the reign of Leo X, he had lost all claim to these qualities on becoming his own master. His policy consisted merely in being evasive and sitting on the fence between the French and the Imperialists, and when he found he could do so no longer he chose the alliance with Francis I because he feared above all things the council which the Emperor wished to assemble and he dared not face. He had not sufficient gratitude to remain loyal to the Emperor to whom he owed his elevation, nor enough foresight to grasp where his advantage lay. Charles V was naturally indignant when he saw what line of conduct the Pope had chosen, openly accusing him of poltroonery; and he even came surprisingly near to wishing Luther good luck. At the battle of Pavia in 1525 the French were completely routed and Francis I made a prisoner. Charles V was now master of all Northern Italy and Clement at his mercy. But the Pope had other enemies besides the Emperor. He had so mismanaged his old foe Colonna that their feud brought about the looting of the Vatican and of several papal churches by the Colonnesi in 1526.

It is no wonder that Clement VII's name is held in greater execration by Italians than that of any other Pontiff, for he himself was directly responsible for the sack of Rome, the appalling and devastating catastrophe which left its mark on the beautiful city for all time, and the horrors of which can never be forgotten. And yet Clement, judged by ordinary standards, was a far better man than most of his contemporaries. Quiet, unassuming, learned, it was not surprising that great hopes had been placed on him—but his qualities were all negative. He was timid, vacillating and small-minded. Drawn by the force of circumstances into the vortex of European politics, he proved himself an incapable ruler, and when he had wrecked the splendid ship he piloted and it was foundering in deep waters, he overlooked the sheet anchors and clutched at straws with childish tenacity. He was indeed only half a Medici. He had none of the magnificence and self-assurance of those princes. He was mean and diffident. The only object he pursued with any continuity of purpose was the establishment of his illegitimate children, but even there he was blundering and futile. Experience taught him nothing. Although he had had to take refuge in S. Angelo when Colonna had raided the Vatican, he still clung to a puerile belief in his inviolability and, having taken no steps whatever for the defence of the city, was waiting quietly in the palace, hoping for the best, while the imperial troops led by Bourbon were actually scaling the walls of Rome. He was rushed through the private passage to the fortress only just in time to escape capture—while the equally optimistic but now panic-stricken cardinals, who had delayed till the last moment to seek shelter, were fighting and scrambling to gain admittance at the gates. When the guards were ordered to drop the portcullis many of the prelates were left struggling outside. Cardinal Pucci, who had been knocked down and injured, was pushed in through a window by his attendants and Armellino was hoisted in a basket on to the battlements. The remainder were left to their fate, and an unenviable one it was.

The occupation of Rome by the barbarian hordes lasted seven months. What, one wonders, can have been the feelings of Clement VII when he caught a glimpse from the fortress of the devastation and sufferings his incapacity had brought upon the city?

When Colonna, Bourbon's ally, entered Rome with his followers he was so awestruck at the sight which met his gaze that, forgetting all past differences and remembering only that he was a Roman, he sent a message to the Pope offering to clear out the intruders and to restore the city to the Holy See. But Clement refused his proffered aid. He preferred to see Rome in the clutches of the Imperialists sooner than to owe its release to Colonna. Meanwhile events were happening in Florence the news of which touched the Pontiff on the raw. The Florentines had overthrown the Medici and proclaimed a republic. Carducci, their gonfalonier, had proposed the election of Jesus Christ as perpetual sovereign of the city. The ensuing ballot had been favourable to the divine candidate, against whom, however, twenty votes had been recorded. The following proclamation was then issued: "Jesus Christ, King of the Florentines, elected by a decree of the people and senate".

The usurpation of his family's prerogatives by this unexpected competitor caused the Pope the most painful surprise. It would appear that he felt this celestial *coup d'état* far more deeply than the sack of Rome or the length and hardships of his captivity, for when it came to discussing terms with the Emperor, he showed much more anxiety to recover Florence for his house than to regain the papal estates for the Holy See. He absolved the imperial troops of all the crimes and atrocities committed by them in Rome and sent them to wreak his vengeance on the Florentines, whose envoys he excommunicated and refused to receive. Florence put up a heroic resistance and held her own for almost a year, but reduced by famine and pestilence, with no allies to give her a helping hand, her downfall was inevitable. She surrendered against a promise of general amnesty from Clement. The Florentines must have known what value to set on it, but they had no choice. The Medici Pope's vengeance was ruthless, and he continued to vent his rancour on the unfortunate citizens during the remaining years of his pontificate, setting far greater store by his family fortunes than by the important issues then at stake in Christendom. Peter's barque was indeed on the rocks and ominously near disruption.

Most of Germany had thrown off the papal yoke, and England had followed her example. It had now become impossible for Clement, who was completely at the Emperor's mercy, to grant Henry VIII the divorce he sought. Charles V, Katherine of Aragon's nephew, could no longer be defied. So Henry broke with Rome, and Clement's excommunication left him unscathed and indifferent. The Church of Rome was now incalculably lowered in authority and prestige, but the Pope did not seem unduly troubled. Up to the last his interests centred in the Medici, and the marriage of his niece Catherine to the son of Francis I filled him with joy and pride; he died with the calm satisfaction of one who has achieved success.

The Romans adopted a primitive method of expressing their contempt and execration for the man who had thrown them to the wolves. If it had not been for the late Pontiff's nephew, Cardinal Medici, whose power was still to be reckoned with, it is likely that Clement's body would have been subjected to every indignity and his monument destroyed. As it was, his tomb had to be cleansed every morning of the pollutions with which it was defaced every night, and a painter kept perpetually at work renewing the inscription. Finally the lettering was cut into the marble; an unnecessary precaution against oblivion, for the name of Clement VII, the Pope responsible for the sack of Rome, is indelibly printed across one of the most ghastly pages of history.

PAUL III AND HIS GRANDSONS
From the painting by Titian in the National Museum, Naples

PAUL III (FARNESE)
1534–1549

❧

TIME had proved to be the "petticoat cardinal's" best friend. So many other and newer scandals, so many important and all-obliterating events had taken place since Cardinal Egidio had made his pitiless indictment against him to the Sacred College, that he felt he could now safely come forward as a serious candidate to the Apostolic See. He had been present at five papal elections and was far too astute not to have benefited by so much experience. He knew the advantage of entering the conclave with an imposing number of avowed supporters and set about collecting them as soon as Clement was dead. Circumstances were all in his favour.

The most important leader to win over was certainly the Cardinal-Nephew—Medici. He disposed of the numerous phalanx of the late Pope's creatures, and whoever could count on their votes was as good as elected. Farnese knew that Medici hated and envied his cousin Alexander, ruler of Florence, and intended to despoil him at the first opportunity. He therefore approached his colleague with a deed ready drawn up, signed and sealed, by which he undertook, in exchange for Medici's support, to give him Ancona with the legation of the Marches, and to help him with all the power a pope could dispose of, to obtain possession of the State of Florence. Moreover, if Cardinal Medici decided to renounce priesthood, Farnese would not only give him all necessary dispensations, but would bestow on him the hand of his daughter Victoria with a regal dowry.

To the Emperor, Farnese sent a solemn assurance that his first thought would be the convening of the council which had been such a bugbear to his predecessor. But Charles V professed himself completely disinterested in the result of the conclave. He had been so disappointed in the two Popes he had helped to make that he probably thought that the Sacred College could do no worse if left to its own devices. Besides, he had now assumed a semi-spiritual authority himself, and affected an attitude of patronising contempt for the Vicar of Christ. He gave no definite instructions to his Roman agents, merely exhorting them to do their best to secure the election of a good pope.

The French party were not opposed to Farnese, especially as Trivulzi, the leader of the pro-French group of Italian cardinals, seemed disposed in his favour. Trivulzi's main object was to secure the election of a pope who would have a short pontificate, as he fully intended to step into his shoes. Farnese, who was aware of the prelate's ambition, made the most of his age and infirmities, also promising to pave the way for Trivulzi to succeed him. Farnese was then sixty-eight and appeared anything but robust. He was bent almost double and walked with great difficulty. His face was positively cadaverous and his breathing laboured. It would have been indeed difficult to find a more suitable candidate. Although his election seemed assured, Farnese was far too old a hand at the game to overlook the importance of details. He knew, better than any, how slippery were the steps leading up to the pontifical throne and how easily a mere trifle might spell success or failure. So when all the Sacred College had assembled in the chapel, after the opening of the conclave, and the Cardinal-Dean was just prostrating himself before the altar, the stillness was broken by the rhythmic tap-tap of a stick on the marble flags. Cardinal Farnese was making his well-staged entry. In the doorway he faltered as though about to drop, with such an expression of lassitude and helplessness, that the nearest cardinals sprang forward to support him and assist him into his stall. The sight of such utter decrepitude moved the prelates deeply. "This is not a Pope" whispered Trivulzi to his neighbours, "but the Papacy in abeyance", and the few cardinals who had still been wavering were completely won over to Farnese. He was unanimously elected and took the name of Paul III.

So beneficent did the invigorating air of the Vatican prove to the palsied veteran, that he survived his elevation fifteen years. Nor were they years of an invalid's living death, but years of crowded ardour and activity. The election of a Roman citizen to the Apostolic See was received in the city with frantic jubilation. As Farnese had been reared in the court of Lorenzo the Magnificent and was rich and lavish, his pontificate seemed to promise a return to the erstwhile gorgeous days of plenty. Paul III was a clever, cultured man, with an easy, conciliating manner which had won him many partisans and disarmed most of his enemies. His policy had always been one of tactful neutrality towards all parties, which however implied no pusillanimity like that of his predecessor. He is described by his contemporaries as "highly bilious" and "tenaciously resentful of injuries". Benvenuto Cellini accuses him of believing in nothing, not even in God. However sceptical he may have been in religious matters, he was however a firm believer in astrology, corresponding regularly with Consarius in Paris and refusing to undertake anything on a day when the influence of the stars was unfavourable.

Trained in the old school of papal supremacy, Paul III considered Charles V's attitude of independent equality insufferable. The semi-pontifical flavour of his Augsbourg "Interims", his perpetual intrusion into matters of dogma, annoyed the Pope considerably. His Holiness made no mystery of his disapproval, but the Emperor remained unmoved. The Holy See no longer held princes in the thraldom of its prestige. Charles had crushed Clement as a giant crushes a pigmy. If, as is argued, temporal power was necessary to Papacy for the preservation of its spiritual independence, to be logical it should have been a sovereignty preponderating over all others—a Colossus that could never know defeat. Such was not the case, and the conqueror's pose of censorious patronage was galling to the would-be theocrat. The secondary and uninfluential position assigned to the Pontiff in European affairs so surprised and disgusted him that Paul III abandoned the field of general politics for the more restricted one of family aggrandisement. His nepotism was unblushing. He bestowed the hat on several of his grandsons, the eldest of whom was barely fifteen. To his infamous son, Pier' Luigi, compared to whom Cesare Borgia was but a playful kitten, he granted Parma and Piacenza, which were possessions of the Holy See and therefore strictly unalienable. Charles remonstrated with him, but to no avail. The imperial agents thereupon incited the citizens of Piacenza to rise against Pier' Luigi and murder him. The people lent a ready ear to these suggestions, as he was considered a monster, and not content with butchering him they mutilated his body and subjected it to ghastly outrages. To escape the Pope's vengeance they then declared themselves subjects of the Emperor to whom righteousness was somehow always profitable. Paul was distracted with grief at the death of the son he loved so passionately and he never forgave the Emperor for his connivance at his murder. It caused him to assume a more friendly attitude towards France, which made Charles say "that most men take the French disease in their youth, but that the Pope caught it in his old age". Paul's resentment was deep and tenacious, for there is evidence in the Florentine archives that he intended to send Charles a mechanical box which discharged a number of shots on being opened, but Duke Cosimo de Medici, having been informed of the plot, prevented the despatch of the murderous tool, thereby earning the Pope's undying enmity. He always had hated the Medici really and had been relieved almost too opportunely of the necessity of fulfilling his promises to Cardinal Medici by that scheming prelate's sudden death. He was poisoned by Alexander, the cousin he had hoped to destroy and who seemed suspiciously confident of impunity. "This is how we rid ourselves of troublesome flies" exclaimed the princely murderer, thus publicly acknowledging his guilt. He himself, we may add, suffered the same fate before long. If he was no friend to Florence, the Pontiff was on equally bad terms with all the other Italian States, as he was ever on the look-out for an opening to seize a city here or there to add to his son's principality.

Two important events marked his pontificate. He summoned the Council of Trent and officially approved of the Society of Jesus: both actions of the greatest moment in the history of the Church of Rome.

His devotion to his offspring, which had been the main interest of his later years, was the weapon chosen by fate wherewith to destroy him. After Pier' Luigi's death, although Piacenza had put herself under the Emperor's protection, the Farnese retained possession of Parma; but seeing that Charles coveted that city, Paul thought it safer to return it to the Holy See and so do away with any excuse the monarch might have had to annex it. His grandson Ottavio, however, openly disregarded his orders and refused to hand it over.

Nor was his insubordination to be the only sorrow he inflicted on the Pope, for the news soon reached His Holiness of an intended alliance between the Emperor, his beloved Pier' Luigi's murderers and Ottavio. That was bad enough, but when he learned that his favourite grandson, Cardinal Farnese, whom he trusted above all, was in league with the culprit, his cup of bitterness overflowed. Paul sent for him and, losing all restraint, snatched the biretta out of the cardinal's hands, tore it to shreds and threw them on the ground. He raved at the traitor and cursed him, his rage only abating as his strength ebbed. He never rallied from the shock and a few hours later was dead.

How, one wonders, would the excessive parental devotion manifested by so many popes have stood the test of the hereditary system? Would their love for a son destined to succeed them have been as blind and overwhelming? If they had felt responsible for their stewardship towards an acknowledged heir, would it not have come between them and resulted in the customary antagonism of sovereigns towards their immediate successors?

JULIUS III (del Monti)

1550–1555

🌸

THE conclave which assembled on November 29th 1549 is one of the most complicated on record and needs considerable simplifying to be comprehensible. The reason for this hopeless-looking tangle is that the various candidates brought forward by the different factions were not really the ones they wished elected, so that the ordinary diplomatic intrigues were underlaid by other more secret and contrary ones creating a state of bewildering confusion. The Duke of Florence, for instance, offered to expend 200,000 crowns to secure the elevation of the Cardinal of Burgos, one of the Emperor's candidates, while he really favoured del Monti. The imperial agent in Rome, while also appearing to support his master's candidates, was secretly working against them for one of his own.

Burgos was an arrogant Castillian of noble birth and secure in the good graces of Charles. He was the natural leader of the Spanish party, but the fact of his being himself a candidate robbed him of most of his authority over his followers, so that they were not really to be depended on. The French group was led by the Cardinal de Guise. It only numbered eight cardinals, but its influence was important owing to the personality of their chief. Guise was an accomplished diplomat and man of the world. Exquisitely courteous, with the exact touch of aloofness, authoritative without peremptoriness, he allied an appearance of frivolity with absolute discretion. Who his protégé was no one knew.

The third faction consisted of the creatures of the late Pope under the command of Farnese, his ungrateful grandson. Although still very young, barely thirty years of age, he had shown great qualities of intelligence and statecraft and had the maturity and judgment of an experienced tactician. It soon became apparent that the proceedings would consist in a contest between himself and Guise. He officially supported Reginald Pole, the Emperor's second selection, commonly called the Cardinal of England. It was very unlikely that a foreigner would be elected, but if such a calamity should occur, Farnese felt convinced that Pole, being a man of rigid principles and opposed to nepotism, would leave the government of the State to him. And at the start it looked quite possible that Rome would have an English Pope, as Pole got twenty-five votes at the first scrutiny, which was very near indeed to the necessary majority, forty-five cardinals being present at the conclave. The French tactics consisted in delaying matters till the arrival of several of their compatriots, who would not only reinforce their party but probably bring an order of exclusion against Pole. The Cardinal de Lorraine in his anxiety to prevent the Englishman's election committed the blunder of trying to buy Farnese privately for a large sum of money; an offer which the latter turned down with scorn, his seeming disinterestedness much enhancing his reputation.

Cardinal Pole would have made an ideal Pope at this juncture, as he was upright and honourable, devout without a trace of bigotry, and both religious and tolerant. Broad-minded and liberal, he would have been the one man capable of grappling with the difficulties which beset the Church of Rome. As it was, he proved to be merely a tool used by Farnese to alarm Guise and oblige him to come into the open. But the French continued to play a waiting game. As, however, the risk of the English cardinal's election must be obviated somehow, Chieti, a Francophile Italian, was commissioned to make an impassioned attack on Pole, accusing him so formally of heresy that the number of his adherents fell to eighteen. Farnese and Trento, his chief supporters, then offered to rush his election during the night, counting on the older cardinals' bewilderment and their difficulty in collecting their wits when only half awake; but the Englishman would not hear of it, protesting that he would not enter the Vatican by the window like a burglar, but solemnly by the open door or not at all, and he quietly but firmly withdrew his candidature.

This dignified attitude struck the Florentine envoy as both opportune and amazing. "What can be done to help a man who will not help himself?" he writes, openly rejoicing at the elimination of a dangerous candidate. Charles was seriously displeased at the way in which his wishes had been disregarded in the conclave, and to all enquiries for further guidance obstinately replied: "Pole or Burgos". But Burgos was impossible—the Sacred College would never elect a Spaniard, especially one whose brother-in-law reigned in Naples and who was uncle to the Duke of Alba. So the Imperialists being at a loss how to obey their master decided to temporise. This policy suited the French, who were awaiting reinforcements, and also Farnese, whose object was to give his cousin Ottavio time to capture Parma, and who knew that delay would be all to his advantage, as the pontifical troops, left without money or food, could not hold out much longer. Thus all parties were unanimous in their wish to gain time.

This state of things resulted in the most unlikely names cropping up at the scrutinies. Most of the cardinals attached no importance to this moonshine voting, but one of them, d'Este, took his chances very seriously. His stupidity was proverbial, and Ruggiero, the Duke of Ferrara's agent in Rome who was working in his interests, must also have been a simpleton. Considering how freely communications passed to and from the Conclave, he seems to have run very unnecessary risks when getting into touch with d'Este, as he complains in his reports of the danger he runs of breaking his neck "climbing by a small ladder on to the roof of the Vatican and slipping about among the tiles, perilous expeditions from which he returned more dead than alive". The Sacred College were well aware of the arduous escalades of the devoted Ferrarese and derived much amusement from them. As to d'Este himself, his misfortunes were a standing joke. His beard and hair were falling out at an alarming rate and his colleagues held a meeting to which he was summoned. They enjoined him with mock solemnity to disclose the nature of his disease. The unfortunate prelate in a fever of apprehension assured them, on his honour, that he had been absolutely chaste for over a year and that the cause of his trouble was the excessive heat of the previous summer. His statement caused much merriment and banter, but d'Este's name did not appear at the subsequent scrutinies. Ruggieri, with perhaps a sigh of relief, acquainted the Duke of Ferrara of the collapse of their schemes: "This little indisposition", he wrote, "has come at an awkward moment for his most reverend Highness, as the cardinals say that it is impossible to elect a Pope attacked with the ringworm".

Meanwhile Cosimo de Medici had been working patiently underground to further del Monti's interests. He attempted to obtain the Emperor's patronage for him, seeing that both Pole and Burgos were out of the question; but the stubborn autocrat refused it with scorn, not thinking the obscure del Monti even worthy of the exclusion.

The French faction had been trying, without success, to gather adherents to the cause of Cardinal de Lorraine, and, failing him, were really at a loss whom to propose. Del Monti cleverly chose this moment to ingratiate himself with Guise, who having no better candidate to hand offered him his support. Several days were then spent in bribing and bargaining, during which Farnese, having agreed to the Frenchman's conditions, unaccountably played him false. Guise indignantly turned on him, and in the presence of the entire assembly called him a liar and a traitor. Had not the Cardinal-Dean hurriedly suspended the sitting there is no knowing to what lengths the quarrel might have gone. As it was, the open break between the two leaders completely engrossed the cardinals' attention to the exclusion of the main business. They noted every phase of the dissension with avid curiosity, commenting excitedly on Guise's refusal to receive Farnese's peace emissaries, and on the various forms of retaliation his resentment was likely to assume.

The Roman citizens, however, cared not one jot about these internal disputes. They wanted a pope and the conclave had been assembled for well over two months without electing one. The city magistrates made the usual expostulations to the guardians, insisting on the Sacred College being put on bread and water rations; but this excessive penalty was permuted to the one-course meal. This measure was an absolute farce, as there was no limit fixed as to the number of dishes this one course, which was the roast, could comprise. The privation therefore was not great and in no way hastened a solution. Days passed, nothing more happened; the Sacred College was still marking time, when it was suddenly roused from its lethargy by the news that Guise had sent for Farnese's peace envoys. Immediately there was a flutter of expectation and events moved rapidly enough. The French leader agreed to meet the Italian on friendly terms; no reference was to be made to their differences. The interview between them took place openly in the long gallery, Guise giving his word and that of the King of France that Parma would be secured to the Farnese. So great was the French cardinal's prestige that Farnese dared not ask him for a written undertaking, but meekly begged him to specify his choice. Guise feigned uncertainty, bringing forward the names of several cardinals before that of del Monti dropped carelessly from his lips.

Farnese fastened on to it as he was intended to do, and the bargain was concluded. Their peering colleagues saw the two former antagonists shake hands, and they knew the Pope was made. Even then del Monti insisted on the greatest circumspection and secrecy, fearing some counter intrigue on the part of the imperialists. But all went well and the next morning he was duly elected and took the name of Julius III.

The new Pontiff had once said jokingly to his colleagues: "If you make me Pope I warn you that the very next day I give you the *Prevostino* for brother member", and he was as good or, rather, as bad as his word. This *Prevostino* was a lad then aged seventeen who was in future to be known as Cardinal del Monte. He was of obscure parentage and his favour had been due to a strange incident. Some years previously, when the Pope was legate at Parma, he happened to have a large monkey as a pet. One day as he was watching its antics from a window he saw it seize on a small boy, and for a few moments it looked as though the animal would kill him. The child, however, managed to free himself, then turning furiously on the monkey attacked it in his turn. The prelate was so delighted with the boy's pluck that he adopted him on the spot, at first giving him the monkey as a playfellow, later making him his own constant companion. Charles V was disgusted with the new Pope, his minion and his monkey; but the Farnese were satisfied, as Ottavio got Parma and Piacenza. As to the French they felt they could have done worse, knowing there was nothing to fear politically from a man whose only ambition was a life of luxury and indolence.

Julius III was a Tuscan, which explained Cosimo de Medici's anxiety to secure his election. He was choleric but had a good-natured and forgiving disposition. The ideal he set himself to realise was an existence of animal gratification untrammelled by any unpleasant duties. He lived mostly in a beautiful villa just outside the Porta del Popolo. As he suffered from the gout and could not resist the temptation of rich and succulent fare, he attempted to counteract the ill effects of these excesses by giving the strictest orders to his attendants never to bring him any disagreeable news of any nature whatsoever, as vexations, he thought, affected the gastric juices and turned them sour.

The five years of his pontificate were spent in hedonistic inaction.

He left the government of the State entirely in the hands of subalterns and spent fabulous sums on feasting and high living. Petruccelli calls him the Heliogabalus of the Church. His language was foul beyond belief. His favourite oath would have seemed coarse enough in the mouth of the lowest ruffian; from the lips of the Vicar of Christ it was so startling a blasphemy that even the loosest-living cardinals were shocked. Their disapprobation did not trouble Julius in the least, he merely made fun of their squeamishness; and indeed the younger ones soon discovered that they had worse things to put up with from him than his oaths. He doted on the *Prevostino*, the Cardinal del Monte. This young scoundrel was so crassly stupid, so debauched, and committed such atrocious crimes that the cardinals were moved to remonstrate with the Pope for having given them such a colleague; but he would not listen to them, flying into a violent passion and telling them that his favourite was worth more than the whole of the Sacred College put together.

Although the Emperor hated and despised Julius, that Pontiff had the proud and rare distinction of having moved the grim monarch to actual hilarity by proposing to make Aretino a cardinal. He refrained, however, from perpetrating such a preposterous piece of buffoonery, but being determined to bestow some especial mark of appreciation on the poet, he kissed him publicly on the lips. Julius enriched and exalted his family in true papal style. Their position was such that the Emperor's illegitimate daughter, the Duchess of Parma, had the greatest difficulty in obtaining an audience from the wife of the Pope's nephew. However carefully he protected his gastric juices against acid reactions, the gout pursued its relentless course, and the Pontiff's sufferings were such that he had perforce to renounce one by one all the exquisite delicacies he so much enjoyed. He gradually became emaciated and painfully feeble and, by an irony of fate, this gormandising epicure practically died of starvation.

MARCELLUS II (Cervini)

1555

🐚

At the conclave which assembled on April 5th, 1555, Julius III's creatures were without a leader. Del Monte was quite incapable of assuming any responsibility and the cardinals had no desire to find him a substitute, for as free lances they could sell their votes to the highest bidder. D'Este was again expending vast sums of money on securing supporters; but his princely birth was a greater hindrance to him even than his denseness. It is evident from his letters to his brother, the Duke of Ferrara, that he had no inkling of his disabilities and considered his chances excellent. The French party wanted a pope whose modest antecedents would ensure his gratitude for their support and who would occupy the Holy See with some degree of decency and dignity. They therefore selected Cervini, Cardinal of Santa Croce, a man of unblemished reputation, and having rallied the drifting cardinals to his cause, he was elected Pope on the fourth day of the conclave and became Marcellus II. His election was a protest against the bestiality of the late pontificate.

The new Pope was the son of a country doctor who dabbled in astrology. Having cast the infant's horoscope, he found that the stars indicated high ecclesiastical honours, and therefore put him into Holy Orders. He was certainly a good prophet and must have been well satisfied with the accuracy of his prognostications. At the time of his elevation Santa Croce was fifty-four, but appeared much older. He was a tall, lean man, bald and frail-looking. His demeanour was quiet and composed; he was not talkative, but very well informed and scholarly. In disposition he was gentle yet firm and resolute, in fact, the very man the Church needed. What good Marcellus might have done is unfortunately merely a matter for conjecture, as immediately after his enthronement he fell a victim to one of those obscure diseases so prevalent in those days, and in spite of being wrapped in the still steaming skins of sheep which had been flayed alive, he failed rapidly and died on the twenty-fifth day of his pontificate.

PAUL IV
From a bronze bust in St. Peter's, Rome

PAUL IV (Caraffa)
1555-1559

THE situation of the various parties was much the same when the conclave assembled after the death of Marcellus II, as it had been at the time of his election, save that Cardinal Farnese had managed to gather round him the leaderless creatures of Julius III and so considerably strengthened his position. Charles V was far too absorbed in his own affairs to give the conclave more than a passing thought. Satiated with power, weary of life, he was about to transfer the government of his immense possessions to his son and stepbrother and retire from the turmoil of politics and warfare. The imperialists, therefore, still led by the aged Burgos, were left much to their own devices and lacked solidarity. The French party, which had lost the Cardinal de Lorraine's guidance, was much perturbed at receiving orders from Henry II to support d'Este, and intended to delay matters until a messenger could be got through to the King informing him what manner of man d'Este really was, and asking for further instructions. D'Este himself was more sanguine than ever; the Duke of Ferrara was in Rome attending personally to his brother's interests; but he had been misguided enough to fall out with Ottavio Farnese over the Parma question, so his canvassing was in reality sheer waste of time and money. To the Farnese the world was simply divided into two sections: those who favoured their occupation of Parma and Piacenza, and those who did not. The former were their friends, the latter their enemies. They admitted of no middle course. It was an obsession with them, an *idée fixe*, outside of which nothing could tempt or even interest them—and their goodwill was a necessity as no candidature could be successful at this conclave without Farnese's support.

On May 15th forty-three cardinals entered the conclave in a very agitated state of mind. They had just been informed that Montluc, commanding the French forces in Italy, had spoken of descending upon Rome, surrounding the Vatican and forcing an election favourable to his country's interests. His well-deserved reputation of ferocity naturally alarmed the prelates, whose fears were in no way allayed by the rumour that Strozzi, the Florentine envoy, not to be outdone by the French, was collecting a strong force both inside and outside Rome to impose an imperial candidate on them. Fortunately the day for these rough-handed methods was over. Montluc was recalled to France, Strozzi received a severe admonition from Florence which cooled his ardour, and the Sacred College were able to proceed to business under ordinary peaceable circumstances. There was still a strong inclination among the majority to bestow the supreme dignity on a man really worthy of it, and Reginald Pole's name was again brought forward. But his absence was a serious obstacle and Farnese had other views. He assured his colleagues that the Englishman would not accept the dignity, and that even if he was prevailed upon to do so, his elevation would entail a long interregnum and the expenditure for his journey to Rome would be enormous. This last argument was a potent one, and no more was heard of the Cardinal of England.

D'Este for the time being had the half-hearted support of the French party and of their Italian adherents, which totalled a respectable number, but Farnese's phalanx was at least as imposing and no pope could be elected without his co-operation. He saw no object in procrastination, and approached d'Este at once, telling him bluntly that he would never consent to the election of an enemy of his house, and that the only solution was to discover a candidate acceptable to them both. D'Este did not feel equal to making a stand against an opponent of Farnese's proficiency and accepted the compromise. Farnese proposed Chieti. He had already settled with him that he would secure his elevation against a written promise that as Pope he would confirm the Farnese's right to Parma, and even extend their territories. Chieti was a Neapolitan of the house of Caraffa, which had always been pro-French, therefore he was acceptable to that party. It was he who had so vehemently accused Pole of heresy at a previous conclave, which had resulted in the election of the blasphemous Julius III. Chieti as Dean of the Sacred College held an important and influential position in the conclave and, all things considered, d'Este thought it wiser to retire in his favour.

The imperialists, who were well aware of Chieti's hatred of Spain, gathered round Burgos, who exhorted them desperately to make a firm stand. Had they all been staunch to their leader, they could have counteracted the Farnese-d'Este coalition, as they were twenty strong, but their inner dissensions and jealousies undermined their strength of purpose. They did not even vote consistently for their official candidate, Morone, whom several of them detested; and Farnese, watching for any sign of disaffection among their ranks, thought the moment opportune to attempt a nocturnal *coup de main*, during which he was confident of sweeping the necessary number of voters off their feet owing to the complicity of darkness, excitement and turmoil. He and d'Este therefore convened their united forces to a meeting that night, from which they all emerged noisily acclaiming Chieti and calling out that they were on their way to elect him by adoration. As the sleepy cardinals appeared at the doors of their cubicles to enquire into the cause of the disturbance, they were forcibly seized upon, surrounded, and dragged along by the Pentecostal pressgang. The hubbub drowned their protests, the darkness concealed their resistance; several had their clothes torn to rags. The tornado swept into Chieti's cell, and bore him in triumph to the chapel, where Farnese was much disconcerted to find that the number of adorers was insufficient by three to form the required majority! He rushed out again, resolved to procure them at all costs, carefully locking the door of the chapel behind him to prevent any further defections.

Meanwhile Burgos had rallied what remained of his party in the Hall of the Consistories and was exhorting them with all the eloquence at his command to remain faithful to the Spanish cause, reminding them that Charles had formally excluded Chieti and that their master's orders were not to be trifled with; but the great Emperor was already a dim and distant shadow to the younger prelates and they were restive and out of hand. Farnese, bursting into their midst took the situation in at a glance, and by promises and cajolery wheedled away the necessary number. Burgos called down all the maledictions of heaven upon the renegades, warning them that they would live to rue their folly; and events proved him a true prophet indeed.

Farnese returned exultantly to the chapel with his recruits and Chieti's election received the necessary canonical sanction. As Pope

Paul IV rose from his stall he appeared to the cardinals inches taller than their old colleague Chieti had been. There was that in his bearing as he looked slowly round which sent a shiver down the spine of some and gave even his most loyal supporters a vague feeling of uneasiness.

Navigero gives the following description of the new Pontiff:

His temperament is dry and bilious. He has incredible gravity and grandeur in his demeanour. He seems born to command. He is very healthy and robust, being all sinews and no flesh. His expression and all his movements have the litheness of youth. Although seventy-nine years old he seems to skim along the ground sooner than to walk. He has two bodily ailments, the flux and the rheum; but the first dispenses him from taking medicine and the second he overcomes by eating Parmesan cheese. He is very scholarly; speaks excellent Latin, Greek and Spanish besides expressing himself in the purest and choicest Italian. His memory is prodigious, and he is an authority on the scriptures etc. His eloquence is remarkable and his private life blameless. He admits of no contradiction; for not only does he consider that as Pontiff his word must be law even to kings and emperors; but he is acutely conscious of his superior learning, his exalted birth and the rectitude of his conduct. He consults no one, treating the cardinals as dust beneath his feet. He is keen in all his pursuits, but in none as much as in the Inquisition. He has no fixed time for meals. He dines whenever he chooses, often in the middle of the night, and expects to be served, with the greatest luxury and punctilio, a number of courses never inferior to twenty-five. He drinks freely and always a coarse Neapolitan wine as thick as broth. At dessert he washes out his mouth with Malmsey. He frequently sits for three hours at his meals, discoursing incessantly. He retires to bed when he is sleepy and remains there till he wakes. No one would be bold enough, under any circumstances, to enter his room before he had rung, whatever the time of day. He never admits anyone into his presence until he is fully dressed which is a lengthy business as he is most meticulous and washes his beard with the greatest care. He spends hours at his devotions and in sleep; and when at last he gives an audience, he talks so persistently that his visitor not daring to interrupt him rarely gets an opportunity of explaining his business. He keeps ambassadors waiting for hours and they rarely manage to see him more than once a year. He is dilatory in all affairs but in those of the Inquisition. Nothing is ever allowed to interfere with the weekly conference he holds on the

Thursday with the Inquisitors, and which seems his greatest interest in life.

Paul's scheme of reforms did not include nepotism, as he invested his nephew Carlo Caraffa, a debauched soldier, with the highest ecclesiastical dignities and the conduct of all affairs both spiritual and temporal. The Pope confiscated all the castles and titles of the Colonna and bestowed them on his nephews; not that he had any affection for them, but he wished, like so many other pontiffs, to make his house all-powerful. Carlo Caraffa had been clever enough to pander to his blind hatred of Spain and to make a pretence of leading a more decorous life. With a show of devotion thrown in, he had completely got round the old man and won his favour. Later, when it came to Paul's knowledge that he had been deceived, his wrath was terrible. He stripped Carlo Caraffa of all his offices and disowned him publicly. His other nephews shared their cousin's disgrace. Paul treated them all with incredible harshness. His maniacal belief in his own infallibility was not shaken, however, by the discovery that Carlo had hoodwinked him so successfully, nor by the subsequent reverses inflicted on him by the imperial forces. If there was not a second sack of Rome it was not because Paul IV averted it in any way, but simply because the Duke of Alba, who was in command of the victorious army, was too devout a Catholic to wreck the Holy City, and was a strong enough commander to restrain his troops from running amok.

It was on a Thursday that the Duke led his victorious army up to the gates of Rome, and had he scaled the walls and entered the town, he would have found the Pontiff presiding at a meeting of the Holy Inquisition and the city at his mercy.

Such, however, was the prestige of the Vicar of Christ to so reverent a servant of the Church as Alba, that when admitted to the presence, the conqueror humbly kissed the Pontiff's feet, and restored to the Holy See all the towns and territories he had won from it. Paul's violence terrified the fearless Spaniard as it terrified all who approached him. He never hesitated to assault those who roused his temper; being angry with the governor of Rome, he boxed his ears and literally kicked him out of the room. He tore the Ambassador of Ragusa's beard out by the roots and insulted the Tuscan envoy, calling his master, Cosimo, a son of the devil. As to the Emperor Charles and King Philip II, there is no term of opprobrium he spared them. All Spaniards, he said, were spawn of Jews and Moors. He treated all monarchs as vassals, refusing to recognise Elizabeth as Queen of England, or Ferdinand as Emperor because he had not been asked to invest them with their dignities. His intolerance was mediaeval, and he was so imbued with his own vice-deity that he sincerely believed all his own opinions to be divinely inspired and therefore infallible. He was scarcely sane on the subject of his omniscience; as to heresy it was to be crushed at all costs and the inhuman methods of Torquemada naturally appealed to his inexorable nature; fire, torture, death; religious arguments which have done service for most beliefs and will always remain more potent than convincing. The cardinals themselves were not secure against the danger of indictment, as the aged Burgos had predicted to the Spanish deserters, and thousands of monks and priests fled to Venice and foreign countries, some even seeking refuge among the Turks. The population of Rome decreased by almost half during this reign of terror.

Paul's other *bête noire* was Spain. He hated that power with equal vehemence as Pontiff, for the humiliations to which the Holy See had been subjected by Charles V, and as a Caraffa for her occupation of Sicily. He thought the moment of the Emperor's abdication an auspicious one to attack a State probably disorganised by such an important change of government and more vulnerable in consequence. He did not hesitate, he, the head of Christendom, to crave Soliman's help against His Most Catholic Majesty of Spain, considering no doubt that Moors were well matched adversaries for a nation of "bastards"! But he soon discovered that he had overrated his enemies' difficulties and underrated their might. The disappointment was a bitter one to his arrogant spirit, but he found solace for his defeat by one enemy in the routing of the other. He pursued his gruesome activities with unabated ardour to the day of his death, adjuring the cardinals with his last breath to maintain the Inquisition in Italy. No sooner did the Romans hear that Paul was dead, than they pillaged and burnt the palace of the Holy Office and liberated all the prisoners from the dungeons, including several cardinals, to whom the hardships of a conclave must have seemed paltry enough after such an experience. The Inquisitors had to fly for their lives, and the Pontiff's statue was mutilated and dragged through the town sewers. As Paul had persecuted the Jews with absolute ferocity, his effigy was capped with their yellow headdress as a crowning insult, and finally thrown into the Tiber.

It is curious, in view of Paul's execration of Spain and most particularly of Charles V and his family, to note the striking affinities he had with Philip II. They were both fanatical bigots, haughty, cruel and relentless. The one sacrificed his son and the other his nephews on the altar of discipline, with self-righteous complacency and no apparent sign of regret or distress. Both Sovereigns were dilatory and procrastinating in affairs of the state, and although the King was taciturn and the Pope loquacious, their outlook was identical. If Philip was the typical Spaniard of his times, then Paul shared the main characteristics of the race he held in such abhorrence.

PIUS IV (ANGELO DE MEDICI)
1559–1565

❧

ON September 5th, 1559, fifty-one cardinals entered the conclave, several of them in a much chastened spirit. Philip II's orders to his countrymen were peremptory and accompanied by a schedule of penalties to be incurred in case of disobedience; ranging from heavy fines to degradation. The Spanish cardinals were to vote for Carpi and no other. Indeed there was no likelihood of insubordination in their ranks for the present; they had found out to their cost what it entailed to elect an enemy of their nation to the Holy See. The French party had received instructions from Catherine de Medici, the Queen Mother, to support d'Este, who obstinately refused to admit the hopelessness of his candidature. Farnese was still at the head of an important group of followers, and by joining forces with Caraffa would wield great power in the conclave. Caraffa's position was a strange one. Although never reinstated in his uncle's favour, he was officially the leader of the late Pope's creatures, amongst whom was his cousin the Cardinal of Naples. Being Caraffas their name was inseparably linked with that of Paul IV, and they not only would have to account to his successor for their own crimes and spoliations; but would also be made scapegoats by all those who had suffered at their uncle's hands. The choice of the new Pontiff was literally a matter of life and death to them, and their line of conduct would therefore be to steer above all for personal safety. The cardinals, who like Morone were held in suspicion by the Holy Office, would strain every nerve to secure a pope antagonistic to the Inquisition; and the Powers would oppose any political or scheming one.

As usual there was a large percentage of cardinals, twenty-two at least, secretly hoping to be themselves elected, which weakened the various parties to which they belonged. The influence of Cosimo de Medici, the Duke of Florence, had also to be reckoned with; his interests were in the hands of an exceedingly able conclavist called Lottino, who by the gradual elimination of other candidates and his own discretion and astuteness was eventually to secure the prize for the Duke's protégé. This candidate, Angelo de Medici, was no blood relation to the powerful Florentine family whose name he bore, but a man of the meanest extraction. His brother had been a stable hand in the service of the Moroni, and being an unscrupulous ruffian had, for a substantial consideration, murdered one of the Visconti against whom his employers had a grudge. The Moroni then attempted to lure Medici into a trap and do away with him, but he was too clever for them, and managed to capture the stronghold in which he should have met his doom. The Duke of Milan subsequently conferred on him the fortress and Marquisate of Marignano in exchange for his original conquest. Angelo's fortunes had risen with those of his brother, but through more peaceful channels. He studied law with success, and his scholarly tastes led him to associate with clerics and men of learning. From being secretary to Farnese, he was soon promoted to become his boon companion; and when Marignano married a relation of his patron's, Angelo was made a cardinal. It is reported that once at a banquet given by Farnese a youth who had entertained the company with songs and improvisations was handed a garland of flowers by the host, and told to present it to whoever among the guests would be Pope some day. The young bard had turned unhesitatingly towards Angelo and deposited the wreath at his feet; then striking the chords of his lyre had sung of his future greatness. The Sacred College unfortunately acted with less decision and promptitude, and the conclave was to drag on for several months before the minstrel's prophecy came true.

During the first weeks it was a struggle between d'Este, backed by the French, and Carpi supported by the Spaniards. Farnese through his animosity against the Ferrarese had gone over to the Spanish faction. He even tried one of his nocturnal surprise stunts in favour of Carpi, but the warier cardinals sent out their conclavists with lanterns to see what was afoot and the movement failed. Then there was the La Queva incident. This cardinal was a general favourite, always ready with an amusing anecdote or a witty sally. He was full of good-natured fun—the "jolly good fellow" of the conclave, and the younger cardinals especially were always flocking to his cell. He considered, perhaps pardonably, that he might as well turn his popularity to some account, and sent his conclavist round to all his friends asking as though on his own initiative for just that one vote, the *voto di onore*, which would give his genial master so much satisfaction. The conclavist accomplished his mission with so much discretion and cleverness that but for a mere accident La Queva would probably have been elected Pope. It happened that a rather inquisitive old cardinal, finding himself among a group of juniors outside the chapel, enquired who they intended to vote for that morning. Most of them returned no answer, but somehow La Queva's name was whispered and amid general hilarity the plot was exposed. Although the more serious members of the Sacred College were indignant at the trick which had been practised on them, La Queva's cronies treated the deception as another of his little jokes and bore him no ill-will.

On September 13th the Cardinal de Guise arrived, and having carefully taken stock of the situation concluded that Caraffa held the key to its solution. He therefore offered him without further ado the sum of 30,000 ducats, the Marquisate of Salerna and a confirmation of all his Italian possessions if he would throw in his lot with the French party. Important as the bribe doubtless was, Caraffa wanted more, and although Guise increased the amount of cash several times Caraffa still hesitated and exhausted the French prelate's forbearance; he broke off negotiations and haughtily refused to have any further intercourse with Caraffa. Time passed. Discipline had never been so lax in any conclave before. Several boards were taken down from the windows, and the cardinals could be seen from outside making signs to their friends and "gesticulating like puppets". A large hole was knocked in the masonry and free intercourse thus contrived with the outer world. As to the Banchi, business was so slack that they had to put up their shutters. November slowly went by without the Sacred College showing any symptoms of awakening from its torpor. Twice a day the regulation scrutiny took place, but most of the voting papers bore the negative "*nemini*". The Paraclete gave no sign.

There were many cases of illness among the cardinals; two of them died and another left the conclave in a serious condition. The days dragged on. The Sacred College looked like settling down to hibernate, when suddenly there was a stir. A letter had arrived from Philip II for Cardinal Colonna informing him that the imperial fief of Palliano was to be restored to his family. It will be remembered that Paul IV had brutally despoiled the Colonna of their castles to give them to his nephews. When he banished these from Rome, the Pontiff had wished to punish them personally for their misdemeanours, but he had no intention of lessening the power of his house. He had therefore allowed them to retain all their ill-gotten riches and possessions. It was very foolish of Vargas, the Spanish envoy, to have made the news public, as Caraffa on hearing of it was naturally enraged and greatly alarmed, breaking definitely with the Spanish faction. He now much regretted having antagonised Guise and tried to propitiate him by advancing a French candidate, the Cardinal of Rheims. He worked so actively that by mid-December he had rallied Farnese to his cause and the other parties began to show signs of anxiety. Vargas was continually appearing at the breach in the wall, sending for the Spanish cardinals and metaphorically shaking the King's fist at them. To the lethargy of the preceding weeks had succeeded a state of frenzied activity. So feverish were the discussions and so violent the disputes that several cardinals, among them Farnese, actually came to blows in the chapel itself. Guise took no part in all this pother. He was not going to have his candidate chosen for him by an outsider, and completely ignored Caraffa's advances. Without the support of his own party Rheims sank as he was bound to do.

There was another tumultuous scene when a Spaniard, Pacheco, was proposed, the Italian prelates crying out that they would not accept a foreign pope, and the Frenchmen leaping on to their stalls and protesting with Gallic vehemence. The pandemonium was such that the scrutiny could not take place, many of the cardinals leaving the chapel as a protest.

It was now Christmas eve, and Cosimo de Medici, kept well informed by Lottino of all the happenings within the conclave, decided that the time had come to start his offensive. He wrote both to Guise and Caraffa recommending his namesake Angelo de Medici to their notice.

He timed his despatch carefully so that its arrival should coincide with that of the Queen Mother's new instructions to Guise. Catherine enjoined him to abandon d'Este and support Medici, and she also sent him a large consignment of gold which proved very useful for buying up a few stray votes.

To Caraffa the Duke gave a solemn pledge, in his own name and Medici's, that he should be secure against all reprisals and that a full pardon should be granted to him and his family. This was what Caraffa wanted above all, and his acceptance disposed of the last obstacle between the Florentine and the Holy See. Angelo de Medici was elected Pope without further parley and took the name of Pius IV.

The new Pontiff was in all respects the opposite of his predecessor. He had none of his arrogance and haughtiness, was on the contrary of an affable, easy-going disposition. His illegitimate children he kept decently in the background, bestowing all his favour on his nephews, the Borromeo, one of whom, Carlo, the Cardinal-Nephew, was a pattern of virtue and was subsequently canonised.

The Pope's gratitude to the Duke of Florence made him very subservient to all Cosimo's wishes. Pius IV was sixty-two years old, of medium height, medium build and medium colouring. He had a pleasant sympathetic countenance, bright eyes and a sprightly manner. He was a tremendous walker and went for long rambles morning and evening. He had remarkable physical energy, was always up and doing. He liked strong wine and coarse food and plenty of both, though the great amount of exercise he took kept him lean. He was straightforward in business and prompt of decision though not always stable. His attitude towards the European princes was also the exact reverse of Paul IV's. He was the first to admit that the Holy See needed their support and was most gracious and amenable in his dealings with them. He was always accessible to their ambassadors whether in his apartments or the Vatican gardens, pacing to and fro with them till they dropped with fatigue. He rose at dawn, and except for his afternoon siesta, never rested. He was not extravagant in his mode of life, rather parsimonious even, his horses being cheap, sorry beasts. But his great hobby—building—swallowed up enormous sums. He was no theologian and not favourably inclined towards the Inquisition; yet he took no steps to suppress the Holy Office or restrain its activities. He himself was safe and happy. He led a life of physical exertion and sensual satisfaction selfishly indifferent to all other concerns. The government of the State he left to his nephews. His foreign policy was one of conciliation; he hated strife and quarrels, and his feeling of obligation towards Cosimo de Medici paled before the risk of displeasing the King of Spain. Philip, in his desire to be revenged on the Caraffa for their uncle's enmity, requested the Pope to bring them all to book for their crimes and depredations. This Pius agreed to do in spite of the solemn promise of immunity he had given them at the conclave. Cosimo de Medici was intensely indignant at such a breach of faith. He upbraided the Pope, reminding him that without Caraffa's support he could not have been elected. He also expostulated with Philip, appealing to him as a fellow sovereign not to bring dishonour on his word, especially as the King in the early days of the conclave had himself promised Caraffa immunity. But Philip was not interested in the Duke's scruples, and Pius wrote with the utmost unction that nothing could ever be allowed to interfere with God's justice.

The Caraffa were therefore committed for trial, and the severity of their sentences must have satisfied even their bitterest enemies. The Duke of Palliano and two of his brothers were condemned to decapitation, and Cardinal Carlo Caraffa to strangulation. All their possessions of course were confiscated. The executions took place on the spot. The Cardinal of Naples seemed at first glance to have been treated more mercifully as he got off with a large fine and a term of imprisonment. But this leniency was only a blind. The Cardinal with cautious foresight had deposited a vast sum of money in the safe keeping of some foreign bankers who would never have handed it over to the Holy See without the owner's consent. He had to live therefore till the money could be transferred to Rome, after which he died in prison. Pius IV's vigorous constitution was gradually undermined by his excesses. He is reported to have drunk as much as twelve pitchers of wine at a single meal, and to have indulged in other exhausting dissipations. He died very suddenly, probably of an apoplectic fit, in 1565.

PIUS V
From a print in the British Museum

PIUS V (GHISLIERE)
1566–1572

AT the time of Pius IV's death, France was in the throes of civil war, and too absorbed with her own difficulties to take a very active interest in the coming conclave. Philip II, confident of his hold over the Holy See, no longer attached a very great importance to the personality of the Pontiff; and the Emperor having no subjects or vassals in the conclave was naturally without influence in the Sacred College. The different factions somehow seemed less clearly defined, less compact. Caraffa's execution had left his uncle's creatures leaderless; Farnese was losing his hold; d'Este, growing old and superseded by his young nephew, was definitely on the shelf and was now known as the Cardinal of Ferrara. The only man of outstanding personality and influence was undoubtedly Carlo Borromeo, the late Cardinal-Nephew. He was an honest, virtuous, narrow-minded man of unmistakable sincerity. Official chief of a large group of followers, his personal prestige was too great to be withstood in such a drifting assembly, and it soon became clear that no serious opposition would be made to any candidate he selected.

Farnese and Ferrara, the erstwhile foes, exchanged civilities and matrimonial projects for their families, which were not intended to materialise, but merely expressed mutual goodwill and a cessation of hostilities.

Borromeo's first nomination was Morone. This appeared a strange choice, as Morone was decidedly in the bad books of the Inquisition, of which Borromeo was a zealous advocate, but he had been Morone's subordinate in Milan and had a profound admiration for that prelate's character and learning. Farnese disapproved of him, however, on the grounds that he had once been Carpi's fortunate rival in some love affair, and Carpi was Farnese's most intimate friend. Nor was Ferrara any more agreeable to his election as years before, when legate at Bologna, Morone had sided with that city against Ferrara in some trifling dispute concerning a water conduit. These two worthies, therefore, put their heads together, and realising that they were not sufficiently powerful to prevent Morone's election by ordinary means, decided to resort to others better fitted to the circumstances. They called on Borromeo, and feigning qualms of conscience appealed to his strictly orthodox convictions against a man suspected of liberal tendencies. The leader, who had never before experienced the intricacies of electoral intrigues and who was himself too straightforward to suspect his colleagues' sincerity, at once deferred to their scruples, and discarding Morone, substituted Alessandrino, whose rigid principles were unimpeachable. This cardinal, whose patronymic was Ghisliere, was the son of a veterinary surgeon, and in his childhood had been employed as a scullion in a Dominican convent. His industry and religious fervour had attracted the attention of the monks, who admitted him to their order at the age of fourteen. His excessive zeal in the cause of the Inquisition had brought him to the notice of Paul IV, who conferred upon him an important post in the Holy Office and the cardinal's hat. Although he led a very retired life, the members of the Sacred College were well aware of his virulent fanaticism. Farnese and Ferrara therefore gasped with horror at the suggestion; but they were hoist with their own petard. They could not possibly take exception to Ghisliere on religious grounds, and they knew Borromeo would be moved by no others. They now sorely regretted their objection to Morone, and the causes of their animosity against him seemed indeed insignificant compared with those that governed their feelings for Ghisliere. Desperately they sought for an escape from the trap, and Farnese hit on the idea of begging Borromeo to accept the pontifical dignity himself; but the future St. Charles' ambitions were not of this world and he firmly declined the honour.

The Sacred College was swept with a wave of apprehension when the name of the new candidate became known. So fearful were the cardinals of appearing remiss that there was a positive rush towards Ghisliere's cubicle. Never did hysterical panic so successfully ape enthusiasm as on January 10th, 1566, when the Cardinal of Alessandrino became Pius V.

Consternation was great in the Papal States at the election of a Pontiff of so forbidding a reputation—especially among the hordes of mendicant friars who infested Rome and the provinces. They well knew that the dreaded command to return to their monasteries and conform to the ascetic rules of their Orders would be the new Pope's first move, and would have to be complied with immediately. As to the cardinals they would be driven not, alas! to a more virtuous life, but to the semblance of it, thereby being compelled to add hypocrisy to the long list of their failings. Good times and a care-free existence were definitely at an end.

Nor were the foreign monarchs any more satisfied. They knew Pius V for an uncompromising upholder of papal supremacy and ecclesiastical prerogatives.

Trained in the pitiless school of the Inquisition, the new Pontiff was inaccessible to compassion. The sight of the most terrible tortures, the cries of agonised humanity left him unmoved. Habit had inured him against sensibility of any sort, and his elevation to the Apostolic See could only mean a renewed impetus to the activities of the Holy Office. He was devoid of any of those weaknesses of the flesh which might have been a point of contact with his fellow creatures. He led the life of an anchorite—was incorruptible and sincere. He was convinced that he had been sent to regenerate mankind and extirpate evil, and was always on the alert to detect signs of it. He held all humanity in suspicion, always ready to pounce on its real or supposed frailties. Wearing a hair shirt himself, he considered physical pain the normal means of benefiting the soul. He has been accused of having taken a sadistic delight in inflicting and witnessing the excruciating torments practised on his helpless victims, but it is far more likely that they produced no reaction whatever on his petrified feelings. He was the monomaniac of forcible salvation.

Pius V had thoroughly disapproved of his predecessor, and showed his contempt for his memory by reversing the findings of the Caraffa's trial, declaring them to have been innocent, and pursuing their accusers and judges with relentless vindictiveness. Considering what unscrupulous villains all the Caraffa were, it is difficult to understand what can have aroused the austere Pontiff's sympathy for them. He was doubly illogical: firstly in vindicating such notorious malefactors, and secondly in invalidating the judgment of Pius IV, who approved of their execution; thus denying his predecessor the universal infallibility he so confidently claimed for himself. He shared Paul IV's arrogant self-assurance to the full, and was very apt to interfere in lay matters that were no concern whatever of his. Even Philip II, who had gained his esteem and approval by the zeal with which he encouraged the burning of his subjects suspected of heresy and the slaughter of Jews and Mussulmans in his dominions, had to remind the Pope pretty sharply that he was quite capable of managing his own affairs.

With Maximilian he was on frankly bad terms. There had been a dispute between the Dukes of Florence and Ferrara about some question of precedence which had been submitted to the arbitration of the Emperor. Without waiting for the monarch's decision, Pius issued a bull deciding the matter in favour of the Medici and concluding with this surprising argument:

> In virtue of the supreme authority with which we are invested and which gives us the right to distribute titles to princes, in the same way as our first father Adam received from God the power to name the animals!

His subjects, naturally, came in for an overwhelming amount of spiritual solicitude. He forbade doctors to attend patients who had not confessed within three days. Blasphemy was punished by heavy fines for the wealthy and flogging for the poor. The Papal States were overrun with spies and informers, even the mentally deficient being subjected to examinations on their orthodoxy and condemned to the rack for their drivellings. Christian love and charity were sadly at a discount in all pontifical procedures. The commander of the small force which Pius sent to assist the French Catholics was instructed by him to take no Huguenot prisoners but to slay them all on the spot.

In his hatred for England, Pius urged Philip II to take command of an expedition against that heretical country, which would, he said, be the most glorious of all crusades. He offered practical assistance by authorising the King to make use of all the revenues due to the Holy See in the Spanish realm, and if the sum was still insufficient the gold chalices were to be melted down and all treasures taken from the churches. But Philip had no men to spare just then even for so admirable a purpose. His armies were fighting in the Netherlands, and the Moors, having risen as a result of the incessant vexations they were subjected to, were giving a good deal of trouble in Southern

Spain. England would therefore have to wait her turn of chastisement.

The Pope was more fortunate in his attempts to form a league with Venice to fight the Turks who had attacked Cyprus. He sent several caravels to join the Spanish and Venetian fleets combined under the command of Don Juan of Austria. They made an imposing array of over 250 vessels, without counting the convoys. Most of the Italian princes had provided men and the force was well armed and disciplined. The Turks had a superior number of galleys but their weapons consisted mainly of bows and arrows, inefficient against armour. The fighting was terrific. The galley slaves begged for their liberty to join in the fray and fought like demons. They liberated their Christian fellow-sufferers in the Turkish vessels, who turned on their captors and considerably hastened the victorious issue of the battle. The sea, says the chronicler, was dyed with blood for leagues around, but the Cross was definitely triumphant over the Crescent, and Don Juan became the most popular hero in Christendom. This signal victory naturally gave Pius V intense satisfaction; all the bells in Rome were rung in jubilation and commands issued for public rejoicings.

The persistent anxiety shown by the great majority of popes during the XVth and XVIth centuries to organise crusades against the Turks was not always the result of unadulterated religious zeal. Venice had long been at war with the Ottoman Empire, who stood in the way of her expansion in the East, and the various Italian States, secretly jealous of her wealth and power, had complacently watched the struggle without ever lifting a finger to help her. When in 1479, the Republic having exhausted her supplies signed peace with Mahomet II, it left the Sultan at liberty to turn his attention to the Peninsula. His fleet besieged and captured Otranto, which his troops occupied for over a year. When news reached the Vatican that Mahomet had sworn "by the only God, to forsake sleep, to abstain from the taste of delicate food or the touch of beautiful things" till he had trodden underfoot the idol of the Christians (the Pope) and stamped out Christian iniquity, then anxiety gave way to panic at the Pontifical Court. The Sultan's sudden death a couple of years later relieved the situation of its most immediate terrors, but the alarm had been a sharp one and danger still lurked in the background. The complete routing of the dreaded foe was therefore a cause of very special jubilation to Italy; but nothing could dispel the gloom which brooded over the Papal States, where every man, woman and child lived in constant fear. The Turkish menace seemed very remote compared to that of the Inquisition.

For a few months more this blight endured, then the Pope fell seriously ill. The despot who had made the sacraments compulsory for the sick had to forgo this ultimate viaticum himself, as the narcotics administered to him for the purpose of allaying his sufferings rendered him unconscious: a more merciful end than that meted out to the unfortunate victims of his fanaticism.

GREGORY XIII (Buoncompagni)
1572–1585

☙

Cosimo de Medici had not waited for the death of the reigning Pontiff to start preparations for the election of his successor; and it. was principally owing to his well-directed efforts that Buoncompagni owed his elevation. The Duke and his candidate had come to an agreement by which the future Pope, in exchange for the triple crown, was to bestow on the Medici the lordship of several important cities. Cosimo's tactics were carefully planned and secure against all mishaps the human mind could foresee. Yet even then Cardinal Ferdinand de Medici thought it advisable to observe all customary precautions, as can be seen by this message written to his father:

> I am without oil or powder [two kinds of poison which Cosimo prepared himself] and also without antidotes. Yet I must have these commodities with me in the conclave to be prepared for any eventuality. Forward me some without delay, also pomanders of strong perfume to hold in the hand so as to counteract the stenches of the conclave.

The cautious prelate was not to be subjected to a long confinement and can scarcely have had occasion to test the virtues of his poisons and antidotes or the potency of his aromatic deodorisers, for the conclave which elected Gregory XIII scarcely lasted forty-eight hours. The only obstacle still left to be overcome by Cosimo's agents, when the fifty cardinals assembled on May 12th, was the candidature of Farnese. That prelate had made a great effort to regain his prestige and had collected round him all the less austere members of the Sacred College whose bond of union was the defeating of Carlo Borromeo's party. Farnese, exerting all his influence and possessing undoubted proficiency at the game, was a serious competitor, but Cosimo was not perturbed. He had bought the Spanish cardinal Granuela, who was to stage so bold a piece of bluff that its very audacity was its guarantee of success.

As soon as the doors of the conclave were closed, Granuela called at Farnese's cubicle and on being admitted drew from within his robe a letter bound with a large yellow ribbon and sealed with the arms of Spain. Then reverently baring his head without uttering a word, he placed the document on the table with deferential solemnity while Farnese watched him spellbound and mystified. Recovering his composure, however, he stretched out his hand to pick up the letter, but Granuela prevented his doing so, edging him away from the table while he explained in cautious whispers that he had only just arrived from Naples bearing the despatch, and that it contained Philip's instructions to the Spanish party. He knew, he added, that the King had pronounced the exclusion against Farnese, but being himself well disposed towards him, wished to spare him an affront which would ruin any future chances he might have of occupying the Holy See; while if an election was arrived at immediately, before he had had time even to deliver his message, there need be no necessity ever to divulge it. It seems incredible that such an experienced conclavist as Farnese should not have suspected a ruse and insisted on verifying the Spaniard's assertions, but somehow Granuela managed to impress him with his honesty of purpose, which proves how judicious Cosimo was in the selection of his confederates. Having achieved this initial and hazardous master-stroke it was child's play for such an able strategist to persuade Farnese that Buoncompagni was his own suggestion, and to send him hot-foot to hasten his election.

The new Pontiff, Gregory XIII, was the son of a small tradesman of Bologna. He had studied law and his remarkable intellectual gifts had earned for him a chair at the university. He had subsequently been employed on various diplomatic missions to which his training and quiet, easy manner particularly fitted him. His open, pleasant countenance invariably disposed strangers in his favour, and his sympathies were all with moderation and tolerance. He owed the hat to Pius IV and on his accession immediately reinstated all that Pope's creatures to the dignities and benefices of which Pius V had deprived them. The Romans and all the subjects of the Holy See drew a deep breath of relief and thanksgiving at the advent of a more human Pontiff, for human he certainly was, and would no doubt have proved himself so had he been at liberty to do it. But he was surrounded by the censorious prelates who had been Pius V's familiars, the Pontiff whose terrifying wraith seemed to haunt the Vatican. The Jesuits also were always at hand, creating an atmosphere of austerity and religious enthusiasm to which the Pontiff offered less and less resistance as time wore on and his natural impulses grew weaker. He was devoted to his illegitimate son, and had at first attempted to shower riches and dignities on him as his predecessors had done for their offspring. But he soon discovered that times had changed and that the Papal Court viewed these signs of parental fondness with such marked disfavour that he had to resign himself to the humiliation of begging patents of nobility and honours for his beloved son from the Venetian Republic and the King of Spain. What his real feelings about the massacre of St. Bartholomew were, no one can tell. The event occurred so soon after his accession that he cannot possibly have been privy to it. Pius V had undoubtedly urged some such measure on Catherine de Medici, but it seems established now that the horrible slaughter was inspired mainly by political reasons and court intrigues. Hatred of Coligny's personality much more than of his convictions was the cause of his murder.

It was an accepted prerogative of sovereigns in those days to dispose of the lives of their subjects. The security of the throne came before all other considerations, and if there was no guilt attached to the slaying of one rebel, logically there was none incurred by the slaughter of many. A proof of how insignificant a part religion played in the matter is given by Lord Acton in his *Essays on Liberty*. He writes that:

> Catherine de Medici proposed to Queen Elizabeth to do to the Catholics of England what she had done to the Protestants of France, promising that if they were destroyed there would be no loss of her goodwill.

So much for the Queen Mother's religious zeal.

As to the Pope he ordered illuminations and processions. The guns of S. Angelo boomed, the churches re-echoed with Te Deums, a medal was struck to commemorate the pious deed and Vasari was ordered to immortalise the event on the walls of the Sixtine Chapel. Could the head of the Church of Rome—the official patron of the Inquisition—show less enthusiasm than Philip II, who not only hailed the event as a second Lepanto, but sent a gift of 2000 crowns to Coligny's murderer? Slowly but surely the Jesuits gained in influence and they ended by obtaining a complete hold on the mesmerised Pontiff's mind.

Under their guidance trouble was fomented in Ireland, plots hatched in London to destroy Elizabeth, and missionaries were actively engaged in promoting civil war in France. The order of the Jesuits under Gregory XIII played the part that cardinal-nephews played in the worst days of nepotism. Their word was law; they completely ruled the State and cost the Papacy fabulous sums, for they were gaining a foothold in every quarter of the globe and the perpetual foundation of new houses and the endowments they necessitated drained the Pope's resources as surely as any rapacious or squandering relations could have done. His finances reached such a low ebb that new means had to be found to levy funds, and he resorted under one pretext or another to arbitrary confiscation of foreign merchandise in the ports of the Papal States, and to the expropriation of barons from their feudal lands. Alleging that the original grants made to the nobles were not hereditary, families who had lived for generations on estates they considered their property, were turned adrift to exist as best they could. They naturally resorted to highway robbery and the country was plunged into a state of mediæval anarchy. Long-forgotten feuds were renewed, and bandits preyed impartially on all parties. Gregory was powerless to restore order, for the Jesuits were much better versed in the art of hatching trouble than in that of coping with it—and he was forced much against his will to grant a free pardon to the outlaws and reinstate some of the robber barons into their possessions.

Gregory's name has earned immortality through his association with the reform of the calendar. He was always partial to scientific pursuits and gave every encouragement to the learned men, who undertook to solve the difficult problem, which they accomplished with such success that their formula for the division of time will probably endure for ever. Left to his own devices the Pontiff would probably have led a life of ease, been tolerant and good-natured, held intercourse with men of culture and found satisfaction in parental affections. But his mentors allowed him no backsliding and no respite, goading him on to an artificial pose of dogmatism and bigotry quite foreign to his nature. Gregory XIII reminds one irresistibly of one of those primitive pictorial efforts intended for Christian propaganda, portraying a troubled-looking mortal being dragged upward on his right by a floating angel, while on his left a crouching devil well anchored to the earth by his talons strains desperately to delay the skyward flight.

SIXTUS V
From a print in the British Museum

SIXTUS V (Peretti)
1585–1590

THE success which had attended the Medici's intrigues in the several elections they had sponsored, encouraged them to further endeavours. The lack of interest evinced by the Great Powers allowed the court of Florence a practically free hand, and gave the Medici the most influential position in the conclaves of this period. All those cardinals who coveted the supreme dignity, and there were many, turned towards the Grand Duke of Tuscany as being the most powerful ruler whose patronage they could obtain. Prestige seems to have been the only benefit the Medici can have hoped to reap for their outlay, as it was notorious that the character and policy of most cardinals underwent quite surprising alterations when they were firmly seated on Peter's throne—and their gratitude was no more to be relied on than that of other mortals. But the Medici were proud of the ascendancy they had acquired in the conclaves and prepared actively to add to their laurels by securing yet another victory.

The Sacred College assembled on April 20th, appearing at first to be broken up into numerous small groups; but the situation soon resolved itself into a pitched battle between Farnese and Medici, the two important parties absorbing most of the lesser ones. Farnese was now an old man; he felt convinced that he was attending his last conclave and that he would never again have the chance of obtaining the supreme dignity. He was therefore prepared for a fight to the death and willing to expend his entire fortune on attaining his object. Besides his natural ambition to crown his career so brilliantly, he was also actuated by a spirit of revenge against those who had tricked him in the last conclave, having since ascertained that Philip was in no way opposed to his candidature, though lukewarm in his support. But Farnese's chances were poor. He had always shown too much aptitude for management; was credited with too marked a personality and the house of Farnese was extremely unpopular. Although the sums he offered to his colleagues were very large, most of the cardinals were too rich themselves to be tempted by mere bribes of money. They were more ambitious of power and honours, and Farnese was not likely to bestow anything in that line outside his family circle. Another serious handicap for him was, that his opponent had managed to keep the name of his candidate secret, which obliged Farnese to adopt defensive instead of offensive tactics, always a more difficult line of action for recruiting adherents.

Cardinal Ferdinand de Medici was throwing all his energies into the contest. Like those street musicians who, bringing every limb and joint into play, draw sounds simultaneously from half a dozen instruments, he touched the chords of the voters' contrasting characteristics with masterly unison. He appealed to their piety, licentiousness, austerity, worldliness, youth, age, idealism and greed practically in the same breath. He negotiated advantageous matrimonial alliances between their relatives, promised extensions of territories in his brother's name, flattered, cajoled and menaced. When he considered the moment ripe for action he unmasked his batteries.

Peretti, Cardinal of Montalto, on whose elevation Medici evidently set so much store, was an obscure unobtrusive individual who had been a swineherd in his childhood. Like Pius V he had been befriended by Franciscan monks and had joined their order as a mere lad. The fervour of some Lenten sermons he had preached in Rome had brought him to the notice of Pius V, who, struck with the similarity of their careers, had made him a cardinal and Grand Inquisitor in Venice.

But Peretti's modesty seemed proof against any honours or distinctions. His manner had remained obsequious, his voice was low and deferential. He made a great show of gratitude for any benefits he had received, not only from the Medici, but also from several other influential prelates. His head was perpetually bowed as in salutation, and mediocrity, which in moderation was undoubtedly an asset, seemed in his case almost excessive. So much so in fact that Medici wrote to his brother: "I had advised our monk to be colourless, but I now find I must gild him to brighten him up and sugar him to make him palatable!"

A few votes were still needed to obtain the necessary majority. There could be no question of rallying Farnese either by fair means or foul, so they had to be obtained from independent prelates whose allegiance to either party was a matter of personal advantage. Here romance played the chief part. Cardinal Sforza was known to be much enamoured with the beautiful niece of his colleague Carpi, a close friend of Medici's. What could be simpler than to beg that lady to use her charms and influence to win him over to Montalto's cause? There was also San Sisto, the late Pope's nephew, of whom Medici wrote that: "He would have elected the devil himself to get out of the conclave and return to the arms of his mistress". But his case was more complicated than Sforza's, for the lady's husband was a jealous irascible fellow who threatened vengeance on the gallant cardinal. As long as his uncle had lived, S. Sisto had been fairly safe, but under a new pontificate the situation might be a dangerous one. There seemed to be only one entirely satisfactory solution, the removal of the troublesome husband. Medici's high station debarred him from treating personally of such sordid matters, so he deputed Alessandrino to convey delicately to S. Sisto that some means might be found to dispose of the spoil-sport as soon as the conclave broke up. S. Sisto hesitated, being naturally apprehensive of a weapon that might either fail to act or hit the wrong target, but in a spirit of sporting optimism finally accepted the bargain. His adhesion, carrying with it the votes of Gregory XIII's creatures, secured the triumph of the Medicean candidate. Farnese, livid with rage and disappointment, his last hopes vanishing for ever, heard Montalto proclaimed Pope under the name of Sixtus V; surely the darkest horse that ever won the pontifical stakes.

It is recorded that immediately after his acceptance of the papal dignity, the new Pontiff threw back his head, which was never to be bowed again, and to the utter stupefaction of the cardinals burst into a vibrant and sonorous hymn of thanksgiving. They could not have been more startled if the angels of the last judgment had suddenly leapt out of the fresco on the chapel wall and blown a blast on their trumpets. Some of the more experienced and cautious among them left directly from the Vatican for places of safety. The bleating sheep had been transformed as if by magic into a ferocious wolf. Sixtus V wasted no time in asserting his authority. Instead of the customary garlands and bunting which adorned the city for every new Pope's enthronement, a row of gallows was erected. On the flimsiest pretexts, without even a trial, poor wretches were mercilessly hanged. A lad of thirteen who had offered some resistance when a couple of Papal Guards attempted to rob him of his donkey was strung up on the Pope's personal orders, and when someone objected that the offender was a mere child, Sixtus said: "Add a few of my years on to his and hang him at once".

The Pontiff was certainly faced with a difficult task in restoring order and stamping out banditry. Gregory XIII had left the country in an absolute state of chaos and Sixtus needed all his energy and determination to cope with the situation. He used any means to hand, force, bribes, treachery, and terrorism, but he gained his object, although only temporarily, for the cure did not prove a radical one.

The most inexorable of despots, he was never known to perform an act of clemency. His pontificate can be likened to a perpetual thunderstorm, as he struck as erratically and ruthlessly as lightning. Having led a life of perpetual subservience he grudged to others even a semblance of the freedom he had himself forgone. As a friar, charity had been his means of subsistence and he had, therefore, no consideration for the wage-earner and tradesman and no understanding or sympathy for their needs. Owing probably to the abject poverty of his early surroundings, gold had a veritable fascination for him. He crushed his subjects under a burden of taxation such as the Papal States had never known. He made a more profitable business of trafficking in ecclesiastical benefices even than his predecessors had done, selling the same office several times over. The millions thus collected he hoarded in S. Angelo. Nominally they were intended for Holy Wars or emergencies, but Sixtus never brought himself to part with a single coin for religious purposes. Even when Philip II, owing largely to his promptings, launched the Armada to destroy heretical England, the only contribution made by the Pope towards the costly expedition was a few bales of *agnus dei* and a supply of indulgences. His policy consisted in playing England against Spain, hoping to exhaust and cripple them equally. He betrayed them both, warning Elizabeth of the projected offensive while he sent his blessing and fiery words of encouragement to Philip.

Sixtus had a great regard for his sister, known as Donna Camilla, who soon acquired a very influential position at court. She had been a washerwoman, and some pasquinade having been circulated on the subject of the lady's past employment, the Pope offered 1000 sequins to the author with a promise of his life if he would come forward. The misguided humorist claimed the money, which was paid to him without demur, but he was then seized, his hands struck off and his tongue slit.

Sixtus treated his nephews with customary partiality, and even intrigued to have one of them adopted by Henry III of France as his heir, in the place of Henry of Navarre the Huguenot Bourbon. The Pontiff never forgave the King for not accepting his suggestion, and when the monarch fell a victim to Jacques Clement's poisoned dagger, Sixtus extolled the murderer and vouched for his salvation. He created many cardinals, but only men sufficiently sycophantic and obsequious never to contradict or criticise him, his butler being one of the very first to receive the dignity. His natural impulses, so sternly repressed for fifty years, once released would suffer no restraint. He became subject to fits of temper so uncontrollable that he shook and trembled as though in an attack of ague. He was self-opinionated, stubborn, and yet irresolute and changeable in general intercourse.

His excommunications and offers of friendship to his fellow sovereigns were practically simultaneous. He showered benedictions and eulogies on Philip II, striving ceaselessly meanwhile to undermine his power. He expressed the greatest contempt for the late Pontiff "who had been cowed by a pack of Jesuits" and set out to prove that a Pope could still be an autocrat, an aim he accomplished most successfully. The immense treasures he had amassed undoubtedly gave him that feeling of self-confident superiority inseparable from the prestige of a solid gold basis.

Having for the time being restored order in the Papal States, Sixtus then turned his attention to improving his capital. This entailed the destruction of many ancient monuments and Roman remains, which sacrifices do not seem to have troubled him. In some cases, however, he turned antiquities to account in an ingenious compromise between paganism and Christianity, as for instance by placing a cross in the hand of the Capitoline Minerva, and hoisting statues of St. Peter and St. Paul on to the summit of the columns of Trajan and Antoninus.

But his great claim to celebrity, and an unquestionable one, was the bringing of the Aqua Felice to Rome. He spared no expense in the accomplishment of this important scheme, insisting on the aqueduct being built on the exact model of the ancient Roman works. He conferred a lasting benefit on the city by making its inhabitants independent of the insanitary water of the Tiber, and insuring an abundant and pure supply to all the beautiful fountains of Rome.

The Pontiff's death was unedifying. With his usual self-assurance he had disregarded his doctor's advice and prescribed for himself a diet of wine and fruit which disagreed with him violently. Although the thirty-two cardinals whom he had created were in perpetual attendance and took it in turns to try and induce him to conform to custom by accepting the sacraments, he obstinately refused to do so. Piety had been a necessary sham to the monk Peretti; it was superfluous humbug for Sixtus V.

Some historians have taken him at his own valuation—or nearly so—and called him a great Pope. To the writer he appears to have combined the characteristics of Judge Jeffreys with those of Baron Haussmann—a blend which may have been effective, but definitely lacks grandeur.

URBAN VII (Castagna)

1590

❧

THE Medicis continue to play such an important part in the history of the conclaves at the end of the XVIth century, that it will not seem out of place to give a few details concerning the events taking place at the court of Florence which have a direct bearing on our subject.

Cardinal Ferdinand, though no doubt unpleasantly surprised at the transformation undergone by his cringing monk when once he had become Sixtus V, never showed the slightest fear, however, of his former protégé. He not only stood his ground with him consistently, but on occasion went as far as to defy the formidable Pontiff. There is a story of Medici having had all the clocks in the Vatican tampered with on a day fixed for the execution of a youth whose life he wished to save. The chronicler relates that the Cardinal presented himself at the Vatican and requested from Sixtus a free pardon for his friend. Hearing the clock strike the hour at which the condemned man should have died, and certain that his orders would be punctually carried out, the Pontiff graciously granted the reprieve, which he signed and gave to Medici with a sardonic smile. When Sixtus realised the trick that had been played on him, he was overcome with rage and ordered the immediate arrest of the culprit. Medici, however, was already approaching the palace surrounded by an armed bodyguard, which accompanied him to the very door of the audience chamber. The prelate faced the Pope with fearless self-assurance, his loosely fastened robes allowing a glimpse of the armour he was wearing beneath. "Is this a cardinal's attire?" spluttered the angry Pontiff.

"*This* is", answered Medici, showing his silken gown. "But *this*", he added, tapping his cuirass, "is the accoutrement of an Italian prince."

"If you are not careful, Cardinal, we will deprive you of your hat", pursued Sixtus.

"Then I shall resume my steel helmet, Holiness", replied Medici, quite unmoved; and taking his leave he departed for Florence, where he had important business to attend to.

His brother, the Grand Duke Francis, had, a few years previously, married his beautiful mistress, Bianca Capello, the "Daughter of the Venetian Republic". She hated Ferdinand for having opposed the marriage and relations between them were decidedly strained. The Grand Duke, however, was on very friendly terms with his brother and since the death of his only son, naturally acknowledged and treated him as his heir. The Cardinal was entertaining the ducal couple one day to an *al fresco* meal in the grounds of his country villa, when one of those accidents occurred, so frequently met with in those times, which always looked so bad for those who benefited by them. Both Francis and Bianca were suddenly taken ill and died in a few hours; the Cardinal being naturally accused of having poisoned them. These generally accredited rumours, however, in no way interfered with his accession to power; those were family matters which did not concern outsiders.

His apologists have averred that far from being the murderer, Ferdinand was in point of fact the intended victim. According to their version of the incident Bianca had herself prepared a fruit tart for which she knew the Cardinal had a special liking, and had had it placed on the table among the other delicacies, by a confederate. Francis, who had not been let into the secret of his wife's delicate attention for their host, upset all her plans with marital perversity, by helping himself to a substantial portion of the pastry. Being powerless to prevent the impending catastrophe, and determined at all costs not to be left defenceless at Ferdinand's mercy, the Duchess stoically ate the remainder. Both versions are equally possible and equally uncertain; but the net result of the tragedy was that Cardinal Ferdinand became Grand Duke of Tuscany, and that the Pope who had threatened to deprive him of his dignity, was now requested to allow him to discard it, as it was imperative that Ferdinand should marry and beget heirs for the house of Medici, a favour which Sixtus V was graciously pleased to grant.

It is this Prince, now the head of an important Italian State and familiar with every ruse and intrigue resorted to in papal elections, who is going to be the *deus ex machina* of the coming conclave.

Concentrating all her energies on internal warfare, France, whose heretical King was not even recognised as her Sovereign in Rome, took no part whatever in the proceedings. But Philip II, with his eye on the golden treasure in S. Angelo, was making a great effort to secure as pontiff an ally who would assist him to pursue his Holy Wars with something more substantial than blessings. As Ferdinand was secretly inimical to Spain he would certainly oppose Philip's candidate whoever he might be. There remained a third party consisting of the creatures of Sixtus V led by his nephew Montalto. This young cardinal, barely twenty-two years of age, had been a mere child when his uncle conferred the hat on him and was still very inexperienced and flighty. He had a pleasant manner, was lavish in his mode of life and extremely susceptible to feminine charms. He was consequently the idol of Roman ladies. His aunts, Donna Camilla and the Signora Felice, had a great ascendancy over him, and urged him to support Colonna's candidature, which he agreed to do much against his inclinations, being very friendly with the Orsini. The entreaties of the favourite sultana of his harem, who also used her influence in Colonna's favour, probably helped considerably to overcome his reluctance. Through Montalto, their willing slave, the women hoped to secure the elevation of Colonna, who was their ideal of the *grand-seigneur* and whose inordinate vanity made him as putty in their hands. He had a regular brood of illegitimate children, all actively intriguing to secure the papal crown for their father, and in themselves a guarantee against any danger of austerity or even of restraint.

The position in the conclave was therefore a clearly defined one. There were three parties, and three candidates officially declared: Como, supported by the Spanish faction, a cantankerous old man so generally unpopular in the Sacred College as to be negligible as an opponent; Castagna, the Grand Duke's choice; and the aforementioned Colonna. Castagna was a Genoese who seemed genuinely kind and unassuming, and whose moderation and rectitude had been proved beyond question.

Medici, ignoring the Spanish party, focussed his attack exclusively on Montalto. He was well aware of that young man's devotion to the fair sex, of his extravagance and his expensive tastes, and naturally concluded that since his uncle's death he must be in need of funds.

So without more ado he instructed his agent to offer Montalto a large sum of money, the fief of Celano, which he knew had taken his fancy, a wealthy marriage for anyone of his relations he pleased to name, and for himself the favours of two ladies, both famous for their beauty, who were willing to sacrifice what remained of their virtue in so good a cause. Montalto was sorely tempted and could not conceal the fact from Colonna, who, preferring an honourable retreat to a mortifying failure, decided to withdraw his candidature. Montalto thus freed from any obligation accepted Medici's offer, and Castagna was elected Pope on September 15th, taking the name of Urban VII.

He was beloved by the Romans for the tolerance and equity he had always shown in his dealings with them. Exceedingly charitable, learned and wise, he believed in attaining his ends through kindness and persuasion instead of the usually adopted methods of craftiness and cruelty. He immediately declared his intention of restricting the activities of certain religious orders, especially the political intrigues of the Jesuits, and it was said that he had thereby signed his death warrant. He certainly fell ill and died within ten days of his elevation; but as he was seventy years of age and of a weak and ailing disposition, the fatigue and excitement of the conclave, which had already proved fatal to others, may well account for his sudden collapse. Mention must, however, be made of a strange incident which happened some years later and might be, according to some writers, connected with this Pope's death.

Under the pontificate of Clement VIII, a man confessed voluntarily to the Grand Penitentiary that he had poisoned two Popes. Considering the gravity of the case, the priest withheld absolution until he had consulted Clement. The Pontiff saw no reason why the sinner should not be shriven, but showed a not unnatural anxiety as to the sincerity of his contrition. To put him out of the way of further temptation he was handed over to the Inquisition, an institution where repentance was allowed to suffer no relapse.

Urban VII lived just long enough to relieve some of the distress among his poorer subjects by a generous distribution of alms, and to grant donations to a few really deserving and needy cardinals. He died before the ceremony of his enthronement could take place, a sad loss for Christendom and the Papal States.

GREGORY XIV (Sfrondato)
1590–1591

🌼

THE ease with which the Grand Duke of Tuscany had secured the election of his candidate in the last conclave now led him to abandon all customary intrigues and precautions. He concluded that it was quite unnecessary for him to expend large sums of money when he need only dictate his orders. His attitude towards the cardinals, which so far had always been one of courteous tactfulness, became overbearing and arrogant. To Vinta, his Ambassador in Rome, he writes on October 11th, that is, two days after the new conclave had assembled:

> In case the cardinals are not docile, you will find in the coffer some small phials full of toxins. Put six ounces into each bottle—there are twenty-four phials, a sufficient quantity for fifty bottles:

and when later on Vinta is preparing to return to Florence, Ferdinand instructs him "to bring back the poison—or what remains of it". This substitution of toxicology for Machiavellism, fascinating as the pursuit may have been in itself, was a bad blunder in this case, as the consequences clearly proved.

Philip II, more eager than ever to lay his hands on the hoard in S. Angelo, had frightened the Spanish party into serious activity. He had sent them a list of seven candidates one of which was to be elected. If they failed, the cardinals would be made to feel the full weight of his displeasure. Their leader, Maddruzzo, finding his own name on the list, was spurred on thereby to even greater efforts.

Montalto, head of the most numerous faction in the conclave, had arrived in a very truculent mood. His aunts had reproved him severely for "taking his orders from Florence", and he had been teased and taunted by the ladies for allowing himself to be treated like a child when he could easily have imposed his own wishes on the Sacred College. They lost sight of the fact that his main object had not been Colonna's election, about which he had always been half-hearted, but the gratification of his own personal desires. Money he still needed and made no mystery of the fact. It was also to the advantage of his fair advisers that he should be well supplied with it; so they suggested to him a scheme by which he could replenish his exchequer and be assured of future benefits by securing the election of a pope who would befriend him. While apparently supporting various candidates, he would back another one in secret, both at the Banchi and by private bets through the agency of confederates. As to the man himself, the very one they needed was providentially to be found in their midst.

Two ladies, at whose feet Montalto was languishing just then, had an uncle, Sfrondato, Cardinal of Cremona, whom nobody certainly would suspect of any ambition to occupy the Holy See. His perpetual smile was child-like and disarming, and he was reported in the conclave to busy himself exclusively "with dressing the altar and sweeping out his cell". Approached on the subject he showed himself more than willing to play the part assigned to him and everything was arranged to his own satisfaction, also to that of Montalto and the charming ladies who had so much to gain by their uncle's election, and so little to lose by paying the price for it.

Maddruzzo, endeavouring to obtain Montalto's support, showed him the list of Philip's candidates. The young man was careful not to commit himself. He had seen a note, below the seven names selected by the King, to the effect that Cremona being a Spanish subject would be acceptable to His Catholic Majesty if all the others failed. The great thing therefore would be to keep in with the Spanish party while destroying the seven candidates' chances. Montalto spoke of his obligations to his own faction, but was as conciliating and friendly as caution would allow.

With the Florentine party, Montalto refused to have any dealings whatever, and in truth Monti, the Grand Duke's agent in the conclave, had little enough to offer him. Ferdinand's crude plan of campaign did not appeal to Monti. He was a clever intriguer, frankly corrupt; an adept at handling bribes, a fair portion of which always stuck to his fingers, but poison was not in his line—it was a dangerous, unhealthy weapon. As a sinister murderer Monti was grossly miscast, and knowing it, he wisely ignored Vinta's instructions and his handy little phials. His efforts to advance the affairs of Santa Severina,

Ferdinand's nominee, were casual and perfunctory. He busied himself with intriguing against every competitor put forward either by the Spanish faction or by Montalto's. For an occasional bit of fun he would create a diversion; as when he re-launched Colonna, shrewdly surmising that he would thereby be causing Montalto much annoyance and embarrassment. Being the former candidate of his own party, Montalto was bound to support him, and the situation gave rise to the most ludicrous incidents. Young Ascanio Colonna was most enthusiastic at the idea of becoming Cardinal-Nephew, and canvassed with so much ardour and success that his uncle's election appeared practically certain. Montalto, confronted with the unusual drawback of having too many followers, could think of no better way of disposing of the surplus than by ordering half a dozen cardinals to conceal themselves as best they could when the bell rang for the scrutiny. This they did by hiding under the beds of any empty cubicles they could find, while young Colonna frenziedly searched the premises for them. He actually discovered one of the deserters and dragged him out by the feet, but as he could obtain nothing more satisfactory from him than groans and grunts he realised that he was faced with a conspiracy to prevent his uncle's election, and abandoned the struggle.

Candidates fell right and left like ninepins. This comedy lasted two months, by which time Cremona alone was left standing. There was no hostility against him within the conclave, but the Grand Duke hated him and abused him openly, calling him an ignorant fool and making sarcastic comments on his broom and his inane grin. The outer world had no inkling of the impending *dénouement*; so well had the secret been kept that twenty-four hours before his elevation, the odds against Cremona at the Banchi were still 10 to 1.

Gregory XIV's election was therefore an excellent speculation for Montalto and his fair friends, but Philip was to reap the greatest benefits of all. The Pope's propitiating smirk had not been assumed for a purpose; he was naturally servile, and the high dignity to which he had attained did not alter the feelings of awe and respect with which Philip, his sovereign, had always inspired him. During the ten months of his reign, the Pontiff contributed two millions out of Sixtus V's precious treasure towards the expenses of the Spanish wars, and obeyed all Philip's behests with exemplary docility. At his instigation he subsidised the League in France and sent a riff-raff army of convicts and mercenaries to assist it under the command of his nephew, whom he had created Duke of Montemarciano. He excommunicated Henry IV and ordered all his Catholic subjects either to take up arms against him or leave the country. He had no personal animosity against Henry IV, but he was told these measures should be taken and he took them.

Against the Grand Duke of Tuscany, however, he needed no urging to show vindictiveness. He encouraged an army of bandits to ravage Tuscany, and cried with vexation when Ferdinand's troops captured Piccolomini, their chief, and hanged him. Neither in the field of diplomacy was he a match for the crafty Florentine. A plot by which the town of Ferrara should eventually have fallen into the possession of Gregory's family was discovered by Ferdinand, who acquainted the cardinals with it, so that when the Pope mentioned Ferrara in the consistory there was such a hubbub that he hastily withdrew his brief. He was completely dominated by his relations and they all reaped a harvest of gold; his nieces even appropriating the revenues of bishoprics and other ecclesiastical benefices. He was considered sound and healthy, and his death in October 1591 caused some surprise. There were many who said that Ferdinand's enmity seemed to undermine the strongest constitution. Ferdinand himself piously ascribed the Pontiff's death to the wrath of God, being a punishment for his wicked plot concerning Ferrara.

INNOCENT IX (FACCHINETTI)

1591

🐚

THE Grand Duke Ferdinand was far too clever to be stubborn. He recognised how mistaken his attitude in the last conclave had been, and reverted without hesitation to his former policy. His letters to Vinta contained no more mention of poison; his orders now were to buy votes without counting the cost. He gave his Ambassador the most detailed instructions as to the different modes of approach for each cardinal. Flattery, promises, grants, ready cash; every individual weakness was to be exploited, and Ferdinand seemed to be intimately acquainted with them all. Monti, once more in his element, would do excellent work, and had in fact already secured the adhesion of Sfrondato, the late Cardinal-Nephew. He was a dull-witted, boorish creature, quite incapable of forming a personal opinion and had fallen an easy prey to the experienced diplomat. As to Montalto, ten months of unbridled dissipation had reduced him to a state of utter hebetude. It was sheer waste to bribe him as he was quite unreliable, and as he had lost the confidence of his followers through his instability, it seemed far simpler to buy them directly behind his back.

Before the conclave assembled Ferdinand had already concluded a confidential pact with Facchinetti, the man he had selected as the future pontiff. He was a whimsical old cardinal, incredibly thin; with the brightest, shrewdest eyes looking out of his corpse-like countenance, so piercing as to be almost uncanny. He was perpetually shivering with cold even in midsummer and practically never got up, lying wrapped in innumerable coverlets, as inseparable from his bed as a snail from its shell.

Matrimonial alliances played the chief part in this secret contract, Ferdinand apparently making no attempt to recover the sums expended on the election, the total of which must have been staggering, as the grant to Cardinal de Joyeuse alone amounted to 270,000 crowns wherewith to pay his debts, besides an annuity of 35,000 ducats!

Philip had nominated Mendoza to the leadership of his party with Maddruzzo as candidate. There were still three millions left in the vaults of S. Angelo, and the King meant to have the spending of them if it could possibly be managed. He was well aware that he would have to purchase the cardinal's votes, a deplorable necessity no doubt, but a customary one to which generations of monarchs had become inured. Philip, however, was afflicted with one of those testy consciences which, like a fretful infant, needed perpetual soothing; so he called a meeting of wise men to discuss the question and decide whether such simoniacal methods were legitimate. The members of the conference after mature deliberation gave the verdict which was expected of them, concluding that the ends justified the means, and that by endeavouring to secure the election of a pope worthy of his high office, the King was benefiting all Christendom, and was therefore entitled to adopt any measures he deemed expedient. His scruples thus exorcised, Philip ordered his agents to distribute bribes on a princely scale, so that one way and another the cardinals left the Vatican a good deal richer than they entered it. The customary intrigues kept the conclave sitting for about three weeks and ended in the election of Facchinetti, who took the name of Innocent IX.

The new Pontiff was a man of great charm and was known to be favourable to a reconciliation with France—but he was too ill and exhausted to embark on any very definite policy, though he firmly refused to give Philip any subsidies whatever, seeming anxious, on the contrary, to restore peace and promote goodwill between the Powers. The hardships of a winter conclave and the emotions and strain of his election proved too much for Innocent in his debilitated condition and he died on December 30th, his pontificate having lasted barely three weeks.

CLEMENT VIII (ALDOBRANDINI)
1592–1605

❦

MONTALTO on leaving the Vatican made several unpleasant discoveries. The new Pope's election had not brought him in a single ducat; his debts totalled four times the amount of his revenues; and he could not obtain credit anywhere in Rome. From the ladies he got no sympathy whatever; their pretty teasing had turned to scornful sarcasm and society cold-shouldered him unmistakably. This succession of shocks completely sobered the young man, who realised that he must make a supreme effort or lose everything that made life worth living. The interdependence of his social and his electoral successes made it imperative for him to regain his former power in the conclaves, and the Pope being a dying man, not a moment was to be lost in setting to work. Montalto had always been on very friendly terms with the Duke of Sessa, Philip's Ambassador in Rome; they had been boon companions in many a revel, and as the Spaniard was easy-going and good-natured, he would not refuse to give him a helping hand. Montalto therefore offered him his services in the coming conclave. He would expect a very large sum of money in exchange; as not only would he have to keep himself afloat, but only by lavish generosity could he regain his hold on his followers. He was quite confident that this could be done if Spain did not count the cost. Sessa submitted the proposal to Philip, who accepted the offer, such an understanding between his party and Montalto's insuring the election of any candidate they jointly supported.

Oddly enough both Philip and the Grand Duke had selected Cardinal Santa Severina. He had promised Ferdinand his assistance for the conquest of Naples, and Philip approved of him as being a rabid Inquisitor.

When the conclave assembled on January 10th, 1592, Santa Severina's elevation to the Holy See seemed a certainty. Officially Montalto and his followers adhered to him as being Philip's candidate; but the terrifying Dominican was the last man Montalto wished to give himself as sovereign master. He was therefore much relieved to find that out of the fifty-two cardinals forming the Sacred College there was quite a numerous group led by Altemps, Sforza and old Colonna who vehemently opposed S. Severina's elevation, and were in sufficient force to make an immediate election doubtful.

Gesualdo, the Dean, had the greatest difficulty in inducing the Ambassadors to take their departure. Vinta, the Florentine envoy, was still busily pottering in and out of the cubicles, and Sessa, Philip's Ambassador and a grandee, was not to be hurried. He had not yet given Maddruzzo, reinstated as leader of the Spanish party, the King's list of candidates, and was having a last talk with Montalto. It was getting late; Montalto asked to be shown Philip's instructions, which the Spaniard handed to him. There were five names mentioned, headed by S. Severina's, and all equally unwelcome to Montalto. With feigned indifference he returned the document to Sessa and bade him good-night, then as an afterthought added: "Will you do me a favour? I had half promised my friend Aldobrandini to propose him; the King could have no objection to him and it would make things pleasanter for me if his name could be added to the list. S. Severina's election is an absolute certainty; by this time to-morrow he will be Pope and Aldobrandini will never even be mentioned; but I would have the satisfaction of being able to tell him that I had not neglected his interests." Sessa good-naturedly complied with such a harmless request, and being now respectfully but firmly pressed to leave by Gesualdo, hurriedly handed the paper to Maddruzzo without making any reference to the matter, and took his departure.

As soon as the doors were closed Montalto and his followers joined the Spanish contingent to ascertain the number of their adherents. Forty voices answered the roll-call, five more than was necessary to obtain the majority. Elation probably kept S. Severina awake and anxiety must have had the same effect on Montalto. The conspirators had decided to proceed to the adoration at daybreak, and at four o'clock several cardinals had already assembled in S. Severina's cubicle, where that prelate in a state of great excitement was embracing his friends, forgiving his enemies, distributing grants and making preparations against the looting of his cell. By six o'clock the whole force was massed in the passage and a start was made for the Pauline chapel where the ceremony was to take place. Unfortunately for S. Severina, his quarters happened to be situated in the Borgia tower, and to reach its destination the column had to ascend a very dark and narrow stairway, and walk through the entire length of the state apartments. Each cardinal carried a taper, but they cast a very feeble and flickering light on the gloom of vaulted recesses. The procession lost a great deal of its compactness on the way and seemed thinned and straggly when it reached the great audience chamber. There the advancing phalanx encountered Gesualdo, who was not affiliated to any party, and an attempt was made to abduct him forcibly. He offered a strenuous resistance, protesting loudly against the outrage. Some conclavists attracted by the noise came to his rescue, and Gesualdo escaped in a dishevelled and battered condition to give the alarm.

In the throne room the posse found Altemps leaning against the doorpost, and thinking that he had come to join them S. Severina rushed towards him with open arms: "Stand back, Pope of the devil!" roared the old man, shaking his crutch at the would-be pontiff. This apostrophe sent a wave of dismay through the ranks, as it was unbelievable that any man should take such a risk, even with an acknowledged enemy, if his election was a foregone conclusion. Altemps must have some information that had been kept from them. They looked doubtfully at one another and their pace slackened. At the entrance to the Pauline chapel, astride a chair sat Colonna the elder, and his sneering comments as they filed past him made many feel sheepish and uneasy.

On entering the chapel Maddruzzo, still leading the way with his candidate, was much concerned to note that the place was practically dark. A few lights burned on the altar, but the rest of the oratory was completely obscure. No candles could be found anywhere; they appeared to have been spirited away. The confusion seemed inextricable; Maddruzzo attempted several times to make a tally, but the cardinals, like a lot of troublesome schoolboys, would not keep their places, and several conclavists were elbowing their way through the shadowy assembly ostensibly bent on searching for their patrons, but suspiciously prone to the accidental extinguishing of a taper here and there. Maddruzzo, however, was of the race of the Conquistadors and showed such indomitable perseverance that he managed at last to attain his ends, making certain of a total of thirty-four supporters.

One more was necessary, and a couple of cardinals dashed out to fetch Della Rovere, who, being an invalid and thinking himself quite safe in his bed, had promised his adhesion both to Maddruzzo and Altemps. They bundled the tremulous prelate into some clothes and carried him along between them. As, bearing their unwilling burden, they brushed past Altemps still on guard at the doorway, the old man's fury at recognising Della Rovere erupted as lava from a volcano. Had he not been himself a cripple, he would certainly have followed them and assaulted the renegade. As it was he cursed and reviled him with such nerve-shattering venom that Della Rovere sobbed with sheer fright, and died four days later, never having recovered from the shock.

Contrary to all mathematical axioms, the arrival of an extra unit did not bring up the total number of voters from thirty-four to thirty-five. So many lights had now failed that the body of the chapel was practically in darkness and the hubbub seemed to increase every minute. The open suffrage only yielded thirty-four votes. Maddruzzo was nonplussed, but after an intensive search Cardinal Cusano was discovered absorbed in pious meditation behind the altar.

Santa Severina, not unnaturally, was feeling the strain. With hysterical insistence he requested the cardinals to dress him in the pontifical robes, assuring them that his election was perfectly canonical—but none came forward to do his bidding.

Meanwhile the opposing forces had mustered in the Sixtine chapel, and just as Maddruzzo was calling for another ballot, a messenger appeared bearing a secret communication for Ascanio Colonna from his uncle. Its effect was immediate.

"God will not have this Pope, nor will Ascanio Colonna" the young cardinal exclaimed loudly, and he burst out of the chapel, falling headlong into a group of conclavists eavesdropping at the door. Someone got hold of him but he managed to free himself and joined the elder Colonna in the Sixtine chapel, where his arrival was hailed with thunderous applause.

Maddruzzo, fearing that such a dramatic defection might be an incitement to others, cautiously turned the key in the lock, pocketed it, and prepared to say Mass. A deputation from the Sixtine, however, were soon banging on the door expostulating against the pressure brought to bear on the suffragists and threatening to declare any election void. The menace was a serious one and Maddruzzo decided to unlock the door and proceed with the service previous to the scrutiny. The dissidents, not to be outdone, also fulfilled the prescribed rites, so that two simultaneous ceremonies took place in the Pauline and the Sixtine chapels, an event never before recorded in the history of conclaves.

It was now almost daylight, and while the cardinals in the Pauline settled down for the scrutiny S. Severina, almost distraught with excitement, bustled round with promises and encouragements to the staunch, and assurances of goodwill to the wavering. Nobody, he declared, need fear his vengeance, and as an earnest of his benevolent intentions he announced his decision of taking the name of Clement. But alas! the scrutiny only yielded twenty-eight votes in his favour; and his cause was irretrievably lost, for no papal candidate is ever refloated after so crushing a defeat. The man who had felt so certain of his triumph staggered back to his dismantled cell. He has himself confessed in his autobiography that his grief and anguish were such that, "incredible as it may seem, I actually broke into a bloody sweat!"

The entire Sacred College then retired to bed and slept the sleep of exhaustion for many hours. When business was resumed Philip's other candidates were found generally unacceptable. The Grand Duke had felt so confident of S. Severina's election that he had neglected to give his party any further instructions and they were uncertain of his wishes. Now was the time for Montalto to bring forward his candidate. He had no difficulty in recruiting adherents for Aldobrandini among the dissidents who had no official nominee, and Maddruzzo, believing in all good faith that he was obeying the King's orders, gave him the support of the Spanish faction.

On January 30th, therefore, Aldobrandini became Pope under the name of Clement VIII.

It had been generally felt that the election of a pontiff likely to occupy the Apostolic See during a certain number of years was highly desirable. In consequence the announcement of Clement's accession was hailed with enthusiasm. He was then sixty-three years old, but having a superstitious dread of the climacteric year, he gave his age as sixty-two. His constitution was healthy and robust. He was scholarly and reserved; tall and inclined to stoutness. His morals were exemplary. Aldobrandini's family was one of moderately high

standing; he had several distinguished brothers, and his own successful career was due in a great measure to his ability and merits. In
disposition he was peaceable and cautious. Having been entrusted
with several missions to foreign courts, his experience of diplomacy
had developed the latter characteristic to excess. He weighed his
decisions with the utmost prudence, consulting every authority he
thought competent to advise him, with the result that business moved
slowly under his pontificate. He was no friend to Philip. Since
Francis I, to regain his freedom, had transferred to Charles V whatever claims he may have had to the duchy of Milan and the kingdom
of Sicily, the French had completely evacuated the Peninsula and
Spanish influence had increased in consequence. The refusal of the
Holy See to recognise Henry IV's sovereignty over France had
deprived Italy of the only ally she could oppose to the crushing might
of Spain. Clement realised that unless the balance of power was re-
adjusted Italy would practically become a Spanish colony. He therefore, after subjecting Henry IV's envoys to various rebuffs and
humiliations, lifted the ban of excommunication and received the
erring monarch back into the fold.

As to Ferdinand, although S. Severina's defeat had been distinctly
galling to his pride, Aldobrandini's election was to prove of great
benefit to him in the end; for the Pope saw eye to eye with the Grand
Duke, and all through Clement's pontificate they collaborated closely
and continuously in an effective anti-Spanish policy.

Clement VIII had never been of a very sociable disposition, but
after his accession he became noticeably more aloof and retiring. The
Duke of Ferrara's envoy to the Vatican, in a letter to his master,
throws some interesting light on the case:

> His Holiness [he writes] lives in perpetual dread of poison. His
> cook has received the most stringent orders never to allow a
> stranger into the papal kitchens. His Holiness even had his slipper
> burnt after the Duke of Sessa had kissed it!

The Pontiff's partiality for seclusion, however, did not extend to
feeding in private. On the contrary, he would never sit down to a
solitary meal, beggars being often brought in to grace the pontifical
board. It is permissible to surmise that, combining caution with
benevolence, Clement will have seen to it that all his guests had their

share of the victuals before the dishes reached him.

The gout from which he had occasionally suffered grew worse with advancing years and seems to have affected his temper, which became uncertain and even violent. He trusted no one except his nephew Aldobrandini to whom he gave his whole confidence. As time wore on he relied on him more and more, and in the end the entire responsibility of government rested on his shoulders. Although his power was absolute, Aldobrandini does not seem to have abused it to the same extent as many of his predecessors, and showed distinct foresight and political ability.

Clement VIII died after a very short illness in 1605. The description of the remedies applied to him at the last are strongly reminiscent of those used by witch doctors in darkest Africa, and are too hauntingly sickening to be inflicted on the reader. In the realms of science, art and literature Italy had so long shone with the brightest lights in Europe that it comes as a shock to find her physicians so far behind the teachings of Ambroise Paré, and having recourse in the XVIIth century to methods so barbarous and revolting as those employed at the deathbed of Clement VIII.

PLAN DU CONCLAVE
et
Description des Solemnités.
qui s'observent à Rome après la mort d'un Pape, et pour
l'élection d'un Successeur.

Galerie de la Benediction

Echelle de 20. Aunes.

Occident.

Midi.   Nord.

Orient.

l'Eglise   de S. Pierre.

apelle
Sixte
V
le
utin
sait

Cour de
Borgia.

Cour de
Leon X.

La Bibliotheque Vaticane.

Belvedere

Sala Ducale

G

Cour de
Pie IV.

Galerie de Leon

La grande Cour
de la Fontaine.

Galerie de Grez XIII.

C C C
D D D

les Tours

les Cuisines

Cour de
Sixte V.

Quartier
du
Suisses.

S. Ange

du Clerge qui va
ers au Vatican
dor au
Papo

le Tibre

Chambres B. pour le
les Maitres des Ceremo
nies Pour le voyage du
Pour la Redocution des
Garde e General et du

Garde pour le Passage du
Pont S. Ange.

XVIIth CENTURY

Leo XI · Paul V · Gregory XV · Urban VIII
Innocent X · Alexander VII · Clement IX
Clement X · Innocent XI · Alexander VIII
Innocent XII

LEO XI (MEDICI)

1605

So many members of the Sacred College were in receipt of pensions from the Spanish Crown that Clement VIII, in an effort to counterbalance their influence at the conclave which would elect his successor, had created a large number of cardinals. Only twenty-eight survived him; a sufficient force, however, to hold the Spanish party in check, and even possibly to have decided the issue of the conclave if Aldobrandini, its leader, had had the necessary experience of the complicated technique of papal elections.

Sixty-one cardinals were present at the conclave. The Spanish faction numbered twenty-five, with Avila, a self-opinionated, quarrelsome prelate in command.

Between the two chief opposing forces hovered several smaller groups; such as the five French cardinals headed by Joyeuse. These would certainly co-operate with the Florentines with whom Montalto had also thrown in his lot. As soon as the conclave had settled in on March 14th Aldobrandini made his first mistake. Without testing the temper of the assembly, or giving himself time to increase his following, he officially declared his candidate and attempted to rush his election. His choice was in itself an open challenge to Spain, as Baronio, his nominee, had quite lately written a book exposing the abuses of the Spanish rulers in Sicily both in the secular and the ecclesiastical spheres. Philip III's dependants would naturally oppose the most strenuous resistance to the elevation to the Holy See of their Sovereign's personal enemy.

Aldobrandini imagined that because the French faction was naturally antagonistic to Spain he could count on its support. Joyeuse had certainly not been sparing of his protestations of friendship and goodwill, but his orders were to join the Florentines in furthering the election of Cardinal de Medici, a relation both of the Grand Duke's and of the Queen-consort of France.

As was to be expected, the mere mention of Baronio's name stung

Avila into taking immediate action. Aldobrandini's candidate, besides being an avowed enemy of Spain, had an alarming reputation for austerity, and among Clement VIII's creatures many were mere pleasure-loving youths; so to them Avila appealed, painting a ghastly picture of the life that awaited them under such a pontiff. He frightened them so successfully that out of the twenty-eight only twenty-three voted for Baronio at the first scrutiny. The abstention of the French prelates and the defections in the ranks of his own followers was an unexpected blow to Aldobrandini; but he persevered stubbornly in proposing Baronio at every scrutiny.

For several days the number of votes in his favour fell and rose from twenty-three to fifteen and up again, like the temperature chart of a feverish patient. Aldobrandini having thus thoroughly advertised the fact that he had no hold over his own creatures, the other parties were not slow to take advantage of the situation. France bought fifteen of his followers for cash, and most of the others yielded to various bribes, such as promises of bishoprics, pensions and women.

Spain and Florence were also showering gold on the suffragists and Cardinal Cosenza unashamedly sold himself to the highest bidder after a spirited auction, the purchaser being Joyeuse. Besides the money, precious stones and benefices dispensed on such grand scale, small but delicate attentions had not been overlooked. The Spanish Ambassador sent 500 crowns' worth of gloves and cosmetics to Cardinal Ginassi, and Vinta, on behalf of Ferdinand, made a liberal distribution of scent and boxes of sweetmeats to the prelates, presenting d'Este with "the specifics His Highness wished for!"

Aldobrandini, powerless to stem the tide of defection and now convinced that the Grand Duke and his French allies were the chief culprits in sapping his authority, gathered round him his few faithful adherents and offered his services to his opponents. Avila received him courteously enough, and accepted a compromise on his formal assurance that Baronio's candidature would be withdrawn. In exchange the Spanish leader agreed to lend his support to one of Aldobrandini's followers; but the choice was restricted and the selection they made unfortunate. Aldobrandini soon realised how impossible their candidate was, and did not even attempt to launch him. Avila, thinking he had been tricked, and resenting the cool way in which Aldobrandini had ignored their agreement, took the first opportunity of challenging him publicly to explain his behaviour. Aldo-brandini was curt and sullen. The Spaniard stormed and threatened— the followers of both parties joined in the argument, which soon degenerated into a *mêlée*. Conclavists attracted by the commotion took sides and threw themselves whole-heartedly into the fray.

The uproar reached such proportions that the guardians outside the closed doors thought that the Pope had been elected by acclamation and started to break the seals. Fortunately Dietrichstein, an imperial prelate who had held himself aloof from all factions, managed to dominate the tumult. Being a good linguist and evidently a diplomat as well, he persuaded the belligerents that a mere misunderstanding was at the root of the quarrel; that Avila and Aldobrandini had interpreted certain words one in the Spanish and the other in the Italian sense, and that no one was to blame. The excitement died down and a reconciliation took place between the two antagonists, but only a half-hearted one probably, as they never resumed their alliance.

Meanwhile the younger element of the Sacred College, and very young indeed some of its members were, was perpetually getting into mischief in an attempt to relieve the tedium of the proceedings. They had of course established external communications with their friends through holes in the wall; and no sooner was one discovered and blocked up than they contrived another. Their meeting-place was in Cardinal Du Perron's cubicle. The witty Frenchman kept them amused with spicy anecdotes and occasional frolics, and thus obtained a great influence over them. The old Italian prelates were disapproving and censorious and complained to Joyeuse of this unseemly merriment. To pay them out for their interference the youngsters organised a series of pseudo adorations. Masquerading cleverly as their elders, coughing, wheezing, bent double and assuming tremulous falsetto voices, they would break in on the slumbers of one of their aged colleagues, dreaming perhaps of the coveted tiara, and prostrating themselves on the floor of his cell hail him as Pontiff. When the deception had taken effect they would burst into peals of laughter, scuttle away and disperse before their victim could recover from his emotion or identify the culprits. Another of their pranks consisted in purloining the sticks and crutches of the cripples under cover of darkness in the chapel, so that the worshippers remained marooned till their conclavists, surprised at such protracted devotions, became suspicious and rescued their masters quivering with impotent rage. Then the young scamps, now completely unmanageable, took to voting for one another, so that four of them, all under twenty years of age, got several voices which sent the old cardinals, who had never had any themselves, into paroxysms of indignation.

By March 31st Aldobrandini had so hopelessly lost control of his party that Joyeuse and Montalto considered the moment opportune to bring Medici cautiously forward. Aldobrandini tried to warn Avila of the impending danger, but the Spaniard would not listen to him, saying that the leaders had assured him there was no foundation to the rumour, and that albeit they were cardinals they were also gentlemen and he trusted them not to break their word. Although the Medicean conspirators were assured of the necessary majority, they decided to play for safety by having recourse to a nocturnal surprise attack. They therefore went the round of the cubicles with a lantern, declaring to the cardinals that Medici was Pope and that they must hurry if they wished to join in the adoration. They met with little opposition until they reached Avila's cell, which they had prudently left to the last. The fiery Spaniard abused them virulently for their duplicity and dashed out after them half-clothed, and flourishing his stick, protested furiously in the name of His Catholic Majesty against Medici's surreptitious election. Screaming and cursing he pursued the crowd of cardinals, running hither and thither like a sheep-dog harrying a flock, his shrill voice actually rising above the hubbub; till a couple of young cardinals having started to mimic him he fell back breathless but still defiant. He entered the chapel last but one. Behind him, solitary and dejected, walked Aldobrandini. As day broke on April 1st, 1605, Cardinal de Medici became Leo XI.

His accession was hailed with the greatest enthusiasm in Florence and Paris, and was celebrated all over France with the utmost pomp and universal rejoicings. But the bells had scarcely ceased pealing when news was received of the Pontiff's death. His enthronement had been a splendid and costly pageant, for Leo had all his family's predilection for luxury and grandeur. He appeared to have an amiable and peaceful disposition and, though rather colourless, had many friends. His death came as a great blow to Ferdinand and to the

French party, who had all founded great hopes on his pontificate. It was too sudden and unexpected to be natural, his contemporaries thought, and the Grand Duke wrote to Vinta: "Move heaven and earth to discover the cook who served Clement VIII and who remained on in Leo's employ, and who has now disappeared". An ominous message, the sequel to which is unknown.

PAUL V

From a print in the British Museum

PAUL V (BORGHESE)
1605–1621

🐚

SUCH a costly and sterile victory considerably damped the ardour both of France and of Tuscany. They had not yet had time to meet the heavy obligations incurred in the last conclave before they found themselves confronted with another. There was a general tightening of purse-strings even on the part of Spain, who only distributed a few paltry gifts such as bottles of sweet wine, and seemed scarcely interested in the proceedings. Through Vinta, Ferdinand received offers of service from Cardinal Serafino, valued by that prelate at "the sum of 1000 crowns down and the complete equipment of the palace he was then building". But the bargain failed to tempt the Grand Duke.

Fifty-nine cardinals answered the Dean's summons on May 8th, three less than at the former conclave, one prelate having died meanwhile and two others being too ill to attend. Aldobrandini himself was in such bad health that he could scarcely drag himself out of bed. He was suffering from an affection of the lungs and throat and could only speak in a hoarse whisper; but he had heard that there was an intrigue afoot to elect Sauli, and to him it was of vital importance to prevent such an occurrence. Sauli was a man of good reputation and had many friends in the Sacred College, but he had been Clement VIII's personal enemy and had openly resented the immense power with which that Pontiff had invested the Cardinal-Nephew. Sauli was quite capable, as Pope, of calling Aldobrandini to account for his stewardship of the State, as Pius IV had done to the nephews of Paul IV; and although he had certainly not committed the same crimes and atrocities as the Caraffa, yet his conscience was probably not quite as clear as it might have been. There was for instance a bagatelle of 3 million crowns which had been consigned to the Emperor and paid out of the papal treasury, but had never left the Vatican and could not be accounted for. The house of Aldobrandini was of too recent a growth to have very deep roots, and ran the risk of total ruin at Sauli's hands.

Goaded by the peril into making a supreme effort, Aldobrandini had managed to rally round him twenty-four followers in whom he could put sufficient trust. The number was adequate to guarantee Sauli's exclusion if Aldobrandini could himself remain on the breach and prevent any backsliding among his creatures.

Montalto, during the *novemdiale*, had been busy forming a union known as the "Knights' League" consisting of members all bearing names notable in papal circles, such as Farnese, Sforza, d'Este, etc. Each one of them disposed of a few votes, so that added to Montalto's creatures their total number about balanced their opponents'. Sauli might quite possibly have been elected by adoration on the first morning, had not Aldobrandini remained up all night, not allowing a single one of his followers to leave his presence—and so, to his immense relief, the attempt failed. It was his turn now to take the offensive, and he proposed Bellarmini, one of his own creatures, who was as obnoxious to Montalto as Sauli had been to himself. These two skirmishes having come to nothing, various names were put forward but only tentatively, till on May 16th Aldobrandini, fearing his strength would fail him, suddenly decided to launch his real candidate—Tosco. What had induced the leader to select such a man among so many others is a mystery. He was both morally and physically the coarsest creature imaginable. His language and manners were those of a vulgar ruffian. Not only was he the most profane of prelates, but he had no more respect for his fellow creatures' feelings than he had reverence for the Church. Yet the candidature of this foul-mouthed, brutal being brought about an agreement between the two contending parties. Montalto and Aldobrandini met in Monti's cell, and the former, having no personal nominee and having noted some symptoms of discord among his "Knights", yielded, though regretfully, to Aldobrandini's persuasions.

In the evening they mobilised their united forces to proceed to the chapel for the scrutiny which was to confer the papal crown on Tosco. From the independent factions such as the French and the Spanish rose cries of protestation and even cat-calls and hisses. The excited conclavists had pushed Tosco out of his cubicle to loot it more conveniently, and as he was ill and could not remain standing for long, he had taken refuge in Dietrichstein's cell, where he remained in the company of his host to await events.

Aldobrandini counting his followers missed Baronio and sent someone to fetch him; but he refused to obey the summons, and as in such circumstances delay is always dangerous the leader decided to proceed without him, and a move was made towards the chapel.

In the audience-chamber the procession came upon the recalcitrant prelate, who faced his colleagues boldly. Not only was he one of Clement's creatures, but in the last conclave, as will be remembered, Aldobrandini had made every effort to bring about his election. There was no amity, however, in the look he gave his former champion. To Aldobrandini's injunctions to fulfil his party obligations, followed by an appeal to their old friendship, he replied with rage and scorn that he would never vote for any man unworthy of occupying the Apostolic See. An unmistakable movement of vacillation followed this bombshell, and Montalto, acting on a sudden impulse, exclaimed "Let us elect Baronio!" Aldobrandini, white with shock and exhaustion, managed to raise the cry of "Tosco, Tosco!" among his followers. It was immediately answered by that of "Baronio, Baronio!" from Montalto's party, who endeavoured to push their way through to the chapel with Baronio in their midst. The young and lusty contingent of Aldobrandini's creatures set upon them with gusto; the conclavists joined in and a moment later the fight was raging furiously.

When at last Baronio's supporters managed to find shelter in the Pauline chapel several disabled combatants remained prone on the battlefield. The Dean, Cardinal San Giorgio, mounted on a stool, hastened to pronounce a general absolution, for old Cardinal Visconti, lying in a dead faint with several broken bones, seemed in a very serious condition and might not recover. Aldobrandini, his rochet hanging about him in shreds, collected his adherents in the Sixtine, and in both chapels conclavists were soon at work disposing beds and making all preparations as for a siege. The French party, who preferred the anti-Spanish Baronio to his brutish rival, had joined Montalto in the Pauline, while the Spaniards siding with Aldobrandini again brought the numbers about level.

Tosco meanwhile, waiting in the German's cell and hearing the distant clamour, sent a conclavist to enquire what was happening; but the messenger did not return. Dietrichstein then sallied out but must have found himself involved in the proceedings, for he also failed to report. Unable to stand the suspense any longer, Tosco, supported by a couple of servants, dragged himself towards the scene of operations, arriving just as the turmoil had subsided.

Aldobrandini came forward to meet him with every mark of the utmost deference and led him into the chapel where a couch was immediately made ready for him. There he lay, surrounded by attentive satellites, enjoying his few hours of pseudo-sovereignty.

Practically all the members of the Sacred College spent the night in their respective strongholds; and excitement having given way to weariness the rank and file in either camp showed signs of discontent with the chiefs who had led them into such an impasse. The French prelates acting as mediators went to and fro from one chapel to the other and a meeting was at last contrived between the two leaders. They agreed to give up their respective candidates, and after carefully considering the qualifications of several others, finally settled on Borghese, one of Clement VIII's creatures, who seemed the most acceptable, having no enemies and being on friendly terms with Montalto. The confederates then sought out Joyeuse, who, having no objection to Borghese, promised his party's votes. The announcement made by the two leaders to their partisans caused surprise, but roused no opposition; both Baronio and Tosco behaving with creditable self-possession and being among the very first to express their approval—and pay homage to the Pope-elect. The belligerents, now the best of friends, swarmed round the new Pontiff, who took the name of Paul V.

Borghese's forebears were of Siennese origin, but had, like the Aldobrandinis, abandoned their native Tuscany to escape from the tyranny of the Medici, eventually settling in Rome. They were not rich or powerful, and Paul had started life in a lawyer's office before embracing the more promising ecclesiastical career. He was a tall, heavily built, handsome man, with a healthy complexion, shiny red gold hair, and his arms and hands were covered with a thick growth of down. The older cardinals gazed with consternation on this Hercules, who was only fifty-nine years of age and might well be expected to see them all into their graves. The Great Powers, who knew nothing of him, reserved their opinion until better informed of the new Pope's character and political views, and only tendered formal and conventional congratulations. As to Paul himself, he loudly proclaimed his conviction that the Holy Ghost had singled him out to fulfil his high office and had miraculously imposed him on the suffragists.

The metamorphosis from a pleasant, popular prelate into an autocratic merciless Pontiff was more marked in Paul V perhaps than in any of his predecessors except in Sixtus V. He demanded undiluted servility from those around him and would not accept even the shadow of a criticism in the consistories. His decisions were purely arbitrary and he refused ever to discuss them, either with the Sacred College in relation to ecclesiastical questions, or with the diplomatic envoys in matters of foreign policy. The strictest of disciplinarians where others were concerned, he insisted on the cardinals who held distant bishoprics leaving Rome to reside in them; the alternative being the loss of their benefices. The dutiful observance of regulations which he exacted from his subordinates would have been more impressive had he himself respected those concerning the abuses of nepotism, but this most self-righteous of pontiffs loaded his family with honours and riches just as blatantly as any of his less sanctimonious predecessors had done.

The Italian States were soon enlightened as to the attitude the new Pontiff meant to adopt, for immediately after his enthronement he started to pick quarrels with them all, interfering in their internal jurisdiction under pretext of ecclesiastical privilege. He took action with such rapidity that, not having had time to organise a concerted line of defence, Genoa, Florence and Ferrara thought it safer to submit for the time being to his outrageous encroachments on their independence. When it came to brow-beating Venice, however, it was quite another matter. The Republic had been used to fighting her own battles and emphatically refused to comply with the Pope's tyrannical orders. She simply ignored his excommunications and her clergy sided with their government. The Jesuits were the only ones to obey the summons from Rome by leaving Venetian territory, which delighted the Council of Ten, who had long wanted to get rid of them and now had an excellent excuse to forbid their return. Had Paul dared to do so he would have declared war on Venice—as it was, he eventually had to come to terms with the Republic through the mediation of the Powers.

Nor was the Duke of Ossuna, Spanish governor of Sicily, in the least intimidated by the Pope's anathemas. He wasted no time on remonstrating with him, but had a scaffold erected opposite the Archbishop's palace, the gallows being moved slightly nearer to it every day. The effect of this device, admirable in its simplicity, was most satisfactory, as in the shortest possible delay an order to lift the ban arrived from Rome, without a single word or note having been exchanged by the parties on the subject of the dispute.

No Pope showed more lack of political sense than Paul V. He found fault with all the reigning monarchs in turn till he had not a friend or an ally left in Europe. Even had he been willing to listen to advice there was no one near the Throne with enough experience or sagacity to help him, as he had dismissed all the previous holders of government posts and offices to appoint his brothers and nephews in their place. Ranke says that:

> as he had employed no arts or intrigues to attain the papal dignity he attributed his elevation entirely to divine inspiration and therefore considered himself God's real vice-regent on earth.

That Paul, a Roman born and bred, should genuinely have developed such a simple-hearted belief in supernatural mass-suggestion after attending a couple of conclaves, is difficult to believe. Is it not more likely that the sudden shock of such unexpected and overwhelming good fortune affected his mental balance? He certainly showed unmistakable symptoms of that peculiar form of aberration which a French writer has called "Cesaritis".

Paul V died of an apoplectic stroke on January 28th, 1621.

GREGORY XV (Ludovisi)

1621–1623

❦

As the older cardinals had only too accurately surmised, Paul V outlived a large proportion of his former colleagues, but not, strange to say, the consumptive Aldobrandini, who, however, was by now at death's door. The conclave which met on February 8th, 1621, was to be a very short one. Borghese, the late Cardinal-Nephew, had such an imposing cohort of followers that he considered his choice of a candidate as good as an election. He had settled on Campori, one of his uncle's creatures who was young enough to occupy the Holy See until he himself was sufficiently mature to step into his shoes. Borghese was well aware that Aldobrandini's days were numbered, and hoped that the hardships of a long journey in the bitter cold weather would either deter him from attending the conclave or put an end to his sufferings.

Montalto was now an ageing and broken man, and although he still disposed of a few stray votes, was not a very formidable opponent. Campori, in his anxiety to gain supporters before entering the Vatican, had made promises and offers of future benefices to several cardinals, so that his candidature was an open secret. This gave his enemies sufficient leisure to prepare their plans for his defeat. His two principal antagonists were the Venetian Republic and Orsini. Venice objected to him on political grounds and the Council of Ten forbade their subjects to vote for him, threatening that in case of disobedience "they and their families would be treated as rebels". Orsini's enmity was of a private nature. Both he and Campori had paid their addresses to a lady of the Borghese family and she had favoured Campori.

Borghese of course was well acquainted with these facts, but his twenty-nine votes gave him complete confidence. He only needed two or three more to reach the required majority, and as the procession of cardinals moved towards the Vatican to enter into conclave he noted with satisfaction that Aldobrandini was not among them, which meant that his few remaining followers would be leaderless and therefore open to parley. He felt himself in a position to defy both Orsini and the Republic and strode forward with great assurance followed by Campori who made no attempt to conceal his elation. They were both badly shaken, therefore, when on reaching the Pauline chapel they caught sight of Aldobrandini, looking ghostly enough certainly but unmistakably present in the flesh and closely surrounded by his five creatures.

Orsini was in command of the opposing faction. He needed two more supporters to make certain of checkmating Borghese, and two cardinals, who had been exiled by Paul V and on whose adhesion he could therefore rely, were due to arrive in the early hours of the morning. If he could prevent Campori's election being carried by adoration during the night, the exclusion of his hated rival (in other fields) was a certainty. France had no desire to see one of Paul V's creatures succeed him, so Orsini persuaded the French Ambassador to spend the night within the precincts of the conclave, which would invalidate any election that might take place.

When Cardinal Varese, whose duty it was to clear the premises of outsiders and close the doors, respectfully pointed out to the French Ambassador that all his colleagues had left and that it was time he did likewise, the diplomat replied haughtily that he would go when he pleased and not a moment sooner. On reiterated attempts being made by Varese, he dared the prelate to interfere with His Most Christian Majesty's envoy; so that against all regulations the doors remained open through the night. In the early hours of the morning the two cardinals whom Orsini was expecting arrived, but before he had had time to exchange a word with them Borghese's creatures rushed forward and attempted to drag them aside. The bewildered travellers, who had had a long and tiring journey and knew nothing of the current events, were tugged this way and that, being unable in the pandemonium to grasp the situation. Sforza, however, managed to enlighten them in a few words and they declared themselves emphatically opposed to Borghese's candidate. The French Ambassador then took his departure, and Campori, acknowledging his defeat, withdrew his candidature.

Through the good offices of Medici, a compromise was reached between all the leaders, who agreed upon the elevation of Ludovisi to the Holy See. He was an aged, feeble old man and his pontificate was not expected to last more than a few months.

The procession which moved towards the chapel to elect him must have resembled those seen at miraculous shrines, for among the cardinals several were too ill to walk and had to be supported or carried on stretchers. Such was the case of Ludovisi himself. Every precaution had been taken while dressing him to prevent his swooning, for his weakness was alarming. Some others, however, were in an even more parlous condition. Aguino, for instance, had to be hurriedly brought back to his cell where he died almost at once, while Aldobrandini, though he managed to live through the electoral sitting, only survived it a few hours.

Ludovisi, who became Gregory XV, reigned for two and a half years and his short pontificate is one of the most important in the history of the Church of Rome. Both the Pope and the Cardinal-Nephew had been brought up by the Jesuits and remained devoted to their interests. Ludovico Ludovisi was a young man of twenty-five when his uncle's accession raised him to the customary position conferring so much power and entailing so much responsibility on its holder. He was extremely handsome, with a commanding presence, and certainly possessed an outstanding personality added to a remarkable aptitude for statesmanship. Historians disagree as to the respective shares taken by the uncle and the nephew in the conduct of affairs, some ascribing all the initiative to Gregory, while others assert that he was a mere cypher, leaving the entire burden of government to Ludovisi. However that may be, the effects of the policy adopted by the Holy See were far-reaching. An extraordinary impetus was given to the promulgation of the Roman Catholic faith all over the world. The Jesuits had already established important settlements in Central America and followed everywhere in the wake of Catholic explorers. But now they themselves acted as pioneers, penetrating boldly into the remotest and most dangerous countries such as China and unexplored parts of Asia. In Japan they founded twenty houses; and a Jesuit at the head of a handful of soldiers practically conquered Abyssinia though his victory bore little fruit. Of the immense number of conversions the Jesuits effected, often by strange and questionable methods, in those distant savage lands, few had a lasting effect on the native populations; but at the moment it looked as though the Pope's authority would soon encircle the globe. Gregory showed his appreciation of the Jesuits' services by canonising Ignatius Loyola, their founder, and Francis Xavier, who had Christianised Goa and the Portuguese Indies.

But there was also important work to be done nearer home, and as the Jesuits were not sufficiently numerous to undertake it unaided, other orders such as the Dominicans, the Franciscans and the Augustines were enrolled as members of "The Society for the Propagation of the Faith". Hordes of them under the leadership of Carlo Caraffa overran Germany, Austria, Hungary and even the Low Countries. Several princes and noblemen, finding that Protestant beliefs tended to the development of socialistic principles, joined the Church of Rome and lent all their support to the proselytisers. A tidal wave of conversions seemed to sweep Europe, and in districts where the populations evinced reluctance to follow the movement pastors were dismissed and their places filled by Catholic missionaries.

An important subsidy was granted by the Pope to the Emperor, and, added to the arbitrary confiscation of much Protestant property, enabled the Crown to support the Catholic propaganda and establish it firmly in the large areas it had reclaimed. The result of this successful coalition between the two Sovereigns was to bring Austria to the forefront both as a European Power and as a bulwark of the Roman Church.

Whatever his share in the foreign policy of the Holy See, Gregory's bulls regarding the observance of regulations laid down for the conclaves must have been entirely of his own devising. Although he probably owed his elevation to the French Ambassador's disregard of those rules, he strove by his edicts to prevent a recurrence of such flagrant abuses, going into the minutest details concerning the ceremonial to be observed, regulations which have been adhered to ever since.

The Ludovisi attitude towards the Great Powers was one of conciliation and courtesy. James I obtained, without conditions, the dispensation he sought for the marriage of the Prince of Wales with a Catholic princess, a favour Paul V had refused even to consider; the result of this concession being that the Catholics in England were treated with much more leniency and toleration. The papal envoys to the court of Madrid were instructed to moderate the royal zeal and discourage religious excesses. In France, where the Jesuits were allowed full scope for their activities, the Huguenots were reduced to a powerless and insignificant party, and Richelieu was rewarded with the hat which he coveted so ardently.

As was natural, the interests of the house of Ludovisi were not overlooked. The family sprang from an ancient and noble stock and Ludovico had all the pride of race of the Neapolitan aristocracy to which he belonged. He certainly added considerably to the fortunes of his house, but he acted with tact and circumspection, always guided by the worldly wisdom he seems to have possessed to an extent surprising in one so young. For instance when the Catholic Valteline, which had broken away from the Protestant Grisons, offered their allegiance to the Pontiff, either as subjects of the Holy See or to form an appanage for his family, the proposal would have proved irresistibly tempting to most ambitious cardinal-nephews, and ambitious Ludovico certainly was. But he had the sense to foresee the inevitable political complications such a measure would entail, and refused the offer both for the Holy See and the Ludovisi. Considering the corrupt times in which he lived, if he did find means of compensating his family for possessions and honours he had forgone, can he really be blamed? Especially as owing to the Pope's precarious hold on life he knew that his tenure of office was bound to be a short one.

More was accomplished during the two and a half years of Gregory's pontificate to restore the power and prestige of the Apostolic See than had been done by any of his predecessors for the past 150 years; but although the papal government had striven consistently to preserve peace among the Powers, when Gregory XV died in July 1623 Europe was on the brink of war, and the policy and disposition of the new Pope would have such an important influence on the trend of events that the result of the coming election could not but be of the greatest interest to all parties concerned.

URBAN VIII
From a print in the British Museum

URBAN VIII (BARBERINI)
1623-1644

GREGORY XV's pontificate had been too short to allow of his creating a great number of cardinals. Richelieu mentions in his memoirs that on his death-bed, as Ludovico was begging the Pope to strengthen his party by a few more nominations, Gregory refused to do so, adding "that he would already have to account to God for having made so many unworthy ones"—an unexpected pronouncement to find recorded by a man who himself owed him the hat!

Ludovisi therefore entered the conclave on July 19th with a number of followers considerably inferior to Borghese's, whose phalanx was still practically complete. But to counteract this deficiency he had the tremendous advantage of a vastly superior intellect and unquestionable prestige. He had only just stepped down from a position of the greatest importance which he had filled brilliantly, and was besides possessed of a remarkably quick and resourceful mind; while Borghese was incapable, effeminate and unreliable. Two of the most prominent members of the last few conclaves had now disappeared: Aldobrandini, whose nephew had been given his uncle's hat, but was still without influence or experience; and Montalto, the erstwhile don Juan, who had recently died. Ludovisi had no difficulty in annexing the few followers who had survived their dead leaders, especially as Bandini, his official candidate, was a creature of Clement VIII's. As usual there were many among the cardinals who openly or secretly coveted the papal tiara. Here are a few of them: the Cardinal-Dean Sauli, the man Aldobrandini had so much feared—his eighty-five years were certainly a point in his favour, but he was known to be completely under the influence of his valet and the man's wife; Monti, the faithful henchman of the Grand Dukes of Tuscany, the most charming cynic in the Sacred College, but too whole-heartedly devoted to Florence; Ginnasio, an inveterate gambler, who had won 200,000 crowns in one night's play at the house of the Duchess of Uzeda when he was Nuncio in Madrid; Araceoli, an austere, fearsome Dominican; Mellini, a double-faced, shifty creature, burdened with numberless debts and nephews; Campori, Borghese's candidate in the last election, badly handicapped by some former scandal of which Orsini held written proofs; Ascoli, a monk who thought uncleanliness a sign of godliness and was generally shunned by his colleagues. There were others besides, too numerous and insignificant to be worth mentioning. The question of the Valteline had now reached a crucial stage, and Italy was looking once more to France to defend her from the bullying of Spain and Austria.

Richelieu, seeing in the election of a Francophile pope an excellent opportunity for France to regain her former influence in northern Italy, was more than willing to play a part in the proceedings, especially as there happened to be present in the ranks of the Sacred College a man whom he knew personally to be genuinely devoted to his interests. This prelate, called Barberini, belonged to a Florentine family which had made a large fortune in trade. Being an orphan, Maffeo Barberini had been sent to Rome as an infant to be brought up by an uncle who was a member of the curia. When the child developed into a most promising young man, the ecclesiastical career naturally suggested itself to the Barberini as the most auspicious field for Maffeo's talents. It was soon apparent that fortune favoured him very especially. He obtained the coveted post of nuncio to the French court and shortly after he was made a cardinal.

This last stroke of luck was due to the fact that Mellini, the Nuncio to Spain, having received the hat, France had immediately requested as a matter of etiquette that a like honour should be conferred on Barberini. Paul V had had to comply with the demand but resented it, and always treated Barberini with great coldness. Borghese had also adopted an attitude of unfriendliness towards him, so although he actually belonged to that leader's faction he was not bound to him by any feelings of gratitude or loyalty. Richelieu, well aware of this state of things, made secret arrangements with Ludovisi and the Grand Duke of Tuscany to support Barberini when their official candidates had failed, which they were bound to do. He also won over d'Este and several Roman prelates; but even then Borghese's forces could hold their adversaries in check and would have to be undermined by some means or other. The means were soon discovered.

In the Spanish faction siding with Borghese was Cardinal Borgia, a clever, crafty diplomat who was thoroughly discontented with his own King for having given the leadership of the party to Zapata instead of to himself, and with Borghese to whom he owed a personal grudge, as Paul V had ordered him to demolish the towers built by Alexander VI to protect the entrance to his Roman palace; and Borgia knew Borghese to have been the instigator of a measure which he considered tyrannical and vexatious. He therefore lent a ready ear to France's blandishments, especially as the secret agreement he drew up with Barberini fully satisfied his thirst for revenge.

Borghese's candidate, Mellini, had been a personal enemy of Gregory XV, and such a choice was equivalent to a declaration of war to Ludovisi, who would oppose his election with the utmost energy. The situation therefore was as follows: Borghese, proposing Mellini but not quite strong enough to secure his election without some outside assistance; the Florentines proposing Monti; and Ludovisi proposing Bandini, both meaning eventually to elect Barberini; the French intending to join their confederates when the time came and lying low meanwhile; the Spanish party siding with Borghese officially, but Borgia at any rate meaning to play him false.

The scrutinies began with a monotonous swing of the pendulum between Mellini and Bandini. As Ludovisi's nominee had been persecuted by Paul V, his situation was identical to that of Mellini. There was not the slightest chance of his being elected, as he was a Florentine hated by the Medici, and had eighty-three nephews to provide for, which was scarcely likely to endear him to his colleagues. Several days went by and from the electoral point of view matters were at a standstill; but the enmity between the two leaders made steady progress. Their attitude towards each other became so hostile and discourteous as to cause embarrassment to their followers, who at last prevailed on them with great difficulty to patch up a reconciliation. They were induced to shake hands and exchange a few civil words, but the good understanding went no further.

The heat was becoming terribly oppressive and the cardinals were appalled at the idea of a long conclave under such exceptionally unhygienic conditions; for not only were many prelates confined to their beds with the ague, but twenty-five conclavists were also laid up and incapable of attending to their duties. The cubicles and the passages were in a condition of nauseating neglect: "the atmosphere being laden with putrid miasmas and sickening smells of decaying victuals that the potent perfumes of the young cardinals could not manage to disguise". To add to the general discomfort, fleas, always plentiful in Rome, appeared in such hordes that the tastiest among their victims were literally being devoured alive.

On August 2nd Borghese had a sharp attack of fever and Borgia decided that time had come for action. After consulting with Ludovisi, Medici and Aldobrandini he approached Farnese, who was also on the sick-list and who was fretting to get back to his palace in Parma. He agreed readily enough to their plan, welcoming any means of escaping from such a gehenna. But even with all these recruits, the coalition was not sufficiently strong to carry an election without Borghese's assent. Barberini undertook to canvass among his own party, and as he was intimately acquainted with his colleagues' foibles and secret ambitions, his offers and promises ranging from matrimonial contracts to archbishoprics were very favourably received. Still as long as Borghese stood out it would have been too hazardous to risk the attempt, and Borghese stubbornly refused to support Barberini, fearing that as Pope he would pay him out for his incivilities. It was a well-known fact to his colleagues that Borghese would never vote for any man younger than himself, so the coalition, pretending to drop Barberini, offered to support any one of three creatures of Borghese whom they named, all of whom were younger than their leader. When Borghese rejected this suggestion the deputation threw up their hands in mock despair. What more could they do? Borghese was so unreasonable that, having sworn to elect none but a creature of his uncle's, he yet refused all those suggested to him!

On August 5th Borghese had another and more severe attack of fever and wrote to the Dean in a panic for permission to leave the conclave. Borgia and Ludovisi, immediately apprised of the fact, called a meeting of the Sacred College to protest against the permit being granted, under pretext that the leader's absence would create a deadlock and that the entire assembly would have to expose their health and lives for the convenience of one man. The prospect of an indefinitely protracted conclave resulted in a unanimous decision against the granting of the exeat.

The Cardinal Prince of Savoya was entrusted with the mission of informing Borghese that the Dean was regretfully obliged to withhold the permit he had applied for. When the invalid had sufficiently recovered from the fit of rage induced by this announcement, it was suggested to him that Barberini's election would be the simplest and quickest way of solving the difficulty. There was nothing Spartan about the fat, self-indulgent, pleasure-loving Borghese, and his opponents knew that now they had him at their mercy. Sooner than face the risk entailed by remaining any longer in the insalubrious atmosphere of the conclave he gave his grudging consent. Immediately Ludovisi ordered the chapel bell to be rung. Borghese himself wrapped in blankets was carried there and Barberini's election took place at once, the new Pontiff assuming the name of Urban VIII. Borghese recovered; but several other cardinals died from the effects of that poisonous claustration, Urban himself being so ill that his enthronement had to be postponed for a couple of months.

Barberini's election was a signal triumph for French diplomacy. Those years of his nunciature at the French Court when he had been young and fêted and enjoyed life to the full had left an indelible impression on his tastes and political outlook. For him France never lost her glamour; he was always to be in sympathy with her aims and antagonistic to her enemies.

Physically, morally and mentally what manner of man was this enthusiastic Gallomaniac that Richelieu had raised to the Apostolic See? Zeno, the Venetian envoy, writes the following description of him to the Senate:

> The new Pontiff is 56 years old. He came out of the conclave in bad health owing to the pestilential atmosphere and the bodily disorders caused by the vehemence of the passions that affect cardinals in those assemblies, disabling some and killing others. His Holiness is tall, dark, with regular features and black hair turning grey. He is exceptionally elegant and refined in all details of his dress; has a graceful and aristocratic bearing and exquisite taste. He is an excellent speaker and debater, writes verses and patronises poets and men of letters.

Urban VIII's chief characteristic was undoubtedly conceit—a self-inflation so colossal as to be positively impressive. So immeasurably superior to ordinary mortals did he consider himself that his exalted sacerdotal dignity scarcely added lustre, in his estimation, to his own personal effulgence. Divine intervention would have been superfluous to bring his merits to the notice of his colleagues, for they were too transcendental to be missed. His candour on the subject of his inherent greatness was almost disarming.

Precedents, regulations, age-old institutions, nothing was ever allowed to interfere with his whims and fancies. He wished to have his statue placed in the Capitol; but there was a law in force that no living pope should have one erected, as scandalous scenes of outrages and mutilation of statues had followed the death of unpopular pontiffs. Urban revoked the decree, countering any objection that might be raised by remarking complacently: "Such a law could not apply to a Pope such as I!" One of his favourite arguments when breaking regulations was: "The decision of a living Pope is worth more than those of all the dead Popes put together". He discarded the ecclesiastical trammels of papacy and adopted the free and martial demeanour of a purely temporal sovereign. He spent his time either studying plans of fortifications and reading theories on strategy, or alternately declaiming the poems of Petronius, or writing verses himself, the nature of which would certainly have startled the Psalmist.

Urban expended vast sums on building the fortress of Castel Franco, or Fort Urbano, near Bologna, the strategic value of which was apparent to no one but himself. He added a defensive wall to S. Angelo and made the passage from the Vatican to the fortress safer and more convenient; he opened a factory for arms at Tivoli and turned the vaults of the Vatican library into an arsenal. He ruthlessly destroyed the antique monuments in the Colonna gardens which stood in his way when he decided to erect a parapet round his residence of Monte Cavallo, and he would have demolished the tomb of Cecilia Metella to make use of the Travertine stones with which it was constructed had not the Roman people risen in revolt and opposed such a menacing resistance that the projected act of vandalism had to be abandoned.

The spirit of contradiction was so highly developed in Urban VIII that he would not fail to run counter to his own opinions if expressed by anybody else. The Venetian envoy turned this characteristic to good account and managed to obtain the most unhoped-for concessions from the Pontiff merely by pleading the opposite of what he wanted. Urban treated the Sacred College with the most withering contempt, never called consistories and completely ignored the *consulta*. His disregard for all accepted forms and traditions was such that his nephew Francesco Barberini, fearful of what the future might hold for him, cautiously refused to take any responsibility concerning the measures adopted by his uncle.

As to the ambassadors, he made it impossible for them ever to introduce a subject however important. He continued with one the conversation begun with another, held forth continually and admitted of no interruption.

The wealth acquired by the Barberini family was fabulous, probably exceeding that amassed by any other pontifical house excepting the Farnese. The regal palace of the Quattro Fontane stands to this day as a witness of the style in which they lived. It was stacked with the finest works of art money could buy, the furniture was sumptuous and all the household utensils of solid gold or silver. The jewels of the Barberini were famous all over Italy and came near eclipsing those of the Medici. It was the invariable custom for the family of the new pontiff to elbow out that of his predecessor, a process which naturally resulted in violent animosities and led to the feuds we have witnessed in the conclaves. But besides falling out with the Ludovisi the Barberini quarrelled with all the other great papal houses as well. Not only would they admit of no superior magnificence but brooked no equality. The Farnese, however, they could not eclipse, and when Duke Odoardo, who had precisely the same notions about his own importance, visited Rome to pay his respects to the Pope, a lively hatred sprang up between the two clans. It resulted later in the seizure of Castro, a Farnese possession, by the papal troops and the excommunication of the Duke. The other Italian States sided with Farnese, as the Pope had already annexed Urbino and they did not intend to let him get hold of Parma and Piacenza as well. Venice also joined the league, and thus assured of the support of his neighbours, Farnese started off on a campaign of his own without artillery or provisions, yet sweeping all before him.

The famous Fort Urbano did not impede his progress, the papal mercenaries offering no resistance, and he marched right up to the gates of Rome, which he might have sacked with the greatest ease had he chosen to do so. But for some unknown reason there he paused; giving

Urban time to enrol a new army which fell on the badly equipped
Farnese troops, dispersing them without difficulty and driving the
Duke out of the Papal States. There followed a stage of desultory and
aimless warfare between the forces of the league and those of the
Holy See, the net result of which was to exhaust the resources of all
the combatants. The pontifical supplies having been the first to give
out, Urban had to turn to France for assistance. Richelieu offered to
mediate, and a peace treaty was drawn up which was certainly not
an advantageous one for Urban. He undertook to restore Castro to
Duke Odoardo and to lift the ban of excommunication he had
laid on him. Several concessions were granted to the other members
of the league, and altogether the conditions he had to accept proved
so galling to the Pope's pride that he actually swooned with mortification after signing the agreement.

His foreign policy was unswervingly Francophile. He treated the
Emperor with persistent churlishness, never lost an opportunity of
slighting him and refused all his requests on principle, however
reasonable they might be. Urban's hostility to Austria led him to
withhold from Ferdinand not only those supplies in men and money
which he naturally expected from Rome, but even the customary
indulgences, which was indeed mean! The Emperor therefore had
to carry on, single-handed and unblessed, the campaign he had
started so enthusiastically with the help and encouragement of
Gregory XV. Urban not only abandoned his predecessor's ally but
even went so far, at Richelieu's instigation, as to favour Gustavus
Adolphus' invasion of Germany. He appears to have been a party to
the intrigues which, by bringing about the disgrace of Wallenstein,
deprived the Empire of the services of the only man capable of
defending her.

The King of Spain, incensed at the Pope's behaviour towards the
Emperor, commanded Borgia to offer a protest to His Holiness,
which the Spaniard did with great spirit and determination. Such
audacity had a galvanic effect on the Pontiff. He sprang from his seat,
burst forth into a torrent of insults and abuse, and as Borgia seemed
prepared to stand his ground and defy Urban's wrath, Cardinal
Barberini, who was young and of powerful build, threw himself on
the Spanish prelate, pinioned him and dragged him from the room.
This incident almost brought about an open rupture between

Philip IV and the Pope, but as just then the King of Sweden's repeated victories in Germany were making him dangerously powerful, Urban suddenly adopted a more conciliatory attitude towards the Spanish-Austrian Powers and the storm blew over.

The Pope's treatment of Borgia caused the greatest indignation among his colleagues, and Ludovisi even spoke of summoning a council to pass judgment on Urban for his manifest indifference to religious matters and his hostility towards the sovereigns who were fighting for the Roman faith. These accusations were certainly well founded, for he had consistently subordinated religion to politics, and by hindering the champions of Catholicism had destroyed most of the advantages obtained by his predecessor, and to him can be assigned a fair share of responsibility in the Thirty Years' War. Ludovisi's motion came to nothing, however, as shortly after returning to his archbishopric of Bologna he died, and no other member of the College of Cardinals had the standing or personality to carry out such a design.

Much no doubt would have been forgiven to Urban VIII had he not gone down to posterity as the Pope who handed Galileo over to the Inquisition. By destroying his writings and condemning the aged scientist to perpetual confinement and supervision, the Holy Office delayed the world's enlightenment, and by approving the sentence the Pontiff assumed responsibility for it. Urban VIII will always be associated with the picture of the cowed and broken genius, brought to his knees to retract publicly and in terms of abject submission the great discovery his contemporaries were not ready to grasp.

Petrucelli says that it was not till 1820 that the Church of Rome officially allowed Catholics to refer to the rotary movement of the earth.

Urban, though not impressed by Galileo's *Dialogues*, was considered a man of culture and literary tastes. He had a magnificent edition of the Roman Breviary printed, as well as a collection of his own poems. Like most Roman pontiffs he wished to leave his mark on the Eternal City, and commissioned Bernini to execute, besides the building of the Barberini Palace, numerous works of art in St. Peter's and elsewhere. But as the artist had a long career of practically uninterrupted favour and success under eight pontificates, Bernini's artistic innovations and achievements have remained entirely his own. The coats of arms of the successive Popes profusely distributed over all his buildings bear testimony to the patronage which enabled him to transform the Rome of the Renaissance and of the counter-Reformation into the Rome we see to-day. But to Urban VIII Bernini was not only the greatest artist of his times, he was also his chosen friend and companion. They both loved theatrical entertainments and the artist wrote witty satirical plays and sketches which were enacted for the Pontiff's amusement. It is difficult to understand how Bernini found leisure to attend simultaneously to the building of palaces, the embellishments in St. Peter's, the chiselling of statuary and the painting of the scenery for his plays, while in constant attendance on Urban. Yet he accomplished this difficult feat, never failing to fulfil any contract he undertook. In addition to the statue which Urban insisted on placing in the Capitol, he also executed numerous busts of the Pontiff, to His Holiness' great satisfaction.

It was Urban VIII who gave the cardinals the title of "Eminence", "most illustrious and most reverend" having been the mode of address in use up to that time. "Eminence" had the great advantage of being both shorter and more adaptable to all languages. The Pope died on July 29th, 1644, calling down all the maledictions of heaven upon his enemies, and accusing them of having robbed him of many years of life through the vexations they had caused him.

INNOCENT X
From the painting by Velasquez in the Doria Gallery, Rome

INNOCENT X (Pamfili)
1644–1655

🐚

Urban VIII's Gallomania had caused a natural reaction in the Sacred College in favour of Spain; the cardinals strongly resented not only the political guidance Italy had been subjected to, but also the inordinate length of the late pontificate. So although the Barberini entered the conclave with forty-eight creatures, which was an enormous following, their position was not as strong as it might appear. Urban VIII had not been content with one Cardinal-Nephew. Acting on the principle that the Barberini must eclipse all other papal houses, he had allowed himself two. To these two men, Antonio and Francis Barberini, the election of the new pope meant either security and the enjoyment of their riches, or ruin and exile and perhaps even death. They would naturally turn for support to France, then ruled by their friend Mazarin under the regency of the Queen Mother Anne of Austria, Louis XIV being but a child. The anti-French tendencies of the conclave, however, made it perilous for them to declare themselves openly and exclusively Mazarin's adherents, for if they failed to secure the election of their own candidate they would find themselves in a desperate situation. They therefore decided on a plan of campaign which would ensure their safety whatever happened. Antonio accepted Mazarin's offer of the leadership of the French party with a life annuity of 32,000 crowns, while Francis treated much on the same lines with Madrid. There existed in the conclave a third independent group of Italian cardinals led by Colonna who, having no official candidate, might be open to negotiations but were distinctly anti-French.

Mazarin's instructions were to further Sacchetti's election—an excellent choice as he was an exceptionally upright dignified prelate, a sound politician, intelligent and highly cultured—but as a protégé of France he was definitely excluded by Spain, and being young, inacceptable to the majority of cardinals.

The Spanish candidate, Pamfili, was also a striking personality.

His private life was not above suspicion like Sacchetti's, as he was known to be slavishly devoted to his widowed sister-in-law, Donna Olympia Pamfili, who for many years now had held him in thraldom; but Roman morals were lax and this long-standing attachment was readily condoned.

Pamfili was silent, reserved and exquisitely courteous. He was certainly not handsome with his bulbous nose, small close-set eyes and thin straggly beard; but his bearing was distinguished and pleasing.

The conclave had been assembled for three weeks before the first scrutiny took place, so busy were all the electors with their intrigues and financial transactions. Antonio Barberini was distributing abbeys and benefices and granting life annuities with a lavish hand, for besides his own vast wealth and possessions he disposed of the large sums of ready money which were pouring in from France.

Heiresses were being bartered against bishoprics and other dignities, a Gaëtano who had a splendid dowry playing an important part in the proceedings. The new Spanish Ambassador's arrival gave a renewed impetus to the bargaining as he made his appearance in a perfect blaze of Oriental splendour, having, he announced, sufficient doubloons in his coffer to buy up the whole conclave. He also had a couple of opulent princesses to dispose of in holy wedlock and fine estates to bestow in the kingdom of Naples. His first move, a very wise one, was to pay Cardinal de Medici's debts, which amounted to 150,000 crowns.

For practically a century now papal interregnums had lost their character of lawless brigandage and become a period of merry-making and carnival masquerades. But while the conclave sat in August 1644 Rome wore no such festive aspect. The Duke of Parma's troops were known to be advancing on the city, and armed bands, levied, it was rumoured, by the Barberini, filled the streets with a martial tumult that could be heard even from the Vatican. The situation was certainly disquieting and the Sacred College began to feel the pressure of circumstances, so on August 29th the voting began in real earnest. Sacchetti's name was put forward by Antonio Barberini, but the result of the scrutiny was disappointing; nor did Francis obtain much better results with Pamfili on the following day.

Foreseeing the dangers of a protracted conclave, the two brothers now sought for means of winning one another over without loss of patronage and security. Antonio made the first move through the agency of M. de St. Chaumont, the French Ambassador. The terms offered were so advantageous that the affair would certainly have been concluded had it not been for the Frenchman's greed. Ten thousand doubloons and the bishopric of Avignon for one of his relations had been agreed upon as his private commission on the transaction, but when the compact was submitted to the brothers for signature, Antonio found that the sum now claimed by St. Chaumont was 20,000 doubloons to be paid immediately in cash or jewels of corresponding value. He was so enraged by this extortionate demand that he broke off all negotiations, much to the French Ambassador's surprise and discomfiture.

It was now Francis Barberini's turn to come forward with proposals from the Spanish party; they were substantial and satisfactory; for Pamfili was not only Philip IV's nominee but he was also acceptable to the Italian party, and in their name as well as in the King of Spain's he guaranteed the safety of the Barberini, giving his solemn promise to protect them from all attacks and reprisals and to obtain for them the Spanish Monarch's patronage. Evidently the dramatic history of the Caraffa did not in any way damp the optimism of the Barberini, for as soon as Pamfili had signed and sealed the document they repaired without demur to Medici's cell. Colonna's party was summoned to a conference and a general agreement reached without difficulty. The next morning Pamfili was proclaimed Pope under the name of Innocent X.

Mazarin was more than displeased both with Antonio Barberini and St. Chaumont. The Cardinal threw all the blame on the Ambassador for having ruined their schemes through his cupidity. St. Chaumont, on the other hand, denied ever having made the demand and accused Barberini of having had the clause inserted without his knowledge so as to have an excuse for going over to Spain. Whatever the truth of the story and whatever Mazarin may have thought of them both, he evidently considered it advisable to remain on good terms with the Barberini. The Ambassador was recalled and France continued to extend her patronage to the late Cardinal-Nephews.

It was soon apparent that they would need all the protection they

could obtain as, in spite of all his promises, the Pope prepared to call
the brothers to account for their depredations and delinquencies.
There was certainly an immense outcry against them, but had they
then and there offered Donna Olympia a sufficiently substantial bribe
there is no doubt that proceedings would not have been taken against
them; but they hated parting with money and thought that, by
affixing the arms of France over the doors of their palaces and paying
a band of mercenaries to defend them, they would escape retribution.
Their enemies, however, were too powerful and too numerous; and
before long they realised their mistake and fled to France. All their
property in the Papal States was confiscated, and they remained in
exile till they had gathered together sufficient resources to purchase
their pardon from Donna Olympia, thus ending where they should
have begun.

The elevation of Cardinal Pamfili to the Holy See pleased all
parties but the French. He was a devoted partisan of Spain, a friend
of the Medici, was related by blood to many illustrious Italian houses,
had aroused no enmities and was seventy-two years old. Innocent X
had great qualities: a kindly, peaceable disposition, frugal habits and
—strange as it may seem in view of his treatment of the Barberini—
a strong sense of justice. He disliked any form of oppression; relieved
his subjects from much of the heavy burden of taxation laid upon
them by his predecessors; constrained the nobles to pay their debts
and considerably reduced the Vatican expenses. His diplomatic
experiences in various European courts had taught him the value of
reticence. He spoke little, was cautious and urbane.

For a short time all went well. Donna Olympia ruled the Papal
States without contest, filling to all intents and purposes the office of
cardinal-nephew. She received the ambassadors, treated with foreign
Powers; no honours were granted or favours obtained but through
her goodwill. Had it not been for her insatiable cupidity, matters
might not have been so bad, as she was a remarkably competent,
shrewd woman, and fully as well qualified to handle the reins of
government as the average cardinal padrone. She had thought it
advisable at first to have a nominal cardinal-nephew, and Innocent
had invested her stepson with the office. But the chance of a brilliant
match having come his way, Donna Olympia decided to dispense
with the figurehead and marry him off to the rich heiress. Camillo

INNOCENT X
From the bust by Bernini in the Doria Palace, Rome

Pamfili may have been a cypher, but his beautiful spoiled young bride certainly was not. She immediately entered into competition with her mother-in-law to capture the Pope's affections and undermine the older woman's influence. A perfect tornado of quarrels and hysterical tantrums now swept the Vatican, and the peace-loving, meditative Pontiff lived in a turmoil of shrill recriminations, vainly striving to restore harmony in the family circle.

It would take far too long to recount the ups and downs of this intestinal warfare: how Donna Olympia imported a distant relation, on whose devotion she thought she could count, to fill the post of cardinal-nephew—so as to hold her daughter-in-law in check; how the young man, gaining ascendancy over the ageing Innocent, played her false and caused her to be banished from the Vatican; how she contrived his downfall, routed all her enemies and returned triumphant and more powerful than ever to reign supreme till the Pontiff's death.

In his foreign policy Innocent was consistently devoted to Spanish interests. It is said that at the time of the Neapolitan rising led by Masaniello the people offered him their allegiance; but he would have no dealings with Philip's rebellious subjects.

Towards France he was openly inimical. He condemned the five propositions of the Jansenists without, according to Voltaire, even troubling to read them, though that is unlikely. He gave the hat to Retz, who had been exiled from France, merely, it was said, to annoy Mazarin, who hated him. He protested, as was to be expected, against the Peace of Westphalia in 1648 which ended the Thirty Years' War by giving official recognition to the Reformation.

With all the Italian States he remained on friendly terms, with the exception of Parma, who had incited the inhabitants of Castro to murder their bishop. These he punished ruthlessly, Castro being razed to the ground. On the site where that unfortunate city had stood he caused a column to be erected bearing the inscription: "*Qui fù Castro*". Those were not merciful times.

Gout caused Innocent such intense sufferings that he was reduced during his latter years to leading an invalid's life, and his end was a sad and lonely one. His entourage shamelessly deserted him and his body lay unattended and unhonoured. All the customary ceremonial and tokens of respect were dispensed with; his family refused to bear the cost of his funeral, Donna Olympia declaring that she was only "a poor widow" and could not even afford the expense of a coffin. At last a humble canon of St. Peter's, outraged at such miserly callousness, himself paid for a pauper's coffin in which to bury the mighty Pontiff.

Two geniuses, Velazquez and Bernini, both at the height of their artistry, have left us contemporaneous portraits of Innocent X. They were both profound psychologists and uncannily proficient, the one with his brush and the other with his chisel, at rendering the personality of their sitters.

Bernini's bust of the Pontiff absolutely conforms to what is known of his character. The eyes have a look of benevolent abstraction; the line of the mouth expresses tolerant scepticism; the shoulders sag as though weighed down by an overwhelming lassitude; an indefinable suggestion of suffering broods over the marble presentment which the sculptor has endowed with such astounding realism.

Not so does Velazquez depict Innocent X. There is no sagging here; the attitude is firm and erect. Did the mild old man really harbour somewhere in the depths of his subconsciousness that streak of malevolent arrogance which exudes from every pore of the repellent features of this saturnine countenance? How can one reconcile these two portraits—both of them immortal masterpieces? Is it a case of dual personality? Perhaps. Yet one cannot help thinking that Bernini knew the Pontiff best. The artist was a familiar of the Vatican; Innocent would have sat quite naturally for him, relaxed and self-revealing. But on the famous Spanish genius he may have wished to make a more stately and conventional impression, an impression more in keeping with his exalted dignity. He may have purposely adopted the attitude which he thought would be expected of him by one used to the haughty, forbidding phantoms which peopled the sinister shadows of the Escorial.

VNVS ALEXANDRO NON
SVFFICIT ORBIS.

ALEXANDER VII
From a print in the British Museum

ALEXANDER VII (Chigi)
1655–1667

🏵️

DONNA OLYMPIA was sufficiently bold and powerful to disregard most precedents; but one thing even she could not attempt, and that was to enter the conclave at the head of the late Pope's creatures. The leaderless group therefore, modestly calling themselves "God's Faction", remained to all appearances independent; but in reality took their orders from the masterful woman ensconced in her palace of the Piazza Navona. The rest of the cardinals formed numerous small cliques, many of them with no definite policy but their own private ambitions and animosities. The Barberini brothers were again to the fore, Antonio siding with the French and Francis with the Spanish as they had done at the previous conclave. They were now on excellent terms with Donna Olympia and their position quite secure. In opposition to "God's Faction", composed mostly of very young prelates, there stood the "Zelanti", an association of the older cardinals. Rarely had a conclave been so multipartite and never had there been one more numerously attended. Sixty-nine cardinals mustered in the Vatican on January 18th, thirty-two of whom were avowed candidates. The Romans of course made tremendous fun of this spate of would-be popes and the daily pasquinades delighted the populace and penetrated even into remote villages. At a hamlet called Arquato, near Ascoli, the yokels dressed themselves up as cardinals and, mimicking the formal ceremonial of the conclave, solemnly elected a shepherd as Pope, crowning him with a cardboard tiara. He published a bull abolishing all millers' fees and salt taxes and was carried in triumph by the villagers. This disrespectful though harmless prank had a tragic sequel, for the culprits were handed over to the Inquisition and in three days' time the unfortunate mock-pontiff was dead.

But to return to the Vatican, the excessive number of candidates was causing serious trouble as it subdivided the already too numerous factions and was bound to result in an unduly protracted conclave.

In effect a fortnight elapsed without any attempt being made at an election. France was again supporting Sacchetti and Spain proposing Castagna—but only half-heartedly, being more occupied with defeating Mazarin's protégé than with forwarding the cause of her own. Tuscany's candidate was Chigi. "God's Faction" with no declared preferences seemed ready to coquet with all parties in truly feminine fashion. Large sums of money were arriving from France, and Terranova, the Viceroy's agent, received 20,000 doubloons from Naples for distribution among the electors. He was accused later by Guarini, the Florentine agent, of having spent only 3000 ducats on bribes and of having kept the remainder for himself! Cardinal de Medici was well provided with funds and valuable gifts, and living up to the family reputation for lavishness and magnificence. As to Donna Olympia, who had an unsurmountable reluctance to putting her hand in her pocket, she was full of testamentary promises bestowing the most munificent legacies, but parting with nothing meanwhile. Her creatures therefore had little influence and, not being bound by any common interest, soon began to drift in different directions, two or three of the most prominent going over to Spain for 1000 doubloons down and a pension of 3000 crowns apiece. Never was simony practised more blatantly than at this conclave. Albizzi, for instance, made no mystery whatever of the fact that he had received 3000 doubloons and a magnificent pair of horses from Falconieri. Antonio Barberini was buying votes quite openly with French gold and French benefices, and offering one of Mazarin's richly dowered nieces as wife to the Duke of Modena. His bribes were so varied and so tempting that when, on February 4th, the first scrutiny took place Sacchetti appeared to have a very good chance of success. Spain continued very lukewarm about Castagna and the number of the lesser aspirants was rapidly dwindling, the general tendency being negative and apathetic.

Nothing is so crushing to a papal candidate as an atmosphere of neutrality, and Sacchetti, with no serious opponent to hamper him, only got thirty-three votes; nor did his following increase by a single unit during the ensuing fortnight though his name was proposed daily and no more suitable alternative was brought forward. The Sacred College then devoted several days to a renewal of active intriguing and bribery. A veritable river of gold was flowing into the Vatican. Conclavists had never had a busier time; they were nightly on the prowl wearing grotesque disguises, their features buried in the luxuriant growth of false beards. Discipline had gone by the board; there was no respect for regulations and members of "God's Faction" scarcely troubled even to feign illness when they left the Vatican to obey Donna Olympia's summons. The Cardinal Landgrave of Hesse, refusing to wear the customary robes and rochet, strode about the conclave in civilian garb and top-boots. When the Dean remonstrated with him he replied arrogantly that he always dressed so to go hunting in swamps. Another cardinal, Carpegna, whose hobby was snaring birds with lime, wandered about the passages imitating the cuckoo's call, which was the usual method of attracting the feathered victims. Being reprimanded for this unseemly disturbance, he gave as an explanation that he was calling the Holy Ghost!

The first days of March brought the distant sounds of the carnival revelries wafting into the depressing precincts of the conclave and the young cardinals almost went mad with the boredom of their seclusion. Their only recreation was gambling. When they had lost all their money they staked their votes or played for forfeits, this last system leading to most unseemly incidents of which the following is an example. The young scamps had discovered that the aged Cardinal Caraffa had contrived a secret passage from his cell to a recess behind the Spanish leader's cubicle, which enabled his conclavists to eavesdrop in all security. The young cardinals thought they would turn their knowledge to account by giving a good fright to the aged prelate whom they much disliked. So one night Maidalchini, who had incurred a forfeit, was wrapped up in a sheet and despatched through the secret passage with instructions to act the spook to the best of his ability. But Caraffa was a bad sleeper and had heard some suspicious sounds, besides which he did not believe in ghosts; he therefore lay quite still when the shrouded form glided in and allowed it to come right up to his bedside, when, with one well-aimed blow of the crutch which he always kept concealed under his bedclothes, he sent the apparition staggering back. Thoroughly disgusted with a part that entailed such painful risks for the actor, Maidalchini fled the way he had come, neglecting in his precipitation to close the door behind him. As Caraffa could not get out of bed unaided, and as he did not wish to expose his methods of obtaining private information by calling for help, he lay all night in an icy draught from which he contracted such a severe chill that he never really recovered.

As had happened in previous conclaves, the juvenile element was up to all sorts of boyish pranks. The youths glued the leaves of the altar missal together, but the prelate who was officiating continued his Mass quite unperturbed. Undaunted by this failure they then sprinkled the leaves with sneezing powder, and scored a complete success, as Cardinal Filomarini had to abandon the service and was assisted out of the chapel in sternutatory convulsions. Other practical jokes consisted in stuffing fishes with tow and introducing laxative powders into custard pies which the conspirators' servants managed to have served up to the bedridden cardinals; but even these pleasant diversions palled after a time and the days seemed interminable.

Suddenly a rumour, starting no one knew how or whence, spread through the conclave. Carpegna was to be Pope! Had he then managed to decoy the Dove after all? Excitement was great at the next scrutiny but only twenty-eight votes bore his name. Still it might be a beginning; in the rudderless condition of most of the factions anything might be possible. The news soon reached Donna Olympia and spurred her into immediate action. She hated Carpegna, whose sister-in-law was one of her most dangerous social rivals, and her orders to "God's Faction" were to prevent his election at all costs and by any means. But his sudden notoriety had been but an air-bubble which subsided of itself. At the next scrutiny, Carpegna's candidature fell ignominiously under a shower of "Nemini".

Meanwhile Chigi, the Florentine nominee, had been gaining ground. Retz, although a Frenchman, had been busily intriguing in his favour. This he did to be revenged on Mazarin, who had banished him from France, and to whom Chigi's elevation could scarcely be pleasing, for when the French Minister had fled before the menace of the "Fronde" and taken refuge in Cologne, Chigi, who was residing there as Papal Legate, had withheld all assistance from the fugitive and had in fact adopted a decidedly hostile attitude towards him. The election of a man he considered as his personal enemy would be a stinging rebuff for Mazarin, whose renewed failure to secure

Sacchetti's election would thus be made doubly mortifying. Sacchetti himself, seeing that Antonio Barberini was deserting his cause, had by now given up all hopes of his own success and modestly faded into the background. He even went so far as to use his influence with the French Ambassador to persuade him into giving his support to his rival. As the Spanish faction was well disposed towards Chigi there now remained only Donna Olympia to win over. She was trapped by a complicated network of falsehoods into withdrawing her opposition and so on April 7th, after a conclave which had lasted for eighty days, Chigi became Pope Alexander VII.

Cardinal de Retz, whose conceit led him to believe that his own zeal and influence were principally responsible for Chigi's elevation, was pained and surprised at Alexander's lack of gratitude and judges him in his memoirs with acrimonious severity. He accuses him of being a hypocrite of the deepest dye and ridicules the rather excessive manifestations of humility displayed by the Pontiff directly after his election; such as refusing to sit in the middle of the altar to receive the cardinals' final obedience, but perching himself instead on the extreme end of it; also by referring perpetually to his unworthiness. His conduct concerning his family is difficult to defend. He refused at first to allow his nephews to come to Rome, but as he was careful not to appoint anyone to occupy State offices and as he himself could never be prevailed upon to attend to business, things soon came to such a pass that the cardinals, the foreign envoys and the courtiers all joined in begging him to conform to precedent and entrust his relations with the management of affairs. He submitted to their entreaties with well-feigned reluctance; but no sooner were his brother and nephews installed in the Vatican than he invested them with all the power, wealth and benefits at his command. Not only did Alexander bestow the most splendid properties, palaces and gifts on his immediate family but even his most distant relations had their share of the spoils, so that in a very short time the Chigi, who had belonged to the modest class of provincial Tuscan nobility, found themselves, through the Pope's favour and the brilliant marriages they contracted, raised to equality with the most ancient and powerful houses in Italy. That Alexander VII should have staged the farce of having his kinsmen imposed on him makes his unscrupulous nepotism far more odious than that of other less pharisaical popes.

After that initial attempt to create a good impression he made no further effort at dissimulation, and once his family was firmly established at the head of the Government he completely threw off the burden of his office. Quirini, who knew him well, says that attainment to the supreme dignity seemed to rob him of all the qualities he had displayed as a cardinal. He lost all power of discrimination, all mental alertness, and the quickness and facility of expression which had formerly distinguished him. His life, both at Castel Gandolfo and at Rome, was one of uninterrupted self-indulgence. He was, says Quirini, *sposò con le delizie* and Pontiff only in name.

His animosity against France occasionally roused him from his lethargy. From the moment of his accession there had been constant friction between Paris and Rome; it culminated in a dispute relating to diplomatic privileges and the Pope was misguided enough to allow his Gallophobia to become so notorious that his Corsican guards, sure of impunity, publicly insulted the French Ambassador's retainers. The Frenchmen drew their swords, the Papal Guards fell upon them, and the Duchesse de Créqui, the Ambassador's wife, only just managed to reach the Embassy in safety, her page being killed on the step of her coach.

The news of the affray caused an immense sensation in Paris, and Louis XIV swore that he would obtain full satisfaction from the Holy See or destroy the temporal power. As Alexander ignored the King's demands for atonement Louis XIV recalled Créqui, turned the Nuncio out of Paris, invested Avignon and ordered his army to be in readiness to march into Italy. Alexander had not expected such prompt and determined action; he took fright, hanged a couple of Corsican guards and dismissed Cardinal Imperiali, the governor of Rome. But these anodyne measures were not sufficient to placate the French monarch.

The Pope could not have chosen a worse moment to defy Louis XIV, as he could hope for no assistance from Spain, which was at war with Portugal, or from the Empire, engaged just then in fighting the Turks; so he had perforce to bow unconditionally to all the terms dictated by France, and bitterly humiliating most of them were. Besides returning Parma and Castro to the Farnese, he was to erect a monument in Rome itself bearing an inscription recalling the outrage, and followed by a record of the Pope's apology expressed in the most abject and obsequious terms. Considering the weakness evinced by most Roman pontiffs, including Alexander himself, for engraving their names and arms on every available stone in Rome, there is a quality of sardonic humour about this stipulation which one cannot but appreciate. This expiatory trophy was duly erected in the form of an obelisk; Alexander, however, did not think it necessary to commission Bernini to execute it. The storm abated; but except for an occasional lull during a couple of short and more friendly pontificates, it raged on and off for the best part of Louis XIV's long reign and resulted at one time in the virtual emancipation of the French Catholic Church from the jurisdiction of Rome.

Alexander VII died on May 22nd, 1667.

CLEMENT IX
From the painting by Carlo Maratti in the Hermitage, St. Petersburg

CLEMENT IX (ROSPIGLIOSI)
1667–1669

✤

LOUIS XIV had determined to give Alexander VII a successor well disposed towards France, and without awaiting the reigning Pontiff's death had commissioned Count de Lyonne, who was well acquainted with Rome and the Sacred College, to find among its members the man most likely to fulfil his purpose. Lyonne had no difficulty in making his choice, for no other prelate could fit in with the King's views more admirably than Cardinal Rospigliosi, whom he had known intimately for several years. Lyonne's selection met with the King's approval and a line of action adopted forthwith. The first move consisted in Lyonne and Rospigliosi affecting a marked coolness in their social relations, soon to grow into a notorious estrangement—while they remained in close touch underhand. No illicit love affair could have been conducted with more precaution or enveloped in more mystery. The success of this amazing piece of bluff was so complete that later on, during the conclave, several of the cardinals actually hesitated to give their votes to Rospigliosi for fear of offending France! The secret had been so well guarded that not one of the Italian cardinals in France's pay knew whom they were to vote for, but had sworn to obey orders blindly at each scrutiny.

There was a dispute between the old and the young cardinals during the *novemdiale* as to where the assembly should be held. The younger element was anxious for the conclave to take place in the Quirinal, the Vatican being considered very unhealthy, more so than ever since Alexander VII had built a playhouse there, the foundations of which were supposed to have displaced and disseminated poisonous miasmas which would be lurking in the long-uninhabited quarters in which the Sacred College would be immured. Certainly the Quirinal was less dismal though scarcely better adapted to the purpose; the building had, however, several advantages which later induced the Sacred College to transfer their sittings there. But in 1667 the older cardinals tended to oppose on principle any motion brought forward by their juniors and, having survived so many conclaves, probably considered themselves immune from infection. Whatever their reasons, they resisted the innovation so strenuously that their opinion prevailed and the conclave assembled as usual in the Vatican on June 2nd.

It was again sectioned into several small groups, and the candidates though less numerous were still plentiful. Francis Barberini himself was now on the ranks; but Spain, to whose party he had always adhered, had placed her interests in the hands of her Ambassador, the Marquis d'Astorga, a brainless old libertine who cared not a fig who became pope and would be of no assistance whatever to Francis. The Barberini anyhow were so unpopular with their colleagues that, whatever promises they may have received, Francis could not count with absolute certainty on any vote but his brother's.

Unlike Spain, France had sent out a clever and active representative in the person of the Duc de Chaulnes, who, besides being supplied with bribes and money galore, had been well primed by Lyonne regarding the intricacies and pitfalls of electoral diplomacy. Mazarin being now dead and Retz in favour once more, that scheming prelate, thoroughly in his element, was let into the secret of Louis XIV's designs and proved a valuable co-operator.

Chigi, the late Cardinal-Nephew, though leader of thirty-four cardinals, had so little personal hold over his creatures that only twenty-four of them really obeyed his orders. As candidate he had chosen d'Elci, a gentle, featureless nonentity who would have needed a far more powerful patron than Chigi to stand any chance of success. Spain it is true had secretly promised him her support, but Astorga was no more interested in d'Elci than he was in Barberini and left his party to follow their own devices.

In addition to Retz two Italian prelates, d'Este and Grimaldi, were working in conjunction with the French, and one of them it was who suggested Rospigliosi to the Spaniards. The proposal was well received by them, as Rospigliosi had made many friends in Madrid during his nunciature and was believed to be on bad terms with France. Chigi was furious at Spain's defection. He accused Harach, her Cardinal Patron, of treachery, and when that prelate replied coldly, "I obey my Sovereign's orders", Chigi, alluding to

Charles II's extreme youth, retorted: "A feeding-bottle, not a Pope, is what your King must have ordered"; but he was not in a position to hold out very long and soon capitulated to Azzolini's blandishments. As a matter of fact Chigi's defeat turned out to be a blessing in disguise for him. He gained far more by Rospigliosi's elevation than he would have done in all probability by d'Elci's, for not only was the very advantageous agreement which he signed so bristling with figures that it looked at first sight as though it were written in numerical cypher, but Rospigliosi, once Pope, treated him with unprecedented generosity and favour.

This conclave, like many others, had an outstanding figure; but one who owed nothing to wealth, influence or party spirit—a man whose original personality, freedom of speech and quick-witted sallies captured the attention of the cardinals and kept them enthralled. His name was Albizzi, and we have seen him in the previous conclave openly boast of the bribes he had received from a colleague. In Lord Arlington's correspondence there are several despatches both from John Finch and from Azzolini (who wrote under the pseudonym of Bayllardy) which are just as concerned with Albizzi's *bons mots* as with the main object of the conclave. This eccentric prelate seems to have been gifted with a ready tongue and a fearless one. Frankly cynical, he treated the most serious subjects with levity, but levity of such a startling cogency that his listeners did not know if they were more aghast at his daring or more exhilarated by the lash of his satirical humour. Both jovial and morose, amiable and waspish, he was the most disconcerting and irresistible jester imaginable. Thanks to him, the inmates of the Vatican never knew a dull moment. Gone were the boredom, the gloom, the petty spitefulness of other conclaves. Laughter echoed through the dim passages, spread from cell to cell; to the noisy hilarity of the younger prelates, their elders responded indulgently with chuckles so protracted that their venerable ribs ached. Spying and horse-play were at a discount.

In the Hall of the Belvedere where Albizzi held his court, cardinals of all parties and all ages congregated in amity clustering round him like a swarm of bees. They hung on his every word, provoking him by a question or well-timed contradiction to ever bolder epigrams or quips. Scarcely could they tear themselves away from the charmed circle to attend the ritual ceremonies or retire to rest. No doubt the fact that Albizzi spared no one added the zest of personal risk to these séances. One's own foibles might at any moment become the subject of some corrosive joke, for he was merciless in exposing his colleagues' most secret defects both moral and physical, not excepting certain ailments of a private nature of which as churchmen they should have had no experience.

Francis Barberini, who in his incurable self-sufficiency thought he had made a friend of Albizzi by tossing him a few patronising compliments, was rash enough to ask him publicly whom he would like to see elected. "Your Eminence", answered Albizzi, "if you were gifted with a little more heart, a great deal more brains, less hypocrisy and a great deal less meanness!" Such brutal candour actually nonplussed Barberini, who beat a hasty retreat and was perhaps better prepared than he would otherwise have been for the crushing defeat he suffered at the next scrutiny.

In his private life Albizzi had never given the slightest cause for scandal, so his position was impregnable and he took a cruel advantage of it. When just before the last scrutiny which was to raise Rospigliosi to the papal throne he was asked what he thought of him he answered: "Urban turned the Holy See into a bank; Innocent into a brothel; Alexander into a tavern; this one will make a playhouse of it". And alluding to Rospigliosi's well-known love of music he added: "He will emasculate the Sacred College by giving the hat to all the castrated singers in Europe!" Many such sayings are on record, and though they are certainly pithy they are painfully crude. Smartness without subtlety scarcely seems wit to our more exacting taste, but no doubt it suited the mentality of the age, for if Lord Arlington's Roman correspondents considered Albizzi's sallies worth consigning *in extenso* in their despatches they must have been confident of their appeal.

Though Albizzi seemed to entertain a scant regard for Rospigliosi, he was not deterred thereby from giving him his suffrage—as he would no doubt have had far harder things to say about all the other *papabili* of the Sacred College. Except for Corsini, the incorruptible, who stood out to the last saying that Rospigliosi was better fitted for making ariettas than bulls, the election was unanimous, and Rospigliosi took the name of Clement IX.

This is how Azzolini describes the new Pontiff in a letter to Lord

Arlington: "Clement IX is 67 years old, he is all charm and kindness; his judgment is experienced and sound. He is an accomplished musician and an enlightened patron of poetry and art. He is subject to heart attacks. The French handled his election with consummate skill outwitting us all; but it is surprising that they did not choose a younger and more vigorous man who would have afforded their King a firmer and lengthier hold over the Holy See."

The Venetian envoy's report contains such a formidable list of diseases with which he says the Pope was afflicted that it seems amazing he should have survived for even two years. He judges Clement without indulgence, accusing him of being verbose and tedious and of deputising his court musicians to transact business with the diplomatic envoys. "The Pope", he continues, "takes a childish delight in giving and receiving presents, and one constantly meets menials in the papal livery walking through the streets of the city carrying trays laden with fruit, flowers and delicacies to the palaces of His Holiness' favoured friends. In fact," adds the Venetian, who had probably not been honoured by any of these fragrant or edible tokens of pontifical regard, "His Holiness is finding his way to the hearts of his subjects through the channel of their stomachs!"

Clement IX may not have been a very great Pope; but he was a gentle and kindly ruler—never committing harsh or unjust actions. He was tactful, generous and moderate in all ways. He invested his nephew with the traditional office but tolerated no abuses of power. If the Rospigliosi rose to prominence and wealth it was due to the prestige which inevitably attended the position they occupied and to the advantageous matrimonial alliances which they contracted, but not to spoliations or the misappropriation of State funds. The Cardinal-Nephew kept his hands scrupulously clean and could not even be accused of the offence known in the French law courts as "traffic in influence".

Music was Clement's passion—he found in its soothing influence a solace to his physical sufferings; but it did not make him neglect the duties of his office. He gave his audiences regularly and visited the hospitals and churches with edifying punctuality. He was the first Pope to show consideration and friendliness to his predecessor's family, allowing Chigi to retain much of his influence, and often consulting him on matters of State. His nephew shared his affable disposition and Clement's pontificate was one of general concord and goodwill. Always on the best of terms with France, he stood sponsor to the Dauphin and his attitude towards Louis XIV was one of gratitude without servility. He gave his whole-hearted support to the Venetians in the war which the Republic was waging against the Turks, and the fall of Candia after a heroic resistance affected him so deeply that it is said to have caused his death, which occurred on December 10th, 1669. Bichi, the Florentine agent in Rome, writing to the Grand Duke a few days later, accuses Clement of having concealed the fact that he was epileptic, which would have debarred him by canon law from exercising ecclesiastical functions; but even if the indictment was correct, which is not proved, it seems a minor transgression easily outweighed by his undeniable qualities.

CLEMENT X (ALTIERI)
1670–1676

❦

As so frequently happened after a very short pontificate, the Great Powers, drained as their exchequers were by continual warfare, showed no inclination to squander vast sums of money again so soon for so uncertain a return. The Count of Peñaranda, who had been sent from Madrid to attend to the business which Astorga continued to neglect, suggested with great good sense that as the cardinals were so treacherous and unreliable, it might be more practical to save up the money, keep aloof from the conclave, and, once the pope had been elected, buy the new cardinal-nephew's goodwill with the totality of the funds. But his idea, breaking as it did with all time-honoured precedents, was rejected by the court of Madrid.

The Italian princes also found the heavy calls made on their budgets by these repeated conclaves too onerous, and economically threw in their lots with either France or Spain, d'Este joining the former and Medici the latter Power.

Beside these two traditional opponents a new party now appeared known as the "Flying Squadron" and acknowledging Queen Christina of Sweden as its guiding star. The circumstances were very favourable for her début as a leader, for had bribery been playing the principal part in this conclave she could not have entered into competition with her rivals. It was in fact her own pressing need of funds which prompted her to take such an active interest in the proceedings; since if the new pope failed to continue the allowance which his two predecessors had granted to the royal and spectacular convert to Roman Catholicism, she would find herself in a very precarious position. Christina was heavily in debt and her Swedish pension, insufficient in itself to meet her expenditure, was paid very irregularly when paid at all. She had set her heart on the election of Vidoni, a pleasure-loving, easy-going cardinal who had obtained the hat through the patronage of the Polish Sovereigns. He was a born courtier and had been an assiduous sycophant of Christina's for many years. He could be relied on, she thought, not only to treat her with generosity, but also to give her favourite, the Marquis del Monte, the captaincy of the Guards and to fall in with her whims generally. The ideal pontiff from her point of view would have been Azzolini, who was her closest friend and had been, so the gossips said, on even more intimate terms with her in the past, but he was only forty-seven years of age so would not be *papabile* for a long time. As her chief of staff, however, Azzolini was invaluable. He was by far the best strategist in the Sacred College, and although he only disposed of six followers, to his skill at sowing dissension within the heart of the contending parties, and to his artful dodges and devices, was certainly due the four months' procrastination which delayed the election.

France had selected Altieri, an old man of eighty, practically senile, and to whom Medici commonly referred as "The Idiot". The greatest secrecy was observed by the French faction, Altieri himself being unaware of their intentions.

Spain openly favoured Odescalchi, a young and ardent churchman whose austerity and religious enthusiasm were unlikely to please any of the other parties.

Louis XIV again entrusted the Duc de Chaulnes with the lay leadership of the French faction and despatched him immediately to Rome, feeling confident of scoring yet another prompt success. But clever and level-headed as he was, the Duke this time was to meet with such complications and unexpected difficulties in the accomplishment of his mission that he practically lost his bearings, and had it not been for a fortuitous circumstance would probably have failed to bring it to a successful issue. To start with, he had left Paris with instructions based on a good understanding between Chigi and Rospigliosi, and arrived in Rome to find that the two prelates had become irreconcilable enemies, which meant an entirely revised plan of campaign. There was nothing to expect from Chigi, who was stubbornly determined to support d'Elci and proved quite intractable. Chaulnes, to guard against all risks, had brought with him the King's exclusion against d'Elci and now congratulated himself on his foresight; but the weapon was only a negative one and Chigi's defection a serious set-back.

The French Ambassador's arrival had been awaited with feverish anxiety by all parties. The conclave had already been assembled for some time when he reached Rome, but no voting had as yet taken place. The entrance of the French cardinals who had accompanied Chaulnes caused great excitement, d'Este as Cardinal Patron of France taking charge of them with officious cordiality.

It was the custom, when a special envoy was due to reach the capital, for the Pope to send welcoming gifts of fruit, pastries and other delicacies to his residence, in readiness for his arrival. Many cardinals seized on the excuse of the interregnum during which they all represented the Holy See, to shower presents of food on the Duke, so that when he alighted he found the hall of his palace transformed into a veritable market-place. Pyramids of fruit, trestles supporting an accumulation of dishes, towers formed of superimposed jars of preserves, flagons of wine, baskets of dainties, boxes of comfits and battalions of cheeses in close formation greeted the surprised and overwhelmed traveller. His embarrassment was intense, for how to dispose of such a plethora of victuals without giving offence to the donors was a serious problem. But this was a trifling difficulty compared to what awaited him at the hands of the ladies; for if Chaulnes was too courteous to risk slighting the cardinals, he was also incapable of meeting any advances from the fair sex with anything but ready response. Christina, who had undertaken with regal self-assurance to win over the French Ambassador to Vidoni's cause, pounced on him without a moment's delay. The Court of Madrid when approached on Vidoni's behalf had been downright inimical and Medici had informed Retz that "The Queen Regent would sooner have the Vatican set on fire than consent to Vidoni's election". Spanish antagonism being considered a sure passport to French favour, much was expected of the effect which the above pronouncement might have on Chaulnes, and Christina could not contain her impatience to set about the gallant Frenchman's conquest.

Whatever his feelings regarding her personality and electoral activities may have been, the Queen's rank commanded Chaulnes' obedient attendance to her summons and, emboldened by his deferential urbanity, she grew daily more possessive and dictatorial. His troubles, alas! did not end with her, for another siren had likewise been lying in wait for him. Marie Mancini, one of Mazarin's famous nieces, who in the capacity of Louis XIV's first love had

distinct claims on his envoy, and in that of wife of the Lord High
Constable Colonna could not be overlooked by a visitor to Rome,
was no less determined on his capture. She also wished to play an
influential part in the conclave and to recruit supporters for her
protégé Bonvisi. Her strategy was devoid of all subtlety as it
consisted in the simple and time-honoured device of seduction.
Attired in the most ravishing and all-revealing Eastern finery, her
golden gauze trousers intended as a parody of her rival's masculine
apparel, Marie Mancini, still young and alluring, received the
pleasantly startled diplomat in her private apartment and managed
without difficulty to keep him there for twenty-four hours! "La
Connetable", as she was generally called, had a vast experience of the
world in general and of men in particular, and the incidents of her
struggle with Queen Christina to secure the allegiance of the bewildered
Ambassador make most diverting reading. She certainly managed to
unsettle him as he made several tentative advances in Bonvisi's
favour, though in a perfunctory and hesitating manner.

No less entertaining is the correspondence between Azzolini
and Christina. Adopting the policy which the French had found
so successful in the last conclave, Azzolini never spoke to Vidoni,
even abusing him to his colleagues on the *agent provocateur* system.
He kept a detailed account of the electors' reactions to these comments and forwarded them every night to Vidoni together with
the reports sent by the Queen from the outer world. Azzolini
treated his royal Ægeria with scant courtesy, begging her curtly
to cease interlarding her letters to him with so many terms of en-
dearment, as it prevented him passing them on to Vidoni and constrained him to the tiresome and unnecessary labour of copying out
the interesting extracts. He also objected to her perpetual entreaties
to him not to touch any food or drink which had not come from her
kitchens, as her solicitude made him the laughing-stock of the Sacred
College. Christina does not seem to have resented her friend's un-
gracious chiding. She was evidently very proud of the way in which
she was hoodwinking the Roman world, and of the caution and discretion she exercised generally, informing Azzolini that to guard
against all risks she had been careful to select a deaf confessor!

Never were the skeins of intrigue more tangled than in this conclave. Even Chaulnes seemed to flounder and lose his footing, so that

his irresolution struck Medici, who reported to the Grand Duke that the French Ambassador's attitude was incomprehensible and that he could not determine whether he was fooling his colleagues or being fooled himself.

There was practically no bribing. Cardinal de Bouillon had brought titles to French benefices worth 15,000 crowns for Rospigliosi himself and the Order of the Holy Ghost for his brother; but these honours were his due in recognition of past services and a mere act of civility on the part of the French monarch.

Owing to the paucity of gold, underlings were to be had at bargain prices. The Duc de Chaulnes' secretary sold his services to Medici and Medici's to Chaulnes; the Marquis d'Astorga's was also bought by France and Chigi's conclavist by Queen Christina. The situation, therefore, was much the same all round and no progress made in any direction.

What in this *galère* had become of Albizzi? There is not a single reference in the accounts of the conclave to his popularity and witticisms, and the omission seems unaccountable till one comes across his name on the list of official candidates. His reserve and circumspection are then readily understood, but one is amazed that a man so clear-sighted about the merits or rather demerits of others should have been so blind as to his own!

When at last the voting began, the first name put forward was d'Elci's, Chigi's friend and nominee. The opening scrutiny yielded twenty-seven votes in his favour, and this was considered such a promising start that an urgent message was sent to Chaulnes, who rushed to the Vatican with the King's exclusion and handed it through the wicket to d'Este with authority to use it at his own discretion. This d'Este did with such precipitancy and so little consideration for the aged candidate's precarious state of health that the shock actually killed him. Chigi immediately replaced him by Bonvisi, Marie Mancini's protégé; but Azzolini made short work of him. The cardinals then amused themselves at playing a cat-and-mouse game with several stray aspirants to the papal tiara, having particularly good sport with Albizzi, whose misguided ambition seemed to have completely deprived him of all acumen, and who was now treated by his former victims to a taste of his own sharp sauce. It must have been galling for him to see how successfully Retz had stepped into his shoes. The Frenchman's memory was prodigious; he had been everywhere and known everybody, and was a versatile and inexhaustible *raconteur*. The cardinals thronged to Medici's cubicle to hear Retz read extracts from his memoirs, which were pronounced far more entertaining than Albizzi's parochial witticisms. Cardinal de Retz had all the ease and charm of manner which stamped the habitué of the court of Versailles, where you might call out a man and kill him on the flimsiest of pretexts, but where brutality of speech would have been an unthinkable lapse of manners and a personal joke concerning physical infirmities utterly beneath contempt.

The French element, composed mostly of prelates of the highest birth and standing, had imposed on this heterogeneous assembly a refinement of tone and expression which some of its members may have found irksome, but to which they all strove to conform. There was an unwonted exchange of small civilities, the cardinals entertaining one another to appetising collations. From Florence Medici obtained an inexhaustible supply of light Tuscan wine called Verdea which was more potent than it looked and was especially appreciated by the French prelates. They themselves produced the finest Burgundy vintages in return, and Chigi provided delicious cream cheeses which his colleagues, especially old Altieri, devoured greedily. Besides his cream cheeses, Chigi's horses were also very popular as they were brought every day to parade under their master's eye on the Piazza S. Pietro, and the cardinals much enjoyed watching the beautiful animals being schooled and put through their paces. This of course was a flagrant infringement of the regulations as the windows should have been boarded up and the outer world invisible to the electors; so Azzolini, who detested Chigi, had no difficulty in inducing the Dean to put a stop to this equine exhibition.

The weeks slipped by without any headway being made by either of the factions though the plotting and scheming proceeded unabated. Bildt says that "the adversaries exchanged lies like rapier-thrusts, without malice or ill-will, as good fencers should"; but Medici, who was better acquainted with the turbid undercurrents, notes that never had he known a conclave where so much hate and deceit underlay such a courteous surface. Azzolini considered that the time had now come to change the Squadron's tactics, and his advice to Christina was: "Tell the truth, it is safest, as everybody will think you are lying—to deceive by honesty is the art of arts".

By April 24th Vidoni's candidature was official, but France had not yet divulged Altieri's name, when a special courier arrived hot-foot from Madrid bearing information of the highest import. The Marquis d'Aitona, a powerful member of the regency council, was dead and his disappearance had caused a complete revulsion in the Government's policy, for the Cardinal of Arragon, who had succeeded him, was devoted to Vidoni's interests. He had managed to overrule the Queen's scruples and the Spanish faction was now ordered to abandon Odescalchi's candidature and support that of the man they had previously been enjoined to oppose most energetically. The abruptness of such a complete change of front, though it left Astorga quite unmoved, was violently resented not only by the Spanish prelates but more especially by their Italian colleagues, who, having joined issue with Spain, had so irretrievably compromised themselves with Vidoni that they could not possibly hope for his favour should he become Pope. Led by Medici they therefore went over in a body to the French party, Chigi for similar reasons following their lead. All night fresh recruits came pouring into the French ranks, even Christina's squadron being carried away by the rising tide, Azzolini alone remaining staunch to Vidoni.

D'Este now disclosed the name of the Pope-elect and without waiting for daybreak the cardinals hurried to Altieri's cubicle to carry him in triumph to the chapel. Here, however, they met with an unexpected check. The aged invalid had no desire whatever to occupy the Apostolic See. His eighty years weighed heavily upon him and he begged and prayed to be allowed to die in peace. He had really lost interest in everything but food and was devoid of all personal ambition; but his electors would brook no refusal. D'Este and Medici, those very prelates who had always been wont to refer to him as "The Idiot", seized him bodily in their arms and, though he clung to the bedclothes with feeble desperation and sobbed piteously, they managed to convey him to the chapel, where he was duly elected, acquiescing out of sheer exhaustion to his proclamation as Pope Clement X. It is amusing to note that when the barriers were removed to permit the ambassadors and officials to pay their respects to the new Pontiff, the first person to fall at his feet with every show of devotion and jubilation was Queen Christina of Sweden!

Clement had no nephews; but his niece having married a Paluzzi he adopted that family as his own and they took the name of Altieri. They filled the usual offices and enjoyed the usual prerogatives, showing no great competence in any branch of affairs but that of their own aggrandisement. Clement's election was not a popular one. His great age, however, augured a short pontificate, so consternation was great when the rumour spread that his father had lived to be 105! His former colleagues' discomfiture on hearing of this strain of longevity in their Sovereign's immediate forebear excited the mirth of the Roman populace and caused much lampooning and derisive banter. Clement was not destined, however, to try his subjects' patience quite so severely as they had feared—but he survived for six years, during which he was kept strictly secluded from business of any kind. His memory was completely gone and he would, if not restrained, bestow the same honours and benefices promiscuously on anybody he came into contact with, his nephew having the ungrateful task of disillusioning the overjoyed recipients of the pontifical favours. He was a harmless, childish old man that France had thought to keep in leading-strings; but she had not foreseen the adoption of the Paluzzis. The new Cardinal-Nephew Altieri was distinctly Franco-phobe and he carefully selected men of the same political opinions to fill all vacancies in the Sacred College.

No outsider was allowed to see the Pope unless accompanied by a member of the Altieri clan; they watched over him and cosseted him with unceasing vigilance, fanning the flickering flame of life which must at all costs be kept burning till they had had time to feather their nests. The object of so much solicitude vegetated happily enough, incurious and indifferent to what happened outside his own restricted world. Meanwhile the Altieri governed and grew rich; they had pinned their faith on a horoscope which gave the Pope nine years of life from the day of his accession, and when he slipped through their fingers three years before the allotted time the Cardinal-Nephew's rage was such that he assaulted the doctors who had attended his uncle, kicking one of them savagely in the stomach. The Altieris, like so many of their predecessors who had prospered and fattened on their relative's pontificate, refused to disburse a farthing for his funeral, and Clement X was buried like a pauper.

· INNOCENTIVS XI ·   ODESCALCHVS PONT
MAX. CREATVS DIE XXI   SEPTEMB. MDCLXXVI
P. Voet pinx.   Jo. V Bruÿn F.

INNOCENT XI
From a print in the British Museum

INNOCENT XI (ODESCALCHI)
1676–1689

❧

ONE is apt to smile at the grandiloquent appellation of "*Roi Soleil*" bestowed by his idolatrous courtiers on the little man in the monstrous peruke who strutted about Versailles on his high red heels; but it is doubtful if since Charlemagne any monarch had exercised such a preponderating influence in Europe; and certainly none had enjoyed such personal prestige.

Louis XIV's desire for cordial relations with the Holy See, apart from his scheme of general ascendancy, was more especially prompted by the hereditary anti-Spanish policy of his house, and Spain, once so mighty and so vast, had now come to such a pass that every well-aimed blow might prove a decisive one. During the XVIIth century the Colossus tottered off its pedestal, crumbling as it fell. Spain lost successively Portugal, many of her provinces in the Netherlands, and those she still held in France. She would have had great difficulty in defending her Italian territories by force of arms and was therefore vitally concerned in securing the election of a friendly pontiff.

To France, on the other hand, stirring up trouble for Spain in Italy meant freedom of action elsewhere. Consequently the political tendencies of the pope were of great moment to the two Powers. They were both equally detested in Italy, but at the close of the XVIIth century France alone was feared. Louis XIV's name was certainly one to conjure with in Rome, so much so that when his Ambassador protested with the Dean of the Sacred College against any election being effected before the arrival of the French cardinals, the conclave, which had assembled on August 2nd, meekly acquiesced and no voting took place before the French contingent entered the Vatican on August 29th. Albizzi, who seemed to have recovered his wits with the discarding of his ambitions, exclaimed: "The Holy Ghost used to be a dove, he has now become a cock!"

The attitude immediately adopted by the French cardinals amazed their colleagues. It was customary for the cardinals created since the last conclave to be officially presented by the Dean to the foreign prelates. But d'Estrées, the leader of the French party, informed this official that by order of the King he and his followers were to have no dealings of any sort with Altieri and his creatures, were not to meet or visit them, were in fact to ignore their existence altogether. He then proceeded to call on all his colleagues, ostentatiously omitting the late Cardinal-Nephew and his creatures.

Such a breach of etiquette, unheard of in the history of conclaves, made a very bad impression. Several well-meaning prelates attempted to act as mediators, among others Cardinal Howard, the most straightforward and God-fearing of men, who addressed Cardinal de Bouillon very civilly in Latin. "My Lord Cardinal," replied Bouillon impertinently, "I am a poor Latin scholar at the best of times, but when it is spoken by an Englishman it is quite incomprehensible to me." Without taking offence at his rudeness, Howard then proceeded with his exhortation in French—laying stress on the fact that all the members of the Sacred College were equals, and that none had a right to set himself above his colleagues and treat them as though they had been rebel subjects: "I who live among heretics", added Howard, "am well aware to what account they will turn these scandalous dissensions, and I beg of your Eminence to behave as becomes a position of such responsibility as ours." But Bouillon brushed these arguments aside with sarcastic brevity.

He and his compatriots were Frenchmen first, churchmen after. The King's favour was the aim and object of their existence; what was the blame or the approval of the Sacred College likely to mean to them? Louis XIV's instructions were explicit and he would countenance no half measures. He meant to bring the full weight of his royal displeasure to bear on Altieri and crush him like an insect. The delinquent was to be severely ostracised during the conclave, and the election of any candidate whose enmity for him could be relied on to endure was to be supported by the French faction. The King's thirst for revenge against Altieri was such that it completely overshadowed his anti-Spanish policy; if a double victory could be scored so much the better, but if that were not possible then Spain must wait her turn. The haughty and overbearing manner which he drove his subjects to adopt and which had been intended merely to humble Altieri, met with such general disapproval that relations became uncomfortably strained. The atmosphere was tense and acrimonious, and Maidalchini, who adhered to the French faction, so exasperated Colonna by his truculent tartness that the latter seized him by the throat and might have strangled him had he not been dragged away in time. All the courtliness and refinement imported from Versailles in the former conclave had melted in the fierce rays of the Roi Soleil's wrath.

Meanwhile the cause of all this pother felt excessively nervous and flustered. He had never expected such systematically organised retaliation, and being apparently gifted neither with brains nor determination, was completely at a loss how to cope with the situation. He shuffled round aimlessly, offering his services to all factions in turn and even sending an envoy to Versailles to make his peace with the King; but Louis XIV, needless to say, refused to see him. Such lack of proper pride earned for him the contempt of all his colleagues and the resentment of those who, having espoused his cause for the sake of principle, felt particularly bitter at his unworthiness.

As though to make amends for its past defection, the Court of Madrid, which had treated Odescalchi so scurvily at the previous conclave, rallied warmly to his support; but the Spanish party was badly led, a prey to division and jealousies, their leaders at loggerheads and their official instructions impossible to comply with, for Madrid wished them both to forward Odescalchi's election and to co-operate with Altieri. Such orders were in hopeless contradiction, as Altieri, who hated and feared Odescalchi, would promote any candidate rather than him, and the last thing Odescalchi himself would wish for was Altieri's patronage as it would inevitably entail exclusion from France. His enmity, on the contrary, proved of the greatest advantage to Odescalchi, for, as his candidature gained in popularity and it became known that Altieri was offering his support to any competitor who would oppose him, the French party began to look upon him with marked favour. They would have preferred Cibo, a prelate entirely devoted to France's interests, but Spain excluded him and Altieri had repeatedly offered to support him.

None of the other candidates was acceptable to Louis XIV. There was Conti, patronised by Queen Christina and the laughing-stock of the Sacred College as his passion for clocks amounted to mania; he

had at least a dozen of them in his cubicle, which made him very
unpopular with his neighbours, nor could he resist the temptation
of pulling the works out of any watch left within his grasp.

Princess Mancini Colonna was concentrating her energies this time
on thwarting any designs Barberini might have, as the High Constable, her husband, had had a dispute with Barberini's nephew on a
question of precedence. Piccolomini was impossible as he had been
turned out of Versailles at the time of the Créqui affair; and Corsini
equally so because Louis XIV had refused to accept him as nuncio.
Therefore France excluded them both. A few other candidates
remained but had various disqualifications which put them out of
court.

Odescalchi seemed the only possible choice, and although most of
his colleagues stood rather in awe of him, he commanded their
respect and grudging admiration. He was the son of a rich banker
of Como, an Austrian subject, and had served with valour in the
imperial army. Severely wounded at the siege of Nimègue and in-
capacitated from further military activities, he had turned towards
religion for help in his adversity and eventually embraced Holy
Orders. The intrepid ardour with which he had fought for his
sovereign he now devoted to the service of the Church. He was
determined to occupy the Apostolic See so as to reform abuses,
exterminate heresy, and restore the primitive ideals of Christianity.
To attain his object he used the necessary means to serve his ends.
Attributing his past failure to his own curt, unbending manner, he
schooled himself to be gracious and pleasant and to conceal the
passionate fervour of his devotion. As he was wealthy and generous
he recruited many adherents during Clement X's pontificate and had
an already important following when he entered the conclave. If
he could obtain the goodwill of the French group his election was
assured. D'Estrées inclined towards this solution, but Retz, more
clear-sighted and more experienced, opposed it. He reminded his
party that France had twice excluded Odescalchi, which he was not
likely to forget, and that he was a subject of the Emperor's and drew
important revenues from Austrian properties; and he managed to
impress on d'Estrées the necessity of imposing stringent conditions
on his offer of adhesion, the most important being that Cibo should
be given the secretaryship of state. When d'Estrées acquainted

Odescalchi with the terms upon which he was willing to support him, the latter, unable to repress his natural abruptness, refused even to consider the question, and the French leader, uncertain how to proceed, sent a messenger to Versailles to report matters to the King and ask for further orders.

Meanwhile business was at a standstill in the conclave. The unpopularity of the French faction grew in proportion to the boredom and discouragement of the electors, who naturally made d'Estrées and his followers responsible for all the difficulties of the situation and treated them with the coldest and barest civility. But the return of the courier from Paris on September 20th suddenly placed the French leader in a position of absolute ascendancy. The tidings were momentous. The siege of Maëstricht had been raised, the Spaniards defeated, and the army of the Prince of Orange was in full flight. The shadow of the victorious monarch fell darkly upon the terrified assembly—and if Retz instead of d'Estrées had been in command of the French party he might have imposed any candidate he chose on the dismayed electors; but d'Estrées had no initiative; the despatches contained the King's approval of Odescalchi's elevation subject to Retz's conditions, and he proposed merely to renew the offer Odescalchi had dismissed so curtly. Too timid, however, to risk another rebuff, he sent for the King's Ambassador, his brother the Duc d'Estrées, to undertake the negotiations. The Duke standing at the wicket had an interview with Odescalchi, who now naturally proved more tractable, and undertook to make all concessions required of him, including Cibo's appointment as secretary of state.

As soon as this agreement became known in the conclave Altieri rushed to Rospigliosi in a perfect frenzy begging him to offer his services to the French for the election of Cibo; but Rospigliosi refused to undertake the mission, telling Altieri that Odescalchi's election was now a settled thing and charitably refraining from any allusion to his ignominious self-abasement. The next morning Odescalchi was proclaimed Pope and chose the name of Innocent XI.

When the news reached Paris it was hailed as a French victory; but the Papal Nuncio shook his head and marvelled at the blindness of the French who thought that their tardy support and the mortifying concessions it had entailed could constitute a title to Innocent's gratitude.

Louis XIV also ignored the facts that Retz had wisely laid stress upon, and deluded himself into believing that his patronage, however reluctantly bestowed, would obliterate all past disfavour and outweigh any claims Spain might have on the Pontiff's allegiance. His illusions, however, were to be rudely dispelled.

The elevation of Innocent XI to the pontifical throne in no way affected his character or resolutions. He remained what his first training had made him; a man of regular habits, just and inflexible, who would admit of no breach of discipline and was scrupulously respectful of it himself. He not only professed to be, but was, opposed to nepotism, for devoted as he was to his nephew Don Livio, he conferred no office upon him, and as he considered his relations sufficiently wealthy to maintain their position without State subsidies, he gave them none. He even wished to publish a bull suppressing nepotism altogether, but deferred to the wishes of the College of Cardinals, who considered the measure inopportune.

He fulfilled his promise to the French faction by appointing Cardinal Cibo Secretary of State, but does not appear to have been much influenced by that prelate's Francophile tendencies. He refunded the money expended by the holders of certain offices on the purchase of their appointments and took measures to prevent the sale of such posts in the future. He insisted on the cardinals altering their mode of life and conforming to their religious duties while reducing their ostentatious expenditure. He entered into every detail concerning ecclesiastical discipline, such as prohibiting the use of snuff for the clergy. In every way he himself practised what he preached, setting an example of rigid self-denial and rectitude. These reforms were not likely to endear him to his subordinates, but when he carried his activities further afield, forbidding ladies to employ male music-masters or to wear masks in public and even legislating on the cut of their bodices, then he really became for the Roman world of leisure one of the most unpopular popes it had ever known.

He was no less exacting where the dead were concerned than he was when dealing with the living, and he could never bring himself to shoulder the responsibility of adding a new saint to the celestial phalanx. He was more at his ease where censure was concerned, condemning without hesitation any writings that did not conform narrowly with his views on orthodoxy. Politically his sympathies were naturally with Spain and the Empire, though his attitude towards France was in no way aggressive till the vexed question of the *régale* brought matters to a crisis between himself and Louis XIV. Both rulers were convinced of the merits of their claim and both determined to fight the quarrel out to the bitter end. The *droit de régale* consisted in an old-established custom by which the French sovereigns received the revenues of bishoprics so long as they were vacant and appointed holders to the dependent livings. This right had always been contested by Rome, but had been exercised on and off for a couple of centuries, and Louis XIV was certainly not the man to relinquish a royal prerogative of any nature whatsoever. He made this perfectly clear to the Pontiff in peremptory terms—but Innocent was equally unyielding and not to be intimidated. He issued a bull solemnly condemning the practice, but which the French Parliament, acting under the King's instructions, declared inoperative. Furthermore Louis XIV called a general meeting of the French clergy to confer on the subject of the dispute.

The result of these deliberations was a foregone conclusion, as the blind submission of the French ecclesiastical body to their Sovereign was such a well-known thing that Condé said that if the King thought fit to go over to the Protestant Church the clergy would be the first to follow him. Their findings therefore were entirely in accordance with the monarch's wishes, and from the declarations drawn up by this assembly sprang the famous Église Gallicane. Innocent of course banned the articles drawn up by these nationalist churchmen, the French Parliament no less inevitably approved them, and the struggle between Rome and Versailles began in real earnest.

So far Louis XIV seemed to have the stronger position, but if the temporary appropriation of ecclesiastical revenues was a matter of minor consequence, the *régale spirituelle*, or nomination by the King to sacerdotal offices and dignities while the Pope withheld canonical institution, was a very different affair, likely to result in immediate chaos and future schism. Europe watched the conflict with interest. The Powers were all in league against France and would willingly have expressed themselves openly in favour of the Pontiff had he given them a chance to do so; but intent only on his mission of reform, he chose that very moment to abolish the privilege of sanctuary claimed by all ambassadors in Rome. This privilege certainly had degenerated into an intolerable abuse, as it had spread from the precincts of the Embassies themselves to all the adjoining streets. Ever since the pontificate of Julius II the exercise of this prerogative had been a source of trouble and disputes, some popes allowing and others denying it, while it had been the primary cause of the Créqui affray. Now Innocent declared that he would receive no ambassadors who had not formally renounced this privilege. Venice immediately recalled her envoy, Spain refrained from sending one, and the Duc d'Estrées having just died, was not given a successor.

The Pope showed no signs of dismay at his isolation, never wavering in his line of conduct and proceeding with the task he had set himself without any apparent misgivings as to its final results. Such serene confidence in the righteousness of his course had a salutary effect on most of the European monarchs, who could not, on mature reflection, fail to admit the justice of the Pontiff's claim and agreed to comply with his demands. The Empire, Spain and England sent ambassadors prepared to concede the point in question, France alone refusing her obedience. The Nuncio in Paris, having exhorted Louis XIV to follow the example given by the other great Powers, was told by that haughty autocrat that he was used to setting examples himself, not to following that of others. He therefore sent off the Marquis de Lavardin as Ambassador to Rome with instructions to claim the privilege all his colleagues had renounced. Innocent immediately gave orders to his officials to ignore Lavardin's arrival and to withhold all the tokens of honour and deference to which foreign envoys were entitled. He also forbade the cardinals to hold any communications whatever with the French Ambassador or his household.

On Sunday, November 16th, 1687, the Romans, thronging the Corso and the Piazza del Popolo, were treated to an unexpected and amazing sight, for Louis XIV's Envoy made his entry into the papal capital not as an ordinary ambassador but as a conqueror investing a fallen city. His escort numbered 200 officers, 300 soldiers, 100 gentlemen and over 100 lackeys. The gilt coach in which sat Lavardin and two French cardinals was drawn by six splendid horses, and followed by another scarcely less resplendent containing the Marquise and her ladies. Forty sumpter mules with blue velvet trappings emblazoned with the royal lilies of France brought up the rear.

As the soldiery reached the approaches of the Farnese Palace they lined the street with drawn swords, sheathing them only when the last of the cortège had disappeared within the portals of the Embassy. Lavardin then issued a proclamation to the effect that if he or his wife encountered in the streets of Rome any cardinals or State officials who failed to show them the customary marks of respect, his escort would deal with them on the spot. The effect of this pronouncement was magical. All means of conveyance used by the Roman aristocracy disappeared from the main thoroughfares during the hours likely to be chosen by the Lavardins for their airing. Day after day the French Ambassador, his wife and their gorgeous suite drove in solitary grandeur through a city whose population seemed to be composed of beggars and shopkeepers. But as soon as the gates of the Farnese Palace had closed on them, word went round that the coast was clear and Rome resumed its normal aspect. This incredible situation actually lasted for nine whole months!

Meanwhile the Pope lying low in the Vatican was made responsible by his disgruntled subjects for the inconvenience they suffered and was accused of cowardice and incompetence. They compared him unfavourably with any of his predecessors, who would have resorted to energetic and violent means of dealing with such an abnormal state of things. But Innocent, though probably aware of these comments, was in no way disturbed by them. He would have found it easy enough to muster his troops, arm the Roman citizens and meet force with force—as a soldier such a course would have been the more congenial to him no doubt—but as the Vicar of Christ, which he now was, such methods seemed to him unsuitable. So he shut himself up in the Vatican and put his trust in Providence.

The Powers who had at first criticised his inaction gradually grew to admire such faith and equanimity, and the imperturbability of his passive resistance so unnerved Louis XIV that he was really at a loss how to proceed. Composedly and methodically Innocent had continued to enact business with all the friendly Powers—and just as composedly and methodically had he continued to oppose Louis XIV. He had excommunicated the French Ambassador and the priests who said Mass for him, and the King had retorted by incarcerating the Nuncio and investing Avignon. The Pope made no further move, and it was evident that he could not be provoked into a single gesture incompatible with his apostolic character. Realising the futility of further bravado Louis XIV decided to recall his Envoy. So early one August morning the gates of the Farnese Palace were thrown open and the Ambassador and his wife, escorted by the officers, soldiers and gentlemen of their suite, and followed by their servants and sumpter mules, clattered through the silent Corso and out of the Porta del Popolo, thus ending an episode probably unique in diplomatic history.

Innocent did not approve of tortures and executions, preferring more persuasive methods of saving sinners from damnation, though his zeal for the suppression of heresy was as great as that of any Inquisitor. More especially did he abhor philosophical sophistry, and he treated Molinos the theologian with exceptional severity. The Pontiff had no liking for the Jesuits, and it is said that when later, Benedict XIV wished to canonise his virtuous predecessor, it was the influence of the Jesuits, exerted through Louis XV, that prevented one of the most worthy and remarkable of pontiffs from becoming St. Innocent XI.

His last illness was a long-drawn-out martyrdom which he bore with admirable resignation and fortitude. He died on August 11th, 1689, and his nephew Don Livio, on whom he had bestowed no honours or riches, gave him a funeral of regal splendour. More exceptional still was the fact that not a single lampoon or pasquinade concerning the dead Pontiff is known to have been circulated in his capital.

ALEXANDER VIII (Ottoboni)
1689–1691

HAD the late Pontiff followed his inclinations he would have distributed no more hats than haloes, for none of the would-be cardinals seemed to him really worthy of the dignity. He was, however, compelled by circumstances to create a few, but at the time of his death there were still ten vacancies in the Sacred College—a most valuable legacy for his successor. Many of the most outstanding personalities of the last few conclaves had now disappeared—such as Barberini, who had outlived nearly all his contemporaries; Azzolini, Queen Christina's friend and adviser; and Albizzi, who had known his day of celebrity as a wit and his day of humiliation as a candidate.

As Innocent had conferred no ecclesiastical dignity on his nephew Don Livio, his creatures were without a leader and unlikely to be held together by any sufficiently strong bond to form a party of their own.

A very reduced assembly entered the Vatican on August 23rd, as out of the sixty remaining members of the Sacred College several abstained from attending the conclave, and the French and German prelates had not yet arrived. Medici was in charge of the Spanish-Imperial factions, and d'Estrées, then living in Rome, at the head of the French. There were a few other small independent groups such as Chigi's and Altieri's, and another, calling itself "The Conscience Squadron", composed mainly of prelates belonging to different Italian States.

Medici's instructions from the Powers he represented consisted mostly of a list of exclusions, to which his father the Grand Duke had also added a few names. From the Emperor, Medici received four different sets of directions: one for general circulation, another to be confided secretly to the independent groups, a third to be whispered within earshot of the French conclavists and so mislead their patrons, and the fourth containing the name of the man the Emperor really wished to see elected.

Louis XIV, now thoroughly under the influence of Madame de Maintenon and in a more conciliatory frame of mind, was sending the Duc de Chaulnes as special envoy to the Holy See. The old nobleman still had many friends in Rome and the choice seemed excellent; but as he was not on speaking terms with the Cardinal d'Estrées, he was to be accompanied by the Marquis de Torcy, who would act as intermediary between the two leaders. All the French cardinals—excepting one who was in disgrace with the King—received strict injunctions to attend the conclave and were provided with the necessary funds to cover their expenses. They were commanded to join Chaulnes at Marseilles, from which port a fleet of twenty-six galleys was to convey them and their retinues to Italy.

The journey proved more protracted than had been anticipated, for a gale of exceptional violence drove the convoy to shelter in the harbour of Porto Venere, where they remained storm-bound for several days. Nor were these tempestuous conditions confined to the elements, as the Duc de Chaulnes, the King's Envoy, and the Duc de Noailles, the Commander-in-Chief of his forces, had a serious quarrel which might have afforded the Marquis de Torcy an excellent opportunity of exercising his talents as go-between, had not Chaulnes in this circumstance been only too willing to do the talking himself!

The incident occurred outside Livorno, which should have been the French fleet's first port of call and where great preparations had been made for its reception. It so happened that the storm which had driven the galleys into Porto Venere had also driven some merchant vessels into Livorno—three English and three Dutch escorted by a battleship. The governor of Livorno, much perturbed at their untimely appearance, sent a message to the captains informing them that he was expecting the French fleet to arrive as soon as the weather improved and that they must be prepared to salute the royal standard of France or take their departure. On receipt of this ultimatum the commanders hastily engaged some extra hands to strengthen their crews, and sailed out to meet the French convoy.

Having sighted the enemy they took up their positions, sails set and colours flying, and prepared for action. Noailles immediately gave orders to open fire; but Chaulnes, who was present, no less unhesitatingly forbade these orders being carried out. There ensued an acri-

monious argument between the two men, Chaulnes insisting that
Noailles' duty consisted in conveying the cardinals safely to Civita
Vecchia, and that he had no right to expose their lives to unnecessary
risks, however tempting it might be for him to add to his laurels by
annihilating a few wretched merchant vessels. Noailles retorted by
proposing to tranship the prelates on to one galley which could take
cover in the port of Livorno, remaining there in perfect safety while
the battle proceeded. He also hinted that it might be advisable for
Chaulnes to accompany his charges to protect them from any further
perils. The old Duke was indignant at such a suggestion and the dispute
between the bellicose field-marshal and the circumspect diplomatist
waxed furious. The latter, however, stood his ground so firmly that
Noailles had to capitulate, but he only did so on receipt of a written
order from Chaulnes commanding him in the King's name to proceed immediately on his journey.

Meanwhile the gallant little fleet's surprise at the evident hesitation
of the French to accept their challenge was changed to stupefaction
when it observed Louis XIV's twenty-six fine galleys veer round and
put out to sea without having fired a single shot, and no doubt the
governor and the inhabitants of Livorno were equally puzzled and
disappointed at the non-appearance of the guests they had prepared
to honour.

At Civita Vecchia the travellers found d'Estrée's coaches awaiting
them, and they made a spectacular entry a few hours later into Rome.
The French prelates were all *grands seigneurs*, but the most resplendent
of them was undoubtedly the Cardinal de Bouillon. There was a
regulation prohibiting cardinals from wearing wigs, and most of the
Italian prelates conformed to it; but this injunction was disregarded
across the Alps, and a contemporaneous portrait of Bouillon depicts
him adorned with a voluminous peruke, his mitre resting on a cluster
of curls, while a *rabat* of beautiful lace escapes frothily from between
his robes and his plump round chin. It is reported of this hierophantic
dandy that he was so obsessed with his exalted rank and ancestry that
when he took the Communion, he would only make use of wafers
stamped with his coat of arms! In the importance attached by all
these aristocratic prelates to their titles and worldly prerogatives
must be found the reason for the disappearance of the old custom
of giving to the members of the Sacred College the appellations of

their sees or of the Roman churches from which they derived their dignities.

There was a general display of magnificence at this conclave, the Italian cardinals belonging to princely houses striving not only to vie with the luxury of the foreign prelates, but more especially to eclipse each other, as evidenced by this letter of Panzuioli, the Duke of Modena's agent in Rome, describing to his Sovereign the ceremonial attending the transference of the Cardinal d'Este's meals from the kitchens which had been assigned to him to the door of the conclave.

I accompanied this morning the dishes of His Highness which were being carried to the Vatican, as do all the courtiers of their Eminences. Two grooms bearing staffs embossed with the Cardinal's arms led the way. Then came the mace-bearer with the Court officials; then the grooms carrying the food in great baskets. Behind them walked His Highness' pages escorting the bread boxes—then the lackeys bearing the wooden support on which are placed the cauldrons to keep the dishes warm. The kitchens which fate has allotted to His Eminence are about a mile away from the Vatican, but they are roomy and convenient, and have been so richly and tastefully decked out with gold and silver plate that there is a constant stream of distinguished visitors to inspect them. Our Cardinal's service is the most sumptuous in Rome not excepting the Medici's. Our liveries also, though they are only the ones used in the country during the winter, outshine all others. By their cut and their striking combination of colours they are far superior to those of the Florentine Cardinal.

The arrival of the French contingent at the Vatican did not immediately tend to speed up the main business of the assembly, for they created a diversion and a hubbub by claiming in their Sovereign's name the privilege of docking his galleys in the port of Civita Vecchia. This pretension gave rise to the most stormy debates— Aguirre, the spokesman of the Spanish party, declaring that Louis XIV, being still under a ban of excommunication, ought not to be accorded deferential treatment by the governing body of the Church. He even proposed that the Sacred College should refuse to recognise Chaulnes' diplomatic standing until such time as the King should have restored Avignon to the Holy See. The more cautious among his colleagues thought Aguirre had gone too far—Louis XIV might be a wayward and rebellious son of the Church but he was still a powerful and victorious monarch who had cowed and humiliated Alexander VII and whom none but a fanatical idealist such as Innocent XI could be daring enough to defy openly. So it was decided that the question would be settled by a ballot, which resulted in forty-two votes out of fifty in favour of acceding to Louis XIV's demands and receiving Chaulnes as his Ambassador.

That matter disposed of, the cardinals were now at liberty to attend to the pope's election. Among the new candidates was Altieri, but with no following but his own creatures and of course excluded by France. This last Power, in alliance with Savoy, was patronising Visconti; but merely to gain time, only Visconti himself taking his chances seriously. The Odescalchi group was scattering in various directions as their private sympathies prompted. The Venetians, who had for so long been kept at arm's length in papal circles, had been busily intriguing for the last few years to obtain a firm and powerful backing for a candidate of their own nationality. There was a strong prejudice, fostered by the autocratic Italian rulers and shared by the monarchical European Powers, against the elevation to the Holy See of a subject of any republican State. Genoese and Venetian candidates had therefore always encountered a stubborn opposition from most of their colleagues. This prevention Venice had set herself to overcome through the agency of her envoys to the various Courts in Europe. Their chief recruit was the Emperor, to whom they had made substantial offers of subsidies to assist him in his campaign against the Turks, and it was the name of their candidate—Ottoboni —which was mentioned in Leopold's fourth and final instructions to Medici. Spain had also been won over to his cause, and Ottoboni's great age would be likely to recommend him to the majority of his colleagues, so his candidature seemed a very promising one.

But before risking his name at the scrutiny, Medici considered it advisable to test the temper of the assembly by proposing another Venetian—Barbarigo—as a *ballon d'essai*. The twenty-nine votes obtained in his favour were considered a sufficiently encouraging result to allow of Ottoboni's name being whispered discreetly within hearing of a few conclavists.

D'Estrées, who distrusted the Venetian, on hearing the rumour of his growing popularity, immediately offered to support him, calculating thereby to draw Spain's exclusion on him. This transparent manœuvre caused considerable amusement to his more wily opponents, as can be imagined. On realising the failure of the plan he had thought so Machiavellian, d'Estrées, caught in his own trap, saw no means of escape but to swallow his pride and appeal to Chaulnes for help. But the Duke was an old friend of Ottoboni's and had already written to the King about him in a favourable spirit, and Louis XIV seemed disposed to patronise him as he had patronised Odescalchi, that is, as a makeshift and subject to the acceptance of certain conditions. There was evidently no way out for d'Estrées, so he bowed to the inevitable, only asking the Ambassador to undertake the negotiations with Ottoboni himself. The terms of the agreement consisted in the Pope's recognition of the *droit de régale* in exchange for which the King would surrender Avignon and his Ambassador would renounce the right of asylum. On this understanding, accepted by Ottoboni, the French party gave him its support and he was proclaimed Pope on October 6th—to be known as Alexander VIII.

The new Pontiff was eighty years old, but of a strong and healthy constitution, and was reputed to be an able and resourceful politician. He only reigned for eighteen months, but during that short space of time he managed to destroy most of his predecessor's good work. All the money saved by Innocent XI was squandered on enriching the Ottobonis. To a cardinal who ventured a word of remonstrance Alexander replied: "I have no time to lose; for me the day is almost done!" And so nepotism flourished once more.

The Pope gave great satisfaction to the clergy and the Roman ladies by revoking all the measures imposed on them by Innocent XI which they considered so vexatious—but he antagonised the Emperor and the King of Spain by filling the vacancies in the Sacred College with subjects of all countries but their own. Nor did France have it all her own way, for Chaulnes, who seemed in no hurry to fulfil his share of their agreement, was informed that he would receive no invitation to the Pope's enthronement unless he made the official renunciation to the right of asylum without delay. The Duke waited till the very last moment but had to comply in the end. Alexander adhered to his own part of the treaty with France, but proved on his deathbed that his conciliatory attitude had been dictated by political caution only; for, seeing himself about to pass beyond the reach of retribution, he issued a manifesto declaring, as Innocent XI had done, that the doctrines and actions of the Gallican clergy were subversive of the supremacy of the Church of Rome and their findings and those of the French Parliament therefore null and void. He further-more retracted his recognition of the *droit de régale*, and having thus eased his conscience and bequeathed a hornets' nest to his successor, passed peacefully away on February 1st, 1691.

INNOCENT XII (Pignatelli)
1691–1700

❧

THE revocation of his concessions to France, made *in extremis* by Alexander VIII, had struck the Duc de Chaulnes a shattering blow. He had taken all along a most sanguine view of the late Pontiff's political leanings, encouraged thereunto by the nomination of a couple of French cardinals and Alexander's strict observance of his undertakings. The Duke's reports to Louis XIV had therefore been written in a spirit of sustained optimism. He was well aware that his Sovereign showed no leniency towards officials who misinformed him, and that a lifetime of faithful and devoted service would weigh as nothing against this blatant error of judgment, so he bowed his head and awaited the storm. But it suited Louis XIV's plans much better to postpone the old courtier's disgrace till after the new pope's election, for he had no need of an·active French agent outside the coming conclave and Chaulnes could still play the part of an imposing figurehead. A new situation had arisen during Alexander's pontificate of which the poor old diplomat had not the faintest inkling, and which was so incredible that none even among the most suspicious members of the Sacred College ever came near to guessing the strange secret.

Altieri, the man that Louis XIV had so vindictively humiliated and persecuted, far from seeking to be revenged upon his ruthless enemy, had made it the aim and object of his life to worm himself into the despot's good graces. Having failed to propitiate any of the members of the French faction in the late conclave, he decided to adopt bolder and more direct methods of approach. Either through the good offices of Louis XIV's confessor or through those of Mme de Maintenon herself, he succeeded in reaching the King's ear. His abject, grovelling apologies for the political errors of his youth were accompanied by protestations of devotion and offers of lifelong and disinterested service. As an earnest of his sincerity he warned the King to put no trust in Alexander's apparent friendliness and prepared him for the recantation which he foretold as a certainty. Louis XIV, realising what a valuable source of reliable information this un-expected ally would prove, and probably flattered in his vanity by such dogged determination to win his favour, entered into a con-fidential and clandestine correspondence, over the heads of his official representatives, with the man he had openly sworn to crush.

Altieri's disposition must have been akin to that feminine type which adores a brutal lover, whose fidelity is fostered by ill-treatment and which licks the boot that kicks it, for Louis XIV, who exacted the blindest submission from those who served him, never obtained more diligent or more faithful allegiance than from this cringing infatuated devotee. Altieri's voluntary bondage, like the fulfilment of a vocation, acted as a strong tonic on his mental faculties. He developed a clearness of insight and a firmness of purpose for which he had shown no aptitude before. Louis XIV's goodwill, which he had contrived to win at the cost of so much self-abasement and treachery to his colleagues, seems to have satisfied all his aspirations. He asked no more of life now but to bask for ever in the warmth of the Roi Soleil's approbation and to worship at his shrine.

On March 19th the French cardinals entered the conclave which had been assembled since February 12th. They were gratified to find that, conforming to the tacit understanding accepted by their col-leagues, no attempt at an election had been made before their arrival. They brought the King's letters for Chaulnes and d'Estrées, those intended for Altieri being enclosed under cover addressed to a lady of the Orsini family. Chaulnes was immensely relieved by the general tone of the missive he received. He had feared an immediate re-call, and though his orders were disconcertingly vague they were not markedly curt or frigid. Had he known what was going on behind his back he would have felt less reassured about the King's feelings towards him!

As to d'Estrées, his instructions were purposely so nebulous and involved that he had not the slightest idea what he was being told to do. He sent a message to Chaulnes to come at once to the con-clave wicket, and after a long and agitated whispered consultation decided to despatch a courier with all haste to Versailles with a note begging in both their names for more explicit guidance.

Louis XIV's communication to Altieri, on the other hand, was as clear and direct as could be desired. Convinced of his ex-bugbear's utter reliability, the monarch actually proposed to raise him to the Holy See! If Altieri accepted the suggestion, orders to support him would be sent at once to the leaders of the French faction. Altieri all but swooned with bliss—not at the prospect of wearing the triple crown, but at such an overwhelming proof of his idol's confidence. He knew of course that the project was impracticable; Louis XIV had overlooked the effect that such an astounding move would produce on the Sacred College. Except for those cardinals under the direct subjection of France, every one of Altieri's colleagues would have turned and reviled him, and the French party alone could not carry his election. So he wrote to the King and Mme de Maintenon, expatiating on his overwhelming gratitude and alluding in ambiguous terms to the insuperable obstacles standing in the way of his own elevation to the Apostolic See. He was ready, however, with the name of a substitute upon whose loyalty the King could rely as firmly as upon his own. So the most trustworthy of messengers who set out on the fleetest of horses from the ambassadorial stables bearing the bewildered leaders' letters to Versailles was followed a few hours later by another, less conspicuous but no less efficient, bound on the identical errand for another master.

The cardinals had agreed to await their French colleagues before proceeding to elect the pope; but they could scarcely be expected to postpone the scrutinies indefinitely; so on April 4th Chigi suddenly proposed the candidature of Barbarigo, and attempted to carry off his election by surprise. D'Estrées, who was by now a more experienced conclavist, far from opposing the Venetian prelate, appeared to be most favourably inclined towards him, and merely asked for time to obtain the King's consent to his elevation. The majority of Barbarigo's partisans were disinclined to grant this delay and had just resolved to call upon the French faction for their decision when news reached the conclave that Mons had fallen and that Nice Castle had been stormed by the French. This double victory of Louis XIV's army placed d'Estrées in too strong a position to be gainsaid. "The Cardinals Nice and Mons have just arrived", wrote Negri to the Duke of Savoy; "if only a few more of their kind follow the conclave will not last much longer!" Barbarigo was not and never could be acceptable to France. He was austere, rigid, intolerant; and the last man to forgo any ecclesiastical privileges or pander to the autocrat of Versailles.

During the interlude which had now been courteously pressed on the French faction to enable them to obtain their Sovereign's consent to Barbarigo's election, the enforced idleness of the cardinals led to a scandalous relaxation of all regulations. The boarding was taken down, the windows thrown open, and the inmates of the Vatican brazenly exchanged greetings with their friends gathered on the Piazza below. Musicians were engaged to serenade the recluses, and their lady friends, "discreetly veiled", says Gubernatis, "made signs with their fingers in the Spanish fashion!"

The evenings were spent at the gaming tables, many prelates gambling far into the night—this unedifying pastime being the cause of an accident which might have led to the most tragic consequences. A light accidentally knocked over by one of the players set fire to the cubicle, and spread in a few moments with alarming rapidity. This is how Cardinal d'Este describes the incident in a letter to his brother the Duke of Modena:

Last night the conclave caught fire, and the conflagration lasted till the early hours of the morning. I cannot tell you the panic it caused among us. The danger was great no doubt, but the burlesque was greater still. I could have held my sides at the sight afforded by my dear colleagues in raiment and attitudes that Jacob under his ladder would never have dreamed of. This one in a camisole, that one in pants, another in a dressing gown, a fourth wrapped up in wadding, others in vests, or shirts, or strange indescribable garments—but all irresistibly comical. Cardinal Marescotti, who had been laid up for four days unable to move with lumbago—miraculously cured by fright—was rushing about half naked, as hairy as a devil, and repeating incessantly: What next, good heavens, what next? Aguirre, who usually needs the support of four attendants, was gambading along the passages like a frolicsome hare. Maidalchini, who is afflicted with a hernia, flew past holding it up in both hands. Bouillon, scratching himself unrestrainedly, was screaming to his servants to save his periwigs. Forbin, under pretext of salving valuable documents, was searching the cells for compromising papers of which he held large rolls under his arms. Colloredo and S. Susanna marched solemnly round holding a crucifix and chanting: *Libera nos Domine.* Ottoboni, in spotless white night attire, his face fresly painted, was cutting capers, joking and laughing like a lunatic.

The incentive of personal danger drove the conclavists to exert so much energy that the fire was subdued. The victims were accommodated in tenantless cells and the whole assembly retired to sleep and rest. Having recovered from their emotion and fatigue, the cardinals resumed the various occupations with which they strove to while away the interminable hours of leisure.

The couriers seemed an unconscionable time returning from Versailles and Chigi was losing patience, testily pressing d'Estrées for a decision concerning Barbarigo. The whole assembly was getting restive and d'Estrées was at his wit's end how to keep the situation in hand. The French leader had not the slightest suspicion of his Sovereign's secret understanding with Altieri nor, for the matter of that, had any of the other members of the Sacred College. Altieri, who knew that Louis XIV's instructions to his party were being held up until matters had been definitely settled between the French court and his protégé Pignatelli, now considered it advisable to step into the breach himself.

He set out to undermine the enemy's forces by detaching the various factions from their allegiance to Barbarigo. His first recruit was Ottoboni, the late Cardinal-Nephew, who had built a beautiful theatre in his palace and feared above all things to see it closed. It was easy enough to persuade him that Barbarigo would never tolerate such a hobby in a cardinal and that some other candidate could be found who would be more indulgent. Altieri then turned his attentions to the Spanish-Imperial party and, being on friendly terms with their leader, Medina-Coeli, he aroused no suspicion by strolling out of ear-shot with him at the first opportunity. He then proceeded to sound him tactfully on his feelings regarding the Venetian candidate and found the Spaniard quite willing to show his hand. The Cardinal Duke of Medina-Coeli was thoroughly worldly; he loved all the good things of life which rank and wealth had put within his reach. Like Bouillon and so many other exalted prelates he ranked his ecclesiastical dignity far below his secular standing, and when Altieri suggested that the austere and bigoted Barbarigo would impose on the cardinals a life of rigorous discipline, he felt alarmed and outraged, and declared himself willing to connive at any scheme to prevent such an objectionable zealot's election. Medina-Coeli had great influence both in Madrid and Vienna, and was in a position to assume the responsibility of deciding on the merits and demerits of any candidate. He therefore wrote immediately to the Emperor to inform him that he had just discovered that Barbarigo was secretly in league with the French, that he was a dangerous enemy of the Empire and should be given the exclusion. Leopold, who had been inundated with the most contradictory reports and denunciations from Rome, was thoroughly disgusted with the whole business, and more than willing to leave the responsibility of selecting a candidate to the Spanish leader, who would presumably have Hispano-German interests at heart. He therefore sent the exclusion against Barbarigo to Medina-Coeli and trusted to his good judgment.

Meanwhile the Sacred College had the mild excitement of a new candidature—that of yet another Venetian called Delfino, who had worked perseveringly to collect adherents, but who was defeated by the "Zelanti" party, whose leader, Negroni, the soul of puritanical fanaticism, did not hesitate to make public the knowledge he possessed of Delfino's exceptionally unedifying past—and so nipped his chances in the bud.

On July 4th the messengers both from Versailles and Vienna reached Rome simultaneously. The Emperor's letter to Medina-Coeli was exactly such as he had expected and all he could wish for, but Louis XIV's orders to Chaulnes and d'Estrées caused their recipients utter stupefaction. They were to refer to Altieri for instructions and follow his lead unquestioningly; which amounted to putting them in a subordinate position to the man they had so far been forbidden even to speak to and against whom the King had declared a lifelong feud. This thunderbolt, hurled straight out of the blue by Louis at his devoted servants without even a premonitory rumbling, must have all but stunned them—but they were both courtiers by birth and training and instinctively composed themselves to conceal even the faintest trace of surprise or resentment. A secret meeting with Altieri was immediately contrived by d'Estrées, who dutifully subscribed to his new chief's plan of campaign.

Medina-Coeli had of course apprised Altieri of the Emperor's answer, so he knew Barbarigo was doomed, but more supporters were needed for his own candidate Pignatelli, and this work Altieri alone could undertake. Louis XIV was putting large sums of money at his disposal, and Pignatelli having no nephews, the most lucrative State appointments could also be offered as baits. The candidate, an apparently weak-minded and rather stupid old man, had accepted all the French Monarch's stipulations concerning the *régale* and other minor points in dispute and seemed as devoted to the King's interests as Altieri himself.

Medina-Coeli's defection had so hopelessly wrecked Barbarigo's chances that when his name was proposed at the scrutiny of July 9th he could only muster five votes—those of the five most fanatical "Zelanti". Altieri, still successfully concealing his alliance with the French party, had no difficulty in rallying the Spanish leader to Pignatelli's cause and now felt confident of victory. But so fearful was he of some last-moment set-back that not until the scrutiny was actually taking place would he permit d'Estrées to disclose his faction's readiness to support Pignatelli. Altieri's masterly strategy met with complete success, and on July 12th Pignatelli was proclaimed Pope under the name of Innocent XII, the group of the five Zelanti alone refusing to give him their suffrage.

The new Pontiff was seventy-six years old and a Neapolitan by birth—therefore a subject of the King of Spain—and it speaks volumes for the confidence evinced by Louis XIV in Altieri's judgment and good faith that he should have agreed to support such an un-promising candidature. Innocent XII's elevation to the Holy See proved to have the same beneficent and quickening effect on his mental faculties as the bestowing of Louis XIV's favour had had on Altieri's! Attainment of the supreme dignity seemed to infuse new life into him—he shook off the torpor and irresolution which had characterised him so far, and to the general amazement gave every evidence of intelligence and good sense. He took up his residence in the Quirinal and started at once to assert his authority. Ottoboni was ordered to disband his troop of comedians and demolish his cherished play-house. Arrests were made in the neighbourhood of the Embassies, and the Pope's relations were officially notified that they were not to enter the Papal States; according to Gubernatis His Holiness would not even employ Neapolitan servants. He rose early, took long walks and devoted himself entirely to his religious and official duties.

Innocent published a bull abolishing nepotism finally and irrevocably
—laying down that every member of the Sacred College should take
a solemn oath in conclave to conform to the edict if he was raised to
the Holy See.

The Pontiff naturally made many enemies, but none could deny
his rectitude, piety and disinterestedness. He fulfilled his obligations
to France by bestowing certain State offices according to the agreement he had accepted, and never failed to prove his gratitude to
Louis XIV when occasion arose. The advice which he pressed on
Charles II to nominate the Duc d'Anjou as his successor to the throne
of Spain, certainly weighed heavily in the balance when the dying
monarch finally gave his decision in favour of the house of Bourbon.
But in exchange for this service he managed, with the help of Mme de
Maintenon and the Père la Chaise, Louis' confessor, to bring that
proud autocrat to renounce of his own accord his pretensions to the
régale and to make a full and unqualified submission to Rome in the
name of the Gallican Church.

True, the Roi Soleil had passed his zenith, he was no longer the
effulgent demigod of former years—an austere odour of sanctity now
pervaded the conjugal apartments where more voluptuous perfumes
had been wont to linger. Mme de Maintenon and her cohort of
spiritual directors played on the King's religious sensibilities, incessantly stressing with ominous premonitions the approach of the
day of reckoning. More experienced than Innocent XI and less
hampered by scruples, Innocent XII was too wise to antagonise the
Jesuits. He made use of them instead, and it was entirely through the
influence that they exerted over the wife of the ageing Louis that
such a triumph was achieved.

The Pontiff's relations with the Emperor were less friendly. He
annulled an edict issued by Leopold claiming sovereignty over all
fiefs constituted in Italy without his sanction, and confident of the
support of France and Spain, made spirited remonstrances to the
Court of Vienna. Leopold, realising that he had incurred universal
odium by promulgating such an anachronistic and preposterous
pretension, withdrew his claim and no more was heard of it.

Innocent XII added his quota to the Roman monuments by
building several palaces and aqueducts. He abolished many scandalous
abuses, but he had to abandon the plan of reforming the religious

Orders, finding it impracticable to take disciplinary measures against rival congregations while showing leniency towards the Jesuits, whose services he could not dispense with.

Innocent XII died on September 28th, 1700, leaving, besides a reputation for sagacity and virtue, a well-filled treasury and the dignity and influence of the Holy See considerably enhanced.

XVIIIth CENTURY

Clement XI   ·   Innocent XIII   ·   Benedict XIII
Clement XII   ·   Benedict XIV   ·   Clement XIII
Clement XIV · Pius VI

CLEMENT XI (ALBANI)

1700–1721

❧

THE pitiable object known to the world at large as King Charles II of Spain took thirty-six years to die. He was born moribund, not attempting to stand or even to lisp till fully five years old. The most sanguine members of his household had never expected him to survive the crucial years of adolescence; yet he lingered on, and by and by, to the general amazement, grew to a state of semi-manhood. More surprising still, having been married to a healthy, normal young woman, the vivacious Louise d'Orléans, he not only managed to out-live her, but was soon clamouring for another wife, his second consort being Anne of Neuburg, a sister-in-law of the Emperor Leopold.

It was common knowledge that Charles could never expect to become a father, and being the last of his line, the competition to provide him with an heir was naturally very keen. Most of the Continental rulers cast greedy eyes on his vast inheritance, the three most important pretenders to his succession being the Duc d'Anjou, representing the claims of France, the Archduke Charles those of the Empire, and the Duke of Savoy standing for his own.

The interested parties, losing patience at Charles' protracted dally-ing on the brink of the grave, threw decency to the winds and held several conferences to discuss the apportioning of his possessions. Surreptitiously, of course, each claimant had brought to bear all the influence he could dispose of through bribery or intrigue, to induce the Spanish monarch to make a will in his favour; and now that he was under the influence of a German queen and getting weaker day by day, the imperial candidate's chances seemed the most promising. But just as Innocent XII had made use of the Jesuits' spiritual ascendancy over Louis XIV to attain his ends, so did Louis XIV make use of the Pope's spiritual ascendancy over Charles II to attain his own. The Holy Father's advice to such a devout, childlike being was to him as the voice of conscience itself. It outweighed his natural inclination towards the Habsburgs—his own house—it outweighed his tremulous resentment of Louis' high-handed methods—it out-weighed the influence of his wife and his distaste for final decisions. It spurred him to the stupendous effort of proclaiming officially his sovereign will that Louis XIV's grandson should be recognised as his heir.

The triumph of the Bourbons would have been unalloyed had Charles, after making this momentous pronouncement and with a due sense of fitness, turned his face to the wall and expired then and there, instead of outstaying his welcome with such provoking persistence, thus encouraging the frustrated competitors to renewed and frantic efforts to regain lost ground. The death of Innocent XII threw all the actors of this tragi-comedy into a fever of expectation; for if a Francophobe pontiff could be elected before Charles II passed away, there was no reason why he should not prevail on the dying monarch to revoke his former will and appoint another heir. The Empire and Savoy therefore were prepared to strain every nerve to hasten the coming election, while France on the contrary would strive by every means in her power to delay it until Charles was safely out of the way.

As was usual in such moments of international crisis the political tendencies of the future pope were considered intensely important, though the Powers must have known that in any case war was now inevitable. Neither Louis XIV nor Leopold was likely to relinquish his claims because the Pope happened to favour his opponent; nor were the Italian rulers more likely to be influenced by his opinion where the repartition of the Spanish territories in Italy was concerned, if Roman sympathies proved at variance with their own interests. Nevertheless they one and all leapt into the electoral arena with desperate earnestness. The Duke of Savoy, under an appearance of reserve and aloofness, was no less eager and agitated than his neighbours. For years his agent in Rome, Count Graneri, had been at work unearthing the candidate most likely to further his master's interests, and was convinced he had now discovered him. Graneri, who was thoroughly conversant with Roman Court intrigues and in personal touch with all the leading members of the Sacred College, had taken Cardinal Barberini into his confidence and together they had selected Cardinal Albani as the man best adapted to their purpose. Albani was young—only fifty years of age—a Roman born and bred, who, never having left the capital, had not been exposed to any foreign influences and was under no foreign obligations. His father had been a steward of the Barberini and he himself had held important offices under the three last pontificates, his charming, courteous manners making him a general favourite. He was known by his intimate friends to hold strong views on the independence of Italy and seemed the very man Savoy needed, his nationalism according admirably with the Duke's dynastic ambitions.

The Prince of Monaco had succeeded Chaulnes as French Ambassador to the Holy See, the poor old Duke having been recalled immediately after Innocent XII's enthronement; but d'Estrées would still be head of the French faction at the coming conclave where Mme de Maintenon was to have her own private representative— Cardinal de Noailles, whose conclavists and attendants had all been selected by the lady herself. The other prelates forming the French faction were Coislin, Le Camus, Rodolevitch, and Arquien, father of the Queen of Poland. As to Bouillon, he was in deep disgrace with the King for having had the audacity to claim the title of "Prince Dauphin". Louis had dismissed him from his office of Grand Almoner, requested him to return the insignia of the order of the Holy Ghost, and banished him from the kingdom. The French cardinals had strict orders to abstain from all intercourse with him; in fact he was to be treated as he himself had treated Altieri in the days of that prelate's disfavour.

Venice seemed disposed to side with France, but was suspected of playing an underhand game to suit her own purpose, under pretext of leaving her subjects free to follow the dictates of their conscience. Leopold, who had had good cause to regret the confidence he had placed in Medina-Coeli's judgment at the last conclave, had now entrusted Medici with his interests thinking that as an Italian he would be better able to discern the real character and political tendencies of his compatriots than could a foreigner. Such reasoning was no doubt sound; but unfortunately for the Emperor Medici was in no mood to trouble himself with anybody's concerns but his own. He was now the last surviving member of his house, and intended, as soon as the conclave was over, to relinquish his ecclesiastical dignities and make a suitable marriage to perpetuate his line. It could not be long before he was called upon to succeed his father Cosimo III as

Grand Duke of Tuscany, and he had his own political aims to foster. Medici had willingly accepted the appointment of Cardinal Padrone of the Imperialists which carried with it important emoluments and an influential position, but it was not on Leopold's account but entirely on his own that such influence would be exerted. Medici like Savoy wanted a nationalistic pontiff who would see eye to eye with the Italian rulers among whom he himself would so soon be called to occupy a prominent position. Leopold had mentioned no names in his instructions to the leader of his party. As Medici could not fail to realise the importance of securing the elevation of a thoroughly Francophobe pontiff, the Emperor had merely written that he would be satisfied, if no better candidate could be found, with a docile, unassuming individual, so long as there was no question of his having had any previous understanding with the French.

Such on broad lines was the situation of the various factions when the conclave assembled on October 10th, 1700, only thirty-eight prelates answering the first roll-call. The French cardinals dribbled in singly at several days' interval, disclaiming any knowledge of the King's wishes, his instructions being entrusted to Cardinal de Noailles, who would be the last, they said, to reach the Vatican. Candidates and exclusions were equally numerous, and d'Estrées raised no objection to a few preliminary ballots taking place to clear the ground for more serious action. Leopold had made some advances to Bouillon who was presumably smarting under the treatment meted out to him by his Sovereign; but whatever his inward feelings may have been the would-be "Prince Dauphin" clung staunchly to his compatriots and always voted with them.

Altieri was the same secret and invaluable ally that he had proved to be at the last conclave. Besides defeating all the efforts of the dogmatic and inflexible Zelante to hasten on an election, he also managed to persuade Medici that as all the chances seemed in favour of a Bourbon reigning in Spain it would be advisable to delay matters till Noailles arrived on the scene with the latest information from Versailles. Rumours were rife that Charles was now dead, in which case it would indeed be rash for the future ruler of Tuscany to make an enemy of Louis XIV. Altieri's advice proved sound enough, for when at last Noailles made his tardy appearance he officially confirmed the news of the Spanish monarch's demise and announced the departure of Philip V for Madrid where he had probably arrived by then. He was also the bearer of a proposal from the French King to the Duke of Savoy offering to exchange Savoy for the kingdom of Sicily, Louis XIV wishing no doubt to wipe the Alps off the map as he had the Pyrenees.

From Medici's letters to the Grand Duke it is quite evident that the Cardinal Patron of the Imperialists was calmly negotiating with the French, utterly regardless of Leopold's interests, nor was he in the least subservient to the wishes of his priest-ridden father, who would have liked a fanatical pontiff to be raised to the Holy See. Medici's views were not likely to coincide with Cosimo's in that respect; the candidates' connections or influence with rich heiresses being of much more interest to him than their religious fervour. Proceeding by elimination Medici and d'Estrées found that only two names now remained on their list—Albani and Acciaioli, the last a great favourite with Mme de Maintenon and also protected by Venice, which made him less acceptable to the Florentine. As to the Spanish party they were like a flock of lost sheep, their shepherd, the Ambassador Duke d'Uzeda, being a timid, irresolute diplomat, incapable of coping with the anomalous situation in which he found himself. He had been appointed by a Habsburg monarch and had not been notified of the change of dynasty. During the reign of Charles II the standing orders of the Spanish faction had been to follow the lead of the imperialists; so much so that we have seen Medina-Coeli apply to the Emperor for orders and exclusions. Uzeda demurred at breaking on his own authority with established custom and tradition, and yet if Spain was now ruled by Louis XIV's grandson he could scarcely throw in his lot with the Emperor!

The prelates were all anxiety to get the election over, and the house of Medici, which would never again have a representative in the Sacred College, made a brilliant exit from the history of conclaves in which it had played such an important part; for now the future Grand Duke took matters entirely in his own hands. Albani seemed the most promising candidate from his point of view, so he set out to persuade d'Estrées to adopt him definitely to the exclusion of Acciaioli. It took Medici the best part of the night to attain his object, but when he separated from the French leader he had his promise of support. Arriving at dawn exhausted, but exultant, in his own cell, he found there his Spanish, Neapolitan and Milanese colleagues waiting to offer him their allegiance. Under his wing they felt secure from the displeasure both of Leopold, who had entrusted Medici with the leadership of the imperialists, and from Louis, whose party were supporting Medici's nominee.

The whole assembly was now in a state of feverish excitement, but Medici needed rest and insisted on having it, postponing the actual election to the morrow. He acted wisely, for his labours and anxieties were not yet over. The prodigies of tact and diplomacy he had expended on inducing the French leader to accept Albani as Pope, he now had to renew so as to induce Albani to accept the supreme dignity. Albani's most noted partisans—Barberini, Ottoboni, and Altieri—gathered round Medici to make a concerted attack: they then took it in turns to try their gifts of persuasion singly on the recalcitrant Pope-elect. Between them they reduced him to a state of collapse, and the officious conclavists having plied him with too generous an amount of restoratives, the overwrought patient showed such alarming symptoms of hysteria that the dispensary had to be ransacked for the most potent sedatives. The majority of Albani's colleagues were convinced that he was acting a part to disarm the suspicions of the French faction; but Graneri in a letter to the Duke of Savoy gives another explanation of his strange behaviour. He says that Albani, having solemnly sworn to renounce nepotism and seeing no loophole of escape from the consequences of his oath, became panic-stricken at the idea of the quarrels and recriminations awaiting him in his family circle. He was burdened with several ambitious nephews and a sister-in-law who dominated him as Donna Olympia had dominated Innocent X. Being a determined and spirited woman, she was likely to make a vigorous attempt to induce him to break his pledge, and he shrank from the encounter.

The entire Sacred College had mustered for the scrutiny, but Medici would not allow the bell to be rung until the doctor, who was in permanent attendance on Albani, had sent him word that his patient was in a more amenable frame of mind. Reports being still unsatisfactory, he requested the cardinals to disperse till further summonses were issued. On September 21st Albani was said to be calmer but still obdurate.

On the 22nd he received a few visitors, his appearance being cadaverous but his manner more normal.

On the 23rd he asked for a conference of theologians to be called who would discuss the subject and determine where his duty lay.

During the conference Albani refused to see anybody, being deep in meditation and no doubt nerving himself to face the verdict. The learned men's decision was that it was incumbent on Albani to accept the papal crown, but that he would not sin in refusing it. When informed of the conclusion arrived at by the casuists, the future Pope is said to have wept copiously, whether from relief or sorrow no one can tell, but as he wept no less copiously at various other moments of his career it was perhaps his habitual manner of expressing emotion. Immediately after his proclamation as Pope Clement XI, however, he dried his tears for the time being and faced his new obligations to the best of his ability. He had little self-reliance, and admitted himself that although he had been considered a good adviser by three Popes he felt unequal to guiding himself. His pontificate was a long and disastrous one. Buffeted this way and that by force of circumstance, he found himself, after having officially congratulated Philip V on his accession, constrained by the victorious Emperor to recognise the Habsburg pretender as the rightful sovereign of Spain. In losing the friendship of the Bourbons he did not manage to gain that of the Habsburgs; he disappointed the Italian States, who had hoped so much of his patriotism, by demurring to join the league they wished to form for the defence of Italian neutrality. He fluctuated perpetually between contradictory policies, always striving to keep in the foreground by officiously offering his mediation where it was not wanted. He soon found himself isolated and ignored by all parties. The Emperor disposed of Parma and other papal fiefs, coolly disregarding Clement's expostulations, and by the Peace of Utrecht Sicily and Sardinia changed hands without any more ceremony. The Pontiff evinced no gratitude towards the Duke of Savoy, Victor Amadeus, who was now King of Sicily. On the contrary he opposed his early patron at every turn, thus laying the seeds of the enmity between the Holy See and the house of Savoy, which endured for over two hundred years.

Even the elements seemed to conspire to add their quota of calamities to this unfortunate pontificate. In 1703 the Tiber overflowed its banks and spread over the Campagna, completely destroying the crops and reducing the peasants to ruin and starvation. Scarcely had the waters receded when a violent earthquake of fifteen minutes' duration shook Rome to its very foundations, the more populous districts of the city suffering the most serious damage. Entire streets disappeared under the crumbling houses and the number of victims was enormous. These cataclysms were followed by an epidemic of "pestilential fevers" which further decimated the population, and the distress and misery were such that the wretched survivors subsisted entirely on grass or on stray animals, as starved as themselves, that they devoured raw. The women were ready to prostitute themselves to any man for a crust of bread, and the more fortunate Romans under pretext of benevolence treated themselves to well-stocked harems.

Clement did his best to remedy this appalling state of things, remitting all taxes to the victims both of the flood and of the earthquake. He also appointed matrons to reclaim and shelter the women who haunted the streets or had found too intimate a hospitality in many ecclesiastical households. But as His Holiness had no reserves of wheat wherewith to make bread and no money wherewith to purchase any food for these erring and ravenous females, the matrons must indeed have been eloquent if they persuaded any of them of the advantages of chastity and an aching void over frailty and repletion. Through the influence of the Jesuits Clement obtained some subsidies from Louis XIV; but France was at war and had little money to spare for philanthropy.

Having joined the league of the Italian States, fighting against Austria, which was completely routed by Prince Eugène, the Pope had perforce to submit to the humiliating terms imposed on him by the conqueror. Louis XIV made no allowances for the difficulties of the situation and, outraged at Clement's recognition of the Archduke as King of Spain, recalled his Ambassador from Rome.

Peace once signed, the imperial troops evacuated the Pontifical States and the Pope immediately set about regaining Louis XIV's good graces. The Bourbon Queen of Spain having just given birth to a son, His Holiness publicly blessed some swaddling-clothes and sent them to Madrid by a special Nuncio with orders to attend the ceremony of the oath of allegiance to the Prince of the Asturias to be taken by the members of the Cortes.

The poor Pontiff was beset with enemies and failed to make any friends. When the Turks threatened to invade Italy, he implored assistance from Venice, Spain, France, Austria and even Russia, but all Europe turned a deaf ear to his entreaties. His last allies in France, the Jesuits who surrounded the King, failed him when Louis died, for the Regent d'Orléans who now governed France was a frank atheist and made a clean sweep of all Mme de Maintenon's ecclesiastical sycophants. The last years of Clement's life were embittered by his disputes with Alberoni, the Spanish Prime Minister and Philip V's favourite, who obtained the hat by a bold and unscrupulous trick and openly defied the Holy See. Before the Pope died, however, Alberoni was an exiled fugitive, ruined and flying for his life, pursued by his ex-master's vindictiveness more spitefully even than by the Pope's.

INNOCENT XIII (Conti)

1721-1724

THERE was now a truce to fighting in Europe; by the Peace of Utrecht and the treaties of Rastadt and Baden some sort of a political equilibrium had been arrived at between the Powers. The Bourbon dynasty had taken root in Spain, an exhausted, ruined Spain which Charles II had left without an army, without a navy and without resources of any kind. Austria's share of the spoils was considerable; comprising part of the Low Countries and the Spanish territories in Italy. France had formally recognised the sovereignty of the house of Hanover in England, and ceased to support the Stuart Pretender; she had also acquiesced in the British occupation of Gibraltar and Minorca. Even Venice and the Turks had ceased fighting, and peace, if not goodwill, prevailed among the nations.

For the first time since the dark ages, French and Spanish interests would not clash at the coming conclave and the two factions would stand side by side as allies, instead of face to face as foes. Although Clement XI had not ventured to raise his nephew to the official position and unlimited power bestowed by his nepotic predecessors on their relations, he had done as much as he dared for his family and given the hat to a young Albani, who in the capacity of Cardinal-Nephew would lead his uncle's creatures into the conclave. As during Clement's long pontificate the Sacred College had been practically renewed, the question resolved itself into the acquisition of Albani's support. Count Kinsky, the Emperor's Envoy, who was evidently not acquainted with the methods of unblushing simony practised in Rome, presented Albani with a ring worth 25,000 florins, but entrusted the large sum of money which should have accompanied the gift to a German prelate called Althan, with instructions to convey it secretly and tactfully to the Cardinal-Nephew. This Althan apparently failed to do, and Albani, disgusted with what he considered the meanness of the Austrians, readily agreed to the proposals made to him by the French party, whose methods were more direct. Their offers consisted of annuities and rich benefices, a particularly tempting item being the convent of the "Ladies of Paradise", a most opulent abbey in the South of France of which the abbess was always chosen from among the most aristocratic families of the country. The candidate selected by the French faction was Conti, a comatose old prelate who had sleepily accepted the Regent's conditions, which were as follows: the hat was to be conferred immediately on Dubois, his Prime Minister; certain Francophile prelates were to be appointed to State offices, and a promise given by Conti to restrain the political activities of the Jesuit order. Albani's adhesion having made a certainty of the election, Conti was proclaimed Pope on May 7th, 1721, under the name of Innocent XIII.

The Emperor was very disappointed at the victory of his antagonists, as he set great store by the new Pope's political sympathies, thinking that the peace of Italy depended on them; but Prince Eugene shrugged his shoulders and is reported to have said that whoever the new Pontiff might be there was no reason to consider him of more importance than any other prince who could only put 8000 or 10,000 men in the field—a force of no significance and which need not trouble the Emperor.

Innocent's disease must have been a very trying one. He hibernated through a pontificate of three years, being occasionally roused from his slumbers to attend to urgent matters of State. He fulfilled all his obligations to France and also instituted an enquiry into Alberoni's misdemeanours, as Clement XI had started proceedings to strip him of his ecclesiastical dignities. This investigation resulted in the unscrupulous ex-statesman being completely whitewashed, a finding which can scarcely have met with Philip V's approval. The Jesuits were treated with less indulgence, or rather they would have been, had the Pontiff not died just as he was about to enforce severe measures against their order, their indiscretions in the East having been fully exposed by the legate Mezzabarba, who had been sent out to investigate the truth of the scandalous reports which had reached Europe from China and elsewhere. In a letter to Lord Carteret dated March 1724, Walton, England's secret agent in Rome, whose mission consisted in keeping an eye on the Pretender, writes:

Innocent XIII might have lived a few years longer had he been more temperate in eating and drinking, and had his doctors been less ignorant. He was an equitable, honest ruler, always kept his word, in fact was inclined to do more than he had promised. He proved grateful to those who had befriended him, a rare quality indeed. He gave few audiences and compared to Clement XI showed little interest in the Pretender. I will have reliable correspondents in the coming conclave who will warn me in good time if any intrigues are afoot which might prejudice the King's interests by favouring the Pretender's.

Innocent XIII died on March 17th, 1724, not as one might imagine, unconsciously exchanging habitual for eternal sleep, but less mercifully after an agony of intense suffering.

Emõ et Rmõ D.D.Nicolao Tit: S.Mª ad Martyres Diac. Card.Iudice S. Palatij Apostolici pro Præfecto.

Cum duorum superiorum Pontificum, quà te Apostolici Palatij praefecturà ornaverunt, Imagines tua auctoritate, atque cura, elaboratæ acceptissimæ fuerint, tertiam quoque insidentis equo BENEDICTI XIII. Cui nuper collatam purpuram accepta refers, utpote te eodem iubente locatam gratissimam, cum tibi, tum omnibus fore confido; praesertim vero iis quibus equitatus celebritati in eà pienda Summæ Dignitatis perfunctione interesse non licuit. Quod tuum igitur est, maiore qua potui diligentia graphio expressam tibi restituo. Datum Romæ Kalendis Augusti, Anno Iubilei MDCCXXV.

BENEDICT XIII
From a print in the British Museum

BENEDICT XIII (ORSINI)

1724–1730

CONCLAVE fever was endemic in Rome, few residents if any escaping at least a touch of the infection. Walton indeed succumbed to a severe attack. It irked him as a loyal Hanoverian to see the Pretender enjoying a well-nigh royal position in Rome and being received at the Vatican with every mark of deference and cordiality. Though known to foreigners in general as the "Chevalier de St. Georges", he was styled "Majesty" by his partisans, of whom Pope Clement XI had certainly been one. The Regent d'Orléans had got rid of his embarrassing guest as he had got rid of the Jesuits. They were all unwelcome legacies of Louis XIV's régime and out of place at the Regent's court.

If a pope could be found who also realised how anachronistic the Stuart claims now were, it would be a signal triumph for King George's agent in Rome. He therefore applied to headquarters for funds and prepared to take a hand at the game, thus creating a new and refreshing diversion for the electors, from the stale and traditional setting with which they were all too familiar. France's attitude of detachment added considerably to Walton's hope of success, as her Ambassador in Rome was declaring openly that his government took no interest in the personality of the new pontiff, for whatever his disposition might be, France had it in her power to bend him to her will. It was indispensable for Walton to secure a confederate in the Sacred College, and after mature reflection, he settled on Alberoni, the erstwhile Spanish minister, who was a free lance and in urgent need of money. Alberoni's whitewash was still so recent that most of his colleagues feared to come in too close contact with him. He had managed, however, to ingratiate himself with the Zelanti by affecting a pious remorse for his past misdeeds, and Walton considered he could not do better than bribe such a shrewd, resourceful man to act in the Hanoverian interests.

Having made an exhaustive study of the tactics successfully

employed in former conclaves, the conspirators laid their plans accordingly. They decided to ignore one another in public and to keep their good understanding a close secret from prying eyes. Furthermore, Alberoni was to ingratiate himself with the Pretender, gain his confidence and publicly pay him the most assiduous court. Their candidate would naturally have to be chosen from among the Zelanti, and Alberoni strongly recommended Imperiali, on whose acquiescence in Walton's conditions he could rely, and who had friends in other parties beside his own.

As the last Pontiff had only appointed two cardinals, Albani remained at the head of an important following, and Alberoni immediately set about obtaining his support—but although not opposed to Imperiali's candidature, Albani was averse to taking any decision before the arrival of his French colleagues, and only gave an evasive reply. As soon as the conclave had assembled Walton, in his inexperience, began to press for an immediate election, and Alberoni, equally eager and over-confident, conceived the scarcely delicate notion of using the Pretender himself as a tool to bring about the election of his enemy's candidate. He actually induced the simple-hearted James to write to the King of Spain begging him to exert all his influence in favour of Imperiali. But by this unscrupulous device Alberoni completely overreached himself, the schemers themselves falling into the trap they had laid for their trusting victim. Their activities had not been nearly so well concealed as they imagined, and when this treacherous manœuvre became known all those, both within and without the conclave, who had nothing to gain by Imperiali's election or were opposed to it, raised a howl of righteous indignation at such unheard-of villainy—and Imperiali's chances vanished like smoke.

On April 20th, a month after the Sacred College had assembled, Cardinal de Rohan arrived from Versailles, and Albani congratulated himself on having kept aloof from Walton's intrigues; for the French leader had the most pleasing proposal to put before him, being no less than an offer to raise his cousin the Jesuit Olivieri to the papal throne!

Albani was exultant, and hastened to draw up an agreement which was immediately signed by all parties concerned, the election being arranged to take place almost at once. But here again the stealthy, insidious secret service proved itself obnoxiously efficient. Within a few hours a copy of the convention was obtained and circulated among the electors. As it was all too favourable to the interests of France and of the Albanis, the imperialists sounded the alarm and were soon joined by all Albani's personal enemies, the most prominent of whom was Cardinal Spinola. This prelate, as spokesman of the party, openly reproached Albani with selling the Holy See to France. The dispute degenerated from home-truths to insults and threats, and ended in blows. Orsini, brandishing a crucifix, attempted in vain to separate the pugilists, getting a liberal share of bruises for his trouble; but where he had failed, Pamphili with a few jugs of cold water was more successful.

Spinola's ardour might be damped but it continued to smoulder, and he would not let matters rest, insisting on an enquiry being made, the result of which proved conclusively that the Jesuits in Vienna, Madrid and Paris had been busily at work to secure their brother-members' election. Notes were discovered signed by Olivieri whereby he made the most questionable promises to France, to Albani and to the General of the Society of Jesus. As most of the electors were inimical to at least one member of this unpopular trio, Spinola had no difficulty in disposing with complete finality of the Jesuit candidates' aspirations.

Such discord now reigned in the conclave, there were such perpetual rows and altercation, that Rohan, who had a gentle disposition and hated scenes, applied for a few days' leave to get a change of air, hoping that by the time he returned the effervescence would have subsided. Being himself only mildly interested in the election, he longed to get away from his fussy and irascible colleagues and mix with ordinary courteous human beings once more. But to his dismay he found the state of affairs in Roman society an exact replica of that in the Sacred College. The lay world was a prey to the same excitement, and seething with the same intrigues—there seemed no escape from the tiresome business, so Rohan determined to bring it to a conclusion as soon as possible, and to that end secured a private interview with Prince Albani, the Cardinal's brother, who had a plan to submit to him.

There happened to be among the conclavists a man called Coscia, who had obtained a tremendous ascendancy over his patron the ardent and mystic Orsini. Coscia was the son of a modest painter of Benevento, a small health resort where Orsini had once been to take a cure. He had lodged with the Coscia family, who had lavished attentions on him, and to make some return for their kindness and solicitude he had taken their son into his service. Now the gossips had it, it was Orsini who was in Coscia's service. To the long list of his self-inflicted penances he had, so they said, added that of waiting on his conclavist hand and foot! It seemed a certainty that, if Orsini became Pope, Coscia would reign, and Coscia had made friends with the Albani. The Dominicans having always been the bitterest enemies of the Jesuits, Orsini as a member of their Order might expect to gather round him all Olivieri's antagonists; and added to Albani's creatures his following should certainly secure for him the necessary majority of votes.

Rohan raised no objection, and Prince Albani having given him a signed assurance that French interests would not be overlooked the prelate returned to the Vatican much relieved at the prospect of an immediate election.

Scarcely had a settlement been reached between himself, Albani, and Coscia than an unrehearsed incident brought matters to a head and saved the French leader any further exertions.

Cienfugos, the Jesuit Cardinal Patron of the imperialists, had not abandoned all hope of leading his party to victory. He planned to carry off the election of his candidate Piazzi by a bold nocturnal attack, and to this purpose had convened all his followers to a secret midnight meeting. The place of assignation he had chosen was the cell of Cardinal Tanari, who had just died and whose body had only been removed that morning. Unfortunately for Cienfugos, one of the late cardinal's servants, worn out with fatigue, had curled himself up behind a heap of packages and fallen asleep. The movements of the conspirators woke him—he listened attentively, heard every word they said; and as soon as they had dispersed to carry out their leader's orders, he rushed to Albani's cell with the story. Albani leapt out of bed, roused his adherents and there ensued one of those *mêlées* in the semi-darkness of the conclave of which we have already witnessed many examples. Insults, blows, imprecations, prayers and comic by-play, the scene conformed to type; but Orsini, who attempted as he had done before to thrust himself and his crucifix between the belligerents, found to his amazement that he was being surrounded, swept off his feet, whisked away to the chapel and elected Pope before he had had time to say as much as an Ave Maria.

Accepting the crown as he would have accepted any other act of God and still clasping his crucifix, he received the homage of the Sacred College, adopting the name of Benedict. As he regarded Peter de Luna as canonical Pope he styled himself at first Benedict XIV, but was prevailed upon to alter the numeral to XIII to avoid profitless discussions.

Benedict's attitude of self-abasement was naturally ascribed to hypocrisy by those who were inconvenienced by its manifestations. He certainly caused considerable embarrassment to the officials in charge of the ceremonies connected with his enthronement by introducing personal touches into the ritual. For instance, he prostrated himself at the door of St. Peter's, to kiss the stone floor, an innovation which completely upset the routine of the ceremonial; the cortège of cardinals having no idea whether they should do likewise or stand about till Benedict rose. The crowd behind, who thought the Pontiff had collapsed, pushed and pressed to get a better view of the incident, causing many accidents and much confusion. Then again, he refused to be carried in the *sedia gestatoria* but insisted on walking through the basilica. The bearers of the empty palanquin, completely nonplussed as to the position they should take up in the procession, started a lively squabble, some being determined to go forward and others insisting on going back, the consequence being a most unedifying and unseemly hubbub. There seems no reason whatever to doubt the sincerity of Benedict XIII's religious fervour. His conduct as Pontiff bears it out in every way. He knew nothing of worldly matters and, as Coscia had expected, left the management of such affairs entirely to him and to the State officials. When consulted on any but ecclesiastical subjects he invariably replied, "Do as you think best—I know nothing about it—I will pray God to guide you".

He confined himself entirely to the settling of clerical problems and issued numerous edicts regarding the regulation of ecclesiastical functions, the vestments to be worn at the different ceremonies and disciplinary measures affecting the clergy. If any objection was raised to these seemingly unnecessary innovations he would refuse ever to discuss them, invariably threatening to abdicate.

His health was bad, he slept but little, ate even less and wore himself out with fasting and maceration of the flesh. He had wished to remain in the Vatican, having no personal fears of malaria, but seeing the consternation of his *entourage* and probably urged to do so by Coscia, he consented to take up his abode in the Quirinal. To Walton's despair he made much of the Pretender, on whom he bestowed a yearly allowance of 18,000 crowns; but the Hanoverian agent countered this irritating set-back by purchasing the services of a cardinal under whose political guidance the Stuart prince had placed himself unreservedly. Walton also made a suitable present to Coscia, who was now all-powerful, and whose first move had been to fit himself with a cardinal's hat. As to Alberoni he was distinctly out of favour with Benedict, who was so scandalised at his wearing a wig that he refused to renew the pecuniary grants made to the exile by his predecessor. Benedict treated the Jesuits as a Dominican naturally would, his hostility being only slightly tempered by Christian charity. Considering the reactionary bent of his disposition, the concordat which he drew up with the King of Sardinia was surprisingly liberal, and he also abolished the tribunal of the Inquisition, an unexpected step for a member of his order to have taken. So strongly did the Pontiff disapprove of games of chance that, having forbidden all betting, he ordered any gambler caught red-handed to be packed off at once to the galleys. He took no notice whatever of his relatives, but unfortunately Coscia's depredations and abuse of power equalled anything ever perpetrated under the régime of nepotism. He took full advantage of the Pope's confidence and simple-mindedness to oppress and despoil his subjects, and richly deserved the hatred and execration which he reaped.

Weak and old as he was, Benedict insisted on officiating at the funeral of Cardinal Ansidei on a cold, wet day of February 1730, and there caught the chill from which he died a few days later, his last hours being in keeping with his edifying life. His restricted outlook and lack of intelligence prevented him from grasping the fact that his duties as Pontiff were concerned with the temporal as well as with the spiritual section of his office and that he was guilty of criminal negligence by allowing Coscia to act as virtual ruler of the Papal States. He noticed nothing himself and no complaints were ever allowed to reach him, as they only emanated from the people; the upper classes, as Giacottazzi says, "being always tolerant of those abuses which they have practised themselves, or hope to practise some day".

As the Pontiff died on a Shrove Tuesday, his death was only made public the next day, so as not to disturb the festivities and also perhaps so as to give Coscia a chance to escape the vengeance of the populace. But this miscreant was laid up at the time with an acute attack of gout and unable to avail himself of the respite, with the result that when he attempted to leave the Quirinal the mob had assembled and surrounded the building, determined to intercept his flight and give him no quarter.

He managed somehow to bribe his servants to carry him away in a pauper's coffin, the crowd uncovering respectfully as what they took to be the remains of a papal scullion passed safely through their ranks. The pseudo-corpse had just been successfully smuggled into the palace of one of Coscia's friends when the people, having scented the ruse, rushed to attack the building. Again the hunted man made a hair's-breadth escape, disguised as an old woman and supported by a couple of retainers dressed in rags. He was suffering so acutely from gout that he screamed with pain at every step he took, arousing the compassion of his pursuers, who never suspected this pitiful old female of being their longed-for quarry. The fugitive thus managed to reach a place of safety, and so as to protect his belongings from pillage and destruction, his friends had them officially confiscated and removed to S. Angelo.

A strange discovery made subsequently in the Quirinal throws a revealing light on the incredible relations existing between Benedict XIII and his confidential adviser and trusted major-domo. A bell was found fastened under the Pontiff's monastical bed, connected to Coscia's room by a rope which hung conveniently to hand from his damask tester. Benedict evidently made a pathetic attempt to put into practice the papal formula "Vicar of Christ and servant of the servants of God".

It is a matter for regret that this well-meaning and self-sacrificing visionary should have been so totally bereft of discrimination.

CLEMENT XII (Corsini)
1730–1740

✤

THE conclave which followed the death of Benedict XIII assembled on March 3rd and lasted four months. Except indirectly, by mowing down with systematic consistency the daily crop of candidates, the activities and intrigues of the Sacred College had little bearing on the ultimate issue.

The Dean, Cardinal Pignatelli, fell ill almost at once and there was no other prelate with sufficient influence over his colleagues to maintain or enforce the necessary discipline during his absence. The weather being oppressively hot, the younger cardinals discarded most of their clothing piecemeal, till the precincts of the conclave must have presented the shocking spectacle of a nudist colony! The windows were opened and free communication established with the outer world; the Marquis de Monteleone, the Spanish Ambassador, was smuggled in through an aperture and spent a whole night in the conclave, a most serious infraction of the regulations. Voting became a mere exchange of civilities, the most surprising names appearing on the forms. Cienfugos, the uncompromising leader of the imperialists, was outraged at such levity: "We might be at the dinnertable paying compliments to the ladies instead of at a conclave to elect a Pope!" he exclaimed, his protest being received with supercilious smiles. But when Coscia's name was read out at the scrutiny, then even the least squeamish waxed indignant, and someone proposed that the slip should be preserved and given to the new pope so that he should deal with the culprit. As, however, there was little likelihood of the humourist having signed his own name to such a compromising document it was eventually burnt with the rest. Coscia was present at this scene, as he had managed to sneak into the Vatican by a side entrance and join his colleagues undetected. His reception had been distinctly chilly and the storm which that unfortunate vote had let loose was an ominous forecast of what the future might have in store for him. He almost fainted with fright and had to be supported out of the chapel, and having been put to bed, thought it wise to remain there for the time being.

The sultry atmosphere was no less damping to the spirits than to the flesh, and the only joke on record turned out to be anything but a merry jest. The victim, an aged prelate called Conti who was monstrously fat and crippled with gout, happened, as he was dragging himself along a passage one morning, to come face to face with Albani. Acting on a mischievous impulse, Albani stopped him, and with exaggerated gestures of precaution whispered in his ear that everything was settled and that he was to be elected Pope that very evening. The poor old simpleton in a frenzy of excitement hastened with frantic efforts to reach his cell; he burst in on his astonished conclavist who was stirring his patron's chocolate, and having managed to stammer out the great news, reeled forward and fell dead of an apoplectic fit.

But the disposing of candidates either by manslaughter or more conventional methods did not bring the Sacred College any nearer to giving St. Peter a successor, and seeing that the electors proved incapable of selecting a pope themselves, it was only to be expected that their duties should be undertaken for them by more enterprising outsiders. The question which was engaging the general attention just then was the Medici succession, as the ex-Cardinal Grand Duke was childless, and Austria, France, Spain and Sardinia were no less anxious to provide an heir for him than they had been in the case of Charles II of Spain. A congress had been held in Seville to examine the various claims, and it had found in favour of Don Carlos, second son of Philip V. The indignant Grand Duke had appealed to the Emperor against this arbitrary decision, which denied to the hereditary Sovereign of Tuscany any say whatever in a matter which he might after all be permitted to consider as of some concern to himself.

The Tuscans naturally resented the idea of being ruled by a foreigner of any nationality, and were strongly in favour of some autonomous form of government on the model of that of Venice or Genoa.

Among the most prominent Florentines both from the point of view of position and of wealth was the Marchese Neri Corsini. He had held diplomatic posts at most of the great European Courts, where he had made many friends; and having lately retired into private life, had settled in Rome to be near his uncle Cardinal Corsini. What more fitting conclusion to a distinguished career could be devised than to become Cardinal-Nephew and finish one's days as an influential member of the Sacred College, or even—perhaps—as Pope!

The circumstances indeed were most favourable; there was little to fear from exclusions and no dangerous rival to defeat; Neri Corsini had powerful connections, much worldly experience, money and feminine support. The Cardinal's personality would also help to further his cause, for among his colleagues he did not appear to have a single enemy. He belonged to the Zelanti faction, but had none of their bigotry and aggressiveness. Without being clever he had a certain political acumen and was recognised as the prototype of the Florentine *grand seigneur*. He had the reputation of being both resolute and broad-minded, was credited with generosity, moderation and good sense, and last but not least, he was seventy-eight years of age.

The centre of electoral activities now shifted from the Vatican to the palace of the Marchesa Acciaioli, the most noted Roman hostess and a close friend of Neri's. She was an invaluable ally with far-reaching influence abroad, and mainly to her efforts was due the Emperor's patronage of Corsini's candidature. Her word of course was law to all the young Roman cardinals, and Prince Albani could refuse her nothing. Neri himself purchased Coscia's vote for 25,000 crowns and sent expensive presents to several of the foreign cardinals. He had always kept in close touch with Florence and had no difficulty in persuading the Grand Duke of the advantage there would be for him in the elevation to the Holy See of one of his own subjects. The Grand Duke himself warmly recommended Corsini to the French, Spanish and Sardinian Monarchs, each one interpreting this proceeding as a sign of special goodwill towards himself. The sympathies of a Florentine pope, the Powers considered, might bear great weight with his compatriots when the time came for a change of dynasty, and Neri Corsini in the post of Cardinal-Nephew would be an invaluable ally. The great thing was to be the first in the field, so as to have the strongest claim on Corsini's gratitude. And so from various points of the compass, messengers bearing the despatches which settled the problem of the pontifical election thundered along the highways, all converging towards the Vatican where the suffragists continued every morning to call perfunctorily on the Paraclete for divine inspiration.

One by one, in the order in which their instructions reached them, the Cardinal-Padrones crept into Corsini's cubicle bringing with them ready-drawn-up agreements across which the old man, who was practically blind, scrawled his illegible signature; Albani under pressure from his brother, followed his colleagues' example; and so on July 12th, 1730, Corsini became Pope Clement XII.

Walton, who does not appear to have taken any active part in this election, was delighted at Corsini's victory. "Under the reign of this Pope", he writes, "the Pretender will enjoy no favour. Clement will govern with caution and sound good sense. He will restore the pomp and splendour which Benedict XIII abolished, for his tastes are very magnificent. He will also encourage literature, having one of the finest and best selected libraries in Europe."

As regards the Pope's behaviour towards the Pretender, Walton was doomed to disappointment, for James managed in time to win Clement's good graces. The Pontiff's caution, or perhaps the lassitude of age, caused him at first to adopt an attitude of neutrality. He evinced little interest in the fate of Tuscany and strove to remain aloof while the Powers flew at one another's throats. But as in the general scuffle several of the papal fiefs were snapped up by one or other of the belligerents, he had perforce to raise his voice in protest, though with little result.

During the ten years of his pontificate many changes took place in Italy, territories continually changing hands either in consequence of treaties or of the fortunes of war. The Papal States were for ever being overrun and plundered by advancing or retreating armies, and finding that expostulations were apt to lead to worse trouble, Clement accepted the inevitable with silent resignation, remaining a passive and impotent spectator of the bartering of papal fiefs between the Bourbons and the Habsburgs. Thus the Emperor exchanged the Two Sicilies with the King of Spain against Parma and Piacenza without even troubling to notify the Holy See of the transaction.

Clement, notwithstanding these slights, made friendly advances to Philip V, bestowing on his third son Don Luis, aged barely eight years old, the cardinal's hat together with the archbishoprics of Seville and Toledo; but he received scant thanks for his affability, the

Queen, Elizabeth Farnese, reproaching him acrimoniously for not doing a great deal more.

He left the administration of the State to his nephew, but insisted on a special commission being appointed to examine and judge Coscia. Benedict XIII's favourite was condemned to ten years' detention in the fortress of S. Angelo and to the loss of all his possessions. He was also excommunicated and deprived of his vote at future conclaves. Just before Clement died, however, his nephews, who felt uncertain as to what might fall to their lot under the next pontiff if such a precedent was allowed, prevailed on the Pope to quash the verdict and sign a decree of rehabilitation which gave Coscia his freedom. His ill-gotten goods were restored to him, at least what could be recovered of them from the safe keeping of his friends.

Heresy was now an accepted calamity. It was confined within certain areas, and although the Church of Rome no doubt deplored the existence of these plague-spots, it no longer felt threatened in its stability. But during Clement's pontificate a new menace known as Freemasonry made its appearance; it caused the Pontiff and his successors acute anxiety, and has not ceased to this day from sapping the foundations of the Catholic Church. This institution had been imported to the Continent from England, the first lodge being opened in Paris in 1725. In the Catholic countries of Southern Europe it spread like wildfire, the aims and spirit of the association developing, however, on totally different lines from those advocated by Christopher Wren and George Payne, and obtaining in the British Isles. Only Anglo-Saxons could accept such a quaint notion as to forward schemes of mutual assistance by adopting mysterious rites and cabalistic signs. Such a thing is incompatible with the Latin temperament. To this race a brotherhood bound by oaths of secrecy whose members were admitted with so much solemnity to the various degrees of initiation, could only have conspiracy as an object and become a destructive instead of a constructive organisation. The English Freemason might be content with symbolic aprons, benevolence, secret signs of fraternity and gargantuan banquets; but the foreigner certainly was not. He eagerly adopted the outward form and structure of the institution with the letter of its regulations; but to expect him to be satisfied with such an anodyne purpose was as

preposterous a notion as it would be with us to ask the members
of a hunt to come to the meet with their pockets full of carrots and,
having fed one another's horses, patted the hounds, sung John Peel
and given the Master the Fascist salute, expect them to jog home
contentedly as though they had enjoyed a good day's sport! No. The
Continental Freemason, like the English hunting man, expects a run
for his money and hopes for a kill.

All those who had a grievance against the existing order of things,
all those who from envy, spite, conviction or altruism were inimical
to the Church of Rome, flocked to join an association in the bosom
of which they could air their views freely, with absolute impunity.
They tasted for the first time the sweets of declamation for which
they have such a remarkable aptitude, and from the Masonic Lodges
no doubt sprang the famous revolutionary clubs of Paris. Although
their bond of union was hatred of "tyranny" in all its forms, their
password was certainly anti-clericalism.

Clement battled energetically against this alarming conflagration
by taking the most rigorous measures against the firebrands. To be
affiliated or to cause anyone to be affiliated to the brotherhood was
punished by excommunication and death. To aid, protect or shelter
a Freemason was scarcely less dangerous, and the Pope's subjects were
obliged under threats of severe corporal punishment to denounce any
member of the society, be he father, brother, husband or son. But
no penalties, however drastic, could stem the movement, which
received stimulus and encouragement from the tone of atheistic
liberalism which pervaded the writings of the most outstanding
intellectuals of the times both in France and in Italy. And so the peril
grew ever more deadly.

Towards the end of his life, however, the unconcerned detachment
of senility saved Clement any further apprehensions, and he died
peacefully on February 7th, 1740.

BENEDICT XIV
From a print in the British Museum

BENEDICT XIV (LAMBERTINI)
1740–1758

❦

NERI CORSINI was well aware that his only chance of winning the coming battle lay in his pursuing the strategy which had proved so successful in the last election. But it necessitated freedom of action and access to his friends which he would lose as soon as he entered the Vatican. He therefore set to work some time before his uncle's death, and in a letter written by him to the Court of Versailles we find a lucid account of the situation. He explains that much as he would like to see one of his own creatures raised to the Holy See, the thing is quite impossible. They are all modern in their outlook; Spain and Austria will certainly exclude them, and their youth will rouse the old cardinals to violent opposition. The new pope therefore must be chosen from among the seniors and yet his sympathies must be with his juniors.

Although these two conditions appeared well-nigh incompatible, Corsini had been fortunate enough to discover the man who fulfilled them both. This paragon was Cardinal Lambertini, whom he describes as a clever, broad-minded, amiable prelate, sixty-five years of age and therefore acceptable both to the young and to the old parties. As soon as he received from Versailles authority to do so, Corsini would treat with Lambertini, whose goodwill towards France he could answer for personally; but he impresses on his correspondent the vital importance of discretion, as only through apparent hostility can the plan succeed.

The Sacred College had now its full complement of members, and Neri was leader of the thirty-two cardinals created by Clement XII; but several of these would not attend the conclave, the young Infante of Spain being among the absentees.

Albani's following consisted of sixteen prelates, an inferior number to Corsini's, it is true, but a more stable and dependable force. Albani had also in his favour the accumulated experience of four conclaves, besides much natural cunning and entire freedom from scruples in the choice of weapons wherewith to defeat his opponents. The struggle promised to be grim and protracted. Corsini had no illusions on that score and quite realised that, face to face with Albani and isolated from his ordinary surroundings, he would be at a serious disadvantage. He was a subtle diplomat, but more familiar with the atmosphere of courts and the *salons* of fair ladies than with that of the ecclesiastical arena of the Vatican. He resolved therefore to enter the conclave with the election of his nominee already assured, and yet to keep the fact so absolutely secret that he should appear to have his own choice forced upon him against his will.

The Court of Versailles had not only given unqualified approval to the Cardinal-Nephew's selection but entered so conscientiously into his scheme of deceit that immediately after Clement's death Louis XV's Foreign Minister wrote to his colleague in Vienna with a proposal of co-operation in the coming conclave. He suggested several candidates, from among which, needless to say, Lambertini's name was omitted. Corsini meanwhile had secured the support of the King of Sardinia and strengthened his position with his own faction, so that when the conclave assembled on February 18th he felt confident of an ultimate victory.

Serious as his misgivings had been regarding his encounter with the veteran conclavist, Corsini soon discovered that he had underrated the difficulties of the enterprise. For six interminable months the contest dragged on, the duellists each in turn advancing, retreating, thrusting and parrying and having recourse to every known trick, feint and artifice of the swordsman. The task of contriving a defeat which under the appearance of discomfiture would in reality be a crowning victory did not, however, prove beyond Corsini's competence, although he had to contend not only with the pitfalls prepared for him by his antagonists, but also with those innocently dug for him by his friends.

Infatuated though he was with the Duchess Salviati, Corsini had wisely refrained from letting her into the secret of his plans, and she, all eagerness to serve him, contrived with the assistance of Tencin, a French prelate who knew nothing of the Lambertini conspiracy, to forward the candidature of d'Elci, a faithful follower of Corsini's. This skirmish of course came to nothing, but it created a most awkward situation for the leader, who must have felt anything but grateful for this ill-timed manifestation of the lady's attachment.

It was consonant with Corsini's policy occasionally to propose a candidate, but he was careful to select those among his creatures who would be more particularly unacceptable to the older faction or to the Emperor. Their downfall alternated with that of Albani's own candidates who were chosen with a view to gaining time, while their leader's spies endeavoured to discover what Corsini's game really was. They failed however to pick up the trail and the situation remained unchanged. But the supply of candidates was not inexhaustible, and gradually through death and elimination only two *papabili* remained standing in the older party: Aldobrandini and Lambertini. It was a well-known fact that Albani detested the former, so Corsini prompted Cardinal de Polignac to propose him, which the Frenchman did at once.

The only excuse Albani could possibly give for refusing to support a member of his own party was that he had already decided on another—and that other could be none but Lambertini! The net was being drawn in, victory was in sight; but the battle was not yet won, for Aldobrandini had many partisans and Corsini had to appear in sympathy with them. Such an unscrupulous enemy as Albani, however, could be relied on to wreck Aldobrandini's chances, and he soon showed what methods he intended to resort to, by forging, or causing to be forged, a letter purporting to be written to him by Aldobrandini, accusing his rival Lambertini of the vilest crimes. Copies of this letter were circulated among the electors, and the most gullible cardinals, without pausing to consider how unlikely it was that a respectable prelate such as Aldobrandini should have been capable of this stupid piece of villainy, immediately called an indignation meeting which resulted in their going over in a body to Lambertini's side.

On hearing the news, Corsini managed to compose his features to an expression of sullen despair so marvellously realistic that it almost defeated his object, as most of his creatures, naïvely believing in his grievous disappointment, declared their intention of organising Lambertini's exclusion at any cost. It took the gifted comedian most of the night to convince his followers of the advisability of bowing to the inevitable, and his relief must have been intense when at last, with bent head and resigned bearing, he led his party to Albani's cell to offer its support to his candidate.

The entire assembly then marched off to Lambertini's cubicle to bear him in triumph to the chapel, but to the surprise of the anxious leaders they found the cubicle empty. The suffragists immediately dispersed to search for the lost sheep so soon to become the shepherd, and he was eventually discovered sound asleep stretched out on a couple of chairs at the remotest end of one of the large halls. On being awakened and asked to explain this strange whim, Lambertini answered very simply that he had wanted to put as great a distance as he could between himself and the vermin which infested his cubicle, and rolling over, begged their Eminences to allow him to resume his slumbers. But there was no more sleep for him that morning; he was hustled off to the chapel, and by nine o'clock had become Pope Benedict XIV.

The part Corsini had so cleverly played in this election soon came to light, for the agreement made with France gave ample proof of it. Besides the office of Secretary of State he was to be given the leadership of the French party with a yearly income of 30,000 crowns. Whatever feelings of resentment those he had so successfully hoodwinked may have harboured against him, his colleagues one and all agreed that a campaign conducted with such consummate ability, discretion and tenacity deserved its reward and few grudged him the fruits of his victory. As to the world at large it soon realised that Corsini had given the Church of Rome the most admirable and popular Pontiff it had ever known.

Benedict XIV was sixty-seven years of age at the time of his elevation to the Holy See. He was a native of Bologna and had made a great reputation as Legal Adviser to the Consistory. He was an expert on canonical jurisprudence and had written many books on the subject. He was also passionately interested in science, art and historical research. He had the most engaging manners, his unfailing cheerfulness was infectious and his charm irresistible. He prepared to govern the Papal States as he had governed his archbishopric—by being a father to his people, protecting the weak and showing tolerance to all. His plan was to restore Papacy to its former glory by rejuvenating the spirit of the institution and bringing it into line with contemporary progress. His accession to the supreme dignity left him unaltered in every way; his whimsicality, his friendliness, his rectitude, his broad-minded piety withstood the test of power, and he remained until Leo XIII's advent the only witty Pontiff on record.

Benedict XIV was situated exactly as his predecessors had been, he had no means at his disposal which they had lacked; and yet he rose immediately to a position of the greatest import, owing entirely to personal prestige. He was the first Pope to acknowledge and accept the inevitable changes time had wrought in Europe, and to adapt himself to the new order of things. He had grasped the fact that among the great nations who ruled the destinies of the world England, Prussia and Russia had come to the very forefront, and that their influence rivalled if it did not outweigh that of the Catholic Powers. He recognised that the practical good sense and the maritime and industrial genius of England had displaced the decadent might of Spain; that Prussian energy and Prussian military organisation would be fatal to Austrian incompetence and that Orthodox Russia was bound to subdue Catholic Poland.

With his Italian neighbours Benedict kept on the best of terms. He ratified the concordat Benedict XIII had signed with the King of Sardinia and which Clement XII had annulled. He conceded to the new King of Sicily, son of Philip V, several privileges he had so far claimed in vain. Only in matters connected with his spiritual realm did he show any symptoms of censoriousness, making new and stringent rules concerning canonisation. He also took energetic measures to prevent the exploiting of the credulous faithful through the agency of pseudo-miracles and pseudo-saints.

A succession of royal visitors appeared at the Quirinal bent on paying their respects to the Sovereign Pontiff. Besides the Kings of Sicily and Sardinia, the Margravine of Bayreuth travelled to Rome bearing messages of deference and amity from her brother Frederick II of Prussia. All the European monarchs vied with one another to obtain his good graces and felt honoured by his friendship. The Empress Elizabeth of Russia always referred to him as "Benedict the Wise", and even Sultan Mohammed sent his Ambassadors to lay sumptuous gifts at the Pontiff's feet. Nothing that a great and liberal ruler could devise to encourage science, art, letters and commerce did Benedict neglect. He was generous and unaffected; he laid aside half his revenues to pay off the debts of the Apostolic Chamber; he kept his relations at a distance, but enriched Bologna, his native city, by building and endowing public institutions.

The whole of Europe sang his praises; even Voltaire the atheist, Voltaire, the relentless foe of the Church of Rome, dedicated a play and several odes to His Holiness! For a time the Pope lost the popularity he had acquired in England, as he was suspected of having assisted the Young Pretender in his disastrous expedition of 1745. If such was the case he would surely have made some attempt to intercede for the Catholic clergy who suffered so severely in the Stuart cause; it is unthinkable that he should calmly have left to their fate subordinates who had merely followed his lead. It is much more likely that the Jesuits used his name to further their own ends. George II, who should have been well informed on the subject, never showed the slightest distrust of the Pope or any animosity towards him. On the contrary, he allowed the bulls which Benedict issued concerning ecclesiastical discipline to be openly published in all the Catholic districts of the kingdom; a thing unheard of since the days of Charles I.

Horace Walpole professed the deepest admiration for the Pontiff, and procured a statue of him from Italy on the pedestal of which he caused the inscription to be engraved:

PROSPERO LAMBERTINI

BISHOP OF ROME

BY THE NAME OF BENEDICT XIV
WHO, THOUGH AN ABSOLUTE PRINCE,
REIGNED AS HARMLESSLY
AS A DOGE OF VENICE.
HE RESTORED THE LUSTRE OF THE TIARA
BY THOSE ARTS ALONE
BY WHICH HE OBTAINED IT,

HIS VIRTUES

BELOVED BY PAPISTS
ESTEEMED BY PROTESTANTS
A PRIEST WITHOUT INSOLENCE OR INTERESTEDNESS
A PRINCE WITHOUT FAVOURITES
A POPE WITHOUT NEPOTISM
AN AUTHOR WITHOUT VANITY
IN SHORT A MAN,
WHOM NEITHER WIT NOR POWER COULD SPOIL.

THE SON OF A FAVOURITE MINISTER,
BUT ONE WHO NEVER COURTED A PRINCE,
NOR WORSHIPPED A CHURCHMAN,
OFFERS IN A FREE PROTESTANT COUNTRY
THIS DESERVED INCENSE
TO THE BEST OF ROMAN PONTIFFS
MDCCLVII

A copy of this inscription was forwarded to Rome and, modest though he was, this "incense" from such an unexpected quarter cannot have failed, one imagines, to gratify the "Bishop of Rome". He read it with a smile, shaking his head in deprecation of so flattering a tribute, and exclaimed: "Alas! I am like the statues of the Piazza S. Pietro—admirable at a distance but monstrous when seen at close quarters!"

Benedict XIV would not have been so lovable had he not been human, and he had his failings as even the best of mortals will have; he could not resist the fascination of cards, and was addicted to profane language, or as one of his early biographers terms it, "unfortunate phraseology". The godly Pontiff never managed to cure himself of this bad habit although he made every effort to do so. As the sight of a crucifix had a restraining effect on his fluency, he had one placed in every room; but even this pious device was not always adequate. There is a story to the effect that, playing cards one day with a hopelessly blundering partner, he found the strain of controlling himself so unbearable that, signing to an attendant to remove the hallowed impediment, he exploded with such a volley of oaths that his terrified partner hid his face in his hands while the other players kept exclaiming: "Holy Father! For God's sake, Holy Father!" in an attempt to drown his voice. Having obtained the necessary relief Benedict recovered his equanimity, the crucifix was brought back and the game resumed. Bridge players, no doubt, will readily condone such an excusable lapse from grace!

The Pontiff always mistrusted the Jesuits and by his last official decree granted to Pombal, the Prime Minister of Portugal, authority to reform the abuses introduced by the Society in the educational and commercial enterprises which were under its control. Benedict never lost his gaiety, good sense and lucidity. To the last his bright blue eyes sparkled with humour and cordiality. He died after a very short and merciful illness, at the age of eighty-three, on May 10th, 1758, after eighteen years of the wisest and most beneficent of pontificates.

CLEMENT XIII
From the statue by Canova in St. Peter's, Rome

CLEMENT XIII (Rezzonico)
1758–1769

🐚

THE Society of Jesus was in dire peril. Times had changed since the days when Ignatius Loyola and his faithful followers had leapt valiantly on to the crumbling walls of the Roman Church to defend its Pontiff. Religious warfare had long since subsided and successive generations of Jesuits had learned to associate the original standards of their Order with an obsolete condition of things; it was therefore inevitable that they should apply their remarkable energies to conquests in other fields. Their statutes had been drawn up on military lines; they took the most binding vows of obedience, the rank and file conforming, as soldiers do, to the orders of their superior officers without question and without incurring any personal responsibility. Many popes had been disinclined to avail themselves of the Society's services, others had frankly disapproved of it—while several had employed them as secret service agents. Such an able and powerful body of men could scarcely be content with the spasmodic and paltry activities altered circumstances had reduced them to; nor could they insist on living up to their founder's ideals, as such Quixotism would have proved most embarrassing for the Holy See. It was necessary, therefore, to find another outlet for their energies, and the obvious one was the aggrandisement of their own Order. This they accomplished through the influence they exerted over the governing classes which they educated, and through the expansion of their commercial enterprises.

They had founded houses all over the world, but the headquarters of the Society remained in Rome, where the General resided. Their organisation was faultless. No sign of talent or ability in a novice was ever overlooked, for talent and ability carefully fostered and developed would prove of the greatest advantage to the community. Unlike those officials in countries where conscription is in force who seem guided by a perverted sense of humour in the distribution of tasks to their newly joined victims, the Jesuits turned to account any qualifications their recruits may have possessed.

They specialised in directing the consciences of the mighty, training picked men for the purpose. Every Catholic monarch had a Jesuit confessor and no lady of fashion would have dreamed of having any other. Consequently they developed through the agency of their penitents an insidious influence which had far-reaching effects. There was no court intrigue or scandal that they were not the first apprised of, and they had a finger in every political pie. The governments of the various Catholic Powers found themselves constantly impeded in their designs by these interfering spiritual advisers, and we have seen how Pombal had appealed to Benedict XIV for an enquiry to be instituted into their educational and commercial methods in Portugal. England had been closed to the Jesuits for well over a century; Russia had ejected them in 1717 and China had done likewise in 1753, forcibly closing down their missions, which had become mere counting-houses.

The chivalrous ideals of Ignatius Loyola had been converted by his later disciples into mere sordid ambitions, thus descending from a plane where few rivals were to be feared into an arena seething with competitors. Things had now come to such a pass that Choiseul in France, Kaunitz in Austria, Pombal in Portugal and the rising Florida Blanca in Spain all agreed that the Society of Jesus was an international menace and must be suppressed. The Jesuits themselves were far too well informed of the trend of events to have any doubt as to what was in store for them at the hands of their enemies and the election of a pontiff well disposed towards their Order had now become for them a matter of life and death. Even if he could not stem the rising tide of execration which threatened the Society, he could at least shelter its members during the storm and give them the moral support which might enable them to weather it.

A new General, Father Ricci, had just been appointed, not perhaps the man best suited to the task at this juncture, but an energetic fighter with an iron determination concealed under a suave and non-committal manner. The hopes of the entire Jesuit community were centred on him, mainly because many of the older cardinals were his penitents and there was reason therefore to believe that his influence in the conclave which was just assembling would be considerable.

The doors were sealed on June 4th, and it immediately became apparent that the issue upon which the election would be fought was first and foremost the Jesuit question. The Sacred College was split into two parties—those who upheld the Society of Jesus and those who were determined on its suppression. The only group which seemed open to compromise was the Spanish one, whose leader, Portocarrero, though under orders to oppose any Jesuit candidate, gave unmistakable signs of vacillation and untrustworthiness. Ricci opened the gambit by instructing his adherents to propose Cavalchini forthwith. Seeing that Portocarrero was wavering in his allegiance to the league of the Powers, the French and Portuguese cardinals took it in turns to stand guard over him to prevent an immediate defection. They alternately threatened him with the anger and vengeance of their respective Sovereigns, or cajoled him with promises of rich rewards, thus managing to gain sufficient time for Luynes, the French leader, to obtain Louis XV's veto against the Jesuit candidate. The precious document, issued under the specious pretext that Cavalchini, being a Sardinian subject, must therefore be inimical to France, arrived in the nick of time and was officially presented to the Dean on the very morning which would in all likelihood have seen Cavalchini's election to the Holy See.

The checkmated candidate took his defeat with great dignity, thanking those who had supported him and causing Luynes much embarrassment by cordially shaking him by the hand.

While Father Ricci was studying his next move, the Sacred College was kept mildly occupied and amused by a couple of ephemeral candidatures. One was Borghese's, his name being put forward by his creditors, who saw in his election their only chance of recovering their money; but in spite of all the efforts made by his interested supporters, Borghese's colleagues refused to take him seriously. The other bubble, Archinto, was longer afloat, being the ladies' nominee. He was a Milanese, therefore an Austrian subject, and had lately been legate in Florence where the feminine element had found him quite irresistible. He was remarkably handsome, wore exquisite clothes, always said the right thing, and his unctuous gestures released whiffs of voluptuous fragrance emanating from his expensive, scented gloves. The Princess Trivulzi, the Infanta Duchess of Parma, the Roman Donna Maria Cenci, in fact all the most aristocratic and fashionable ladies in Italy, were anxious to see their favourite raised to the papal throne. They could of course boast of a number of willing slaves in the Sacred College, and Portocarrero, who was particularly susceptible to feminine influence, now seemed far more eager to please the ladies than to serve either the Jesuits or the Powers. Father Ricci, however, was not the man to be thwarted by a perfumed jackanapes. He had his adherents well in hand, and an intensive campaign was started through the gratings of the Roman confessionals, which promptly resulted in Archinto retiring from the fray.

Meanwhile Ricci had selected a new candidate, the Venetian Rezzonico, who had been educated by the Jesuits and had remained in close touch with them all his life. Warned by his first failure, the General was careful not to show his hand this time; he had also thought it advisable to secure a few more votes, and as the Society disposed of great wealth he bought Borghese's and Malvezzi's suffrage by paying their debts, so Borghese's creditors were satisfied after all. As to Malvezzi, he cared about nothing but horses, and was so used to living with stable lads and felt so bored and out of his element in the Vatican that he had actually brought one of his jockeys as a conclavist so as to have at least one congenial companion in his unaccustomed surroundings. To Portocarrero, Ricci promised the secretaryship of state, and to the Cardinal of York, who was attending his first conclave, practical support for the Stuart cause. All this was done with the utmost promptitude and discretion, for it was most necessary that Rezzonico should be elected as soon as his name had been proposed, so as to obviate the possibility of a veto being obtained against him as it had been against Cavalchini. Therefore the moment the requisite number of votes was safely assured the General issued his commands, and before his antagonists could recover from the shock and surprise Rezzonico had been elected, chosen the name of Clement XIII and been clothed in his white robes of state!

The new Pontiff was not popular. His own compatriots looked upon him as an upstart, his name having only lately been inscribed in the Republic's "Golden Book", an honour he owed exclusively to his wealth. As to the Romans, they were greatly disappointed at being given a Pope who was reputed to be bigoted, ignorant and stupid. He was certainly devoid of any knowledge of statecraft and obstinate and inflexible in his opinions; but these very limitations exactly suited the requirements of his black-robed mentors, giving them a sense of security and a foretaste of power. Physically Clement XIII was undersized and slightly deformed, having one shoulder higher than the other. His manner was quiet and pleasant; he was neither too young nor too old and appeared to have a healthy, sound constitution.

His first official act was to revoke Benedict XIV's bull approving the enquiry into the Jesuits' misdemeanours in Portugal, which had already been acted upon. All through his pontificate he proved a staunch champion of the Society of Jesus and was entirely governed by its General. The Powers ignored both the white and the black Popes and pursued their relentless course. The Jesuits were banished from Portugal in 1759. In France a financial scandal sealed their doom in 1767, owing to the bankruptcy of one of their Martinique counting-houses of which the Père Lavalette was director. It had resulted in the closing down of an important bank in Marseilles and in the consequent ruin of a large number of private investors, giving Choiseul an excellent excuse to turn all Jesuits out of the kingdom. The same year Charles III, convinced that they were hatching a plot to depose him, ordered their immediate expulsion from Spain. They were arrested simultaneously all over the country and marched off to various seaports. They were then put on board a fleet of ships whose captains had orders to disembark them in the Papal States. But thousands of Jesuits had already been deported to Italy and the Pope's subjects not only protested violently against a further influx of refugees but took their own measures to prevent it. France was still driving the exiles across the Alps; from the Two Sicilies they were being despatched northwards and from Parma hustled south. Clement issued bull upon bull excommunicating all those responsible for the exodus, but that helped in no way to solve the problem of how to feed, house and occupy these hordes of clerics.

As fast as they were pushed over the border into the Papal States as fast did the exasperated inhabitants push them out again. As to Charles III's ships they cruised about the Mediterranean finding it impossible to land their human freight. All ports were closed against them as though they had flown the sinister plague flag. It was in vain that the Spanish officers implored the authorities for leave to disembark at least the sick and dying; nowhere could they get a hearing, and so with their 6000 unfortunate passengers crowded to suffocation in the sweltering summer heat, perishing with hunger, thirst, exhaustion and misery, they continued to roam the seas for weeks during which time many of their charges died and others lost their reason. The frenzied captains, not daring to return to Spain with their cargo still aboard, would probably have been driven to unload it on to some deserted spot of the African coast had not the Corsicans taken pity on the surviving wayfarers and allowed them free access to the island.

The "Family Pact" signed by the Bourbons in 1761, though chiefly prompted by their common enmity towards England, came first into operation over the Jesuit dispute. The Bourbons now reigned in France, Spain, Parma and Sicily and bound themselves by this blood alliance to concerted policy and action. This Family Pact inaugurated a system which was later adopted by certain Jews in another sphere of business with perhaps more substantial and certainly more lasting results. But to return to the Bourbons; as excommunications seemed to leave them unmoved, Clement decided to give them a more tangible proof of his apostolic wrath. The Duke of Parma being the least formidable and the most vulnerable member of the coalition, the Pontiff suddenly revived the old claim of the Holy See to his territories and sent his troops to invade the duchy.

Immediately, France, Spain and Naples were up in arms. Louis XV seized Avignon, Ferdinand IV invested Benevento and Charles III manned his fleet. The terror-stricken Pope, not knowing where to turn for help, appealed to the pious Maria Theresa; but all he obtained from her was a quotation from a message, sent in like circumstances by Urban VIII to the Emperor Ferdinand, to the effect that affairs of State and affairs of religion were two different things. This blighting proof of the Empress' erudition so discouraged the Pope that he recalled his army and made peace overtures to his opponents. The Bourbons now pressed their advantage, insisting on the dissolution of the Society of Jesus, which at first Clement stubbornly refused to consider. He even issued a bull praising the Jesuits for their zeal and efficiency, an inconsiderate move which brought matters to a crisis. The Bourbons immediately adopted a menacing attitude, while Clement, confronted with the consequences of his foolhardiness and overwhelmed with the responsibilities he was too weak to shoulder, sought desperately for a loophole. He decided at last to call a consistory to examine the question. There is little doubt that this assembly, carefully selected, would have been in complete sympathy with Clement's views; but it was destined never to meet, as the day before that fixed for the opening of the consistory —February 4th, 1769—the overwrought Pontiff died suddenly.

The news caused the greatest sensation, as he had shown no signs whatever of failing health—and on the night of his death had eaten an excellent supper and, though worried and harassed, appeared perfectly fit. However, as he sat on his bed while his servant drew off his stockings he suddenly clutched his side with a cry of pain, reeled over and was dead within a few minutes.

Rezzonico, the Cardinal-Nephew, who was also Camerlingo, though having been informed at once of the catastrophe, allowed three hours to elapse before coming to his uncle's bedside. No one meanwhile had presumed to interfere with the dead Pope's body, so when Rezzonico made his tardy appearance he found Clement still lying much as he had fallen; his white satin coatee half on and half off, and the tumbled bedclothes, soaked with the blood he had vomited, not even having been removed. Groups of cardinals conversed in agitated whispers while others, restless with excitement, flitted this way and that. The great room was in darkness save for the feeble light of the lanterns carried by the prelates, which cast dancing, fantastic shadows on the ceiling and walls of the death chamber. As they clustered round the Camerlingo and watched him remove the fisherman's ring from the late Pope's finger, few among them doubted that its destruction would symbolise the ruin of the Jesuit cause.

CLEMENT XIV
From a print in the British Museum

CLEMENT XIV (GANGANELLI)

1769–1774

❧

THE Catholic Powers, who had at first been content with expelling the Jesuits from their territories, were determined since Clement XIII's aggression on Parma to obtain from the Holy See the total suppression of the Order. They demanded it as a reparation for the outrage inflicted on the reigning Duke, which they attributed to Ricci's influence over the late Pope.

Choiseul, the able and tireless antagonist of the Jesuits, had been entrusted by the allied Sovereigns, long before Clement's death, with the devising of the plan of campaign to be adopted at the next conclave. They could not have placed their interests in better hands, for besides being the wiliest diplomat in Europe, Louis XV's minister had had, when Ambassador in Rome, ample opportunity to study ecclesiastical psychology; and no experience was wasted on Choiseul. The opinion of his foreign colleagues had been that a species of ultimatum should be presented to the new pope requesting the immediate dissolution of the Society of Jesus; but to this he would not agree. Pressure should certainly be brought to bear on the Holy See, but the Pope could not be actually coerced into signing a decree which, if it was to have a permanent effect, must be prompted by his own conviction and proclaimed as such to all Christendom.

Choiseul therefore repudiated all idea of brutal intimidation. "When one has a favour to ask of a Pope", he wrote, "and one is determined to obtain it, one must ask for two. The irresolution which results from the possibility of a choice lessens the vigour of resistance. Half is granted as an escape from granting the whole!" Choiseul's suggestion, therefore, was that, together with the suppression of the Society, France should request the cession of Avignon and the Comtat Venaissin; Spain that of Benevento and Ponto Corvo; Naples an extension of territory on the frontier of the Papal States; and Austria an immediate and final settlement of the vexed question of Parma and Piacenza. The new pope would therefore find himself

267

confronted either with a concession for which he could not but be prepared, or with a serious mutilation of the patrimony of the Holy See. There seemed little doubt which of the two alternatives the pontiff would decide on; but if by an incredible chance he chose the latter, the material advantages gained by the Powers would be more than sufficient compensation for their wounded pride.

The cardinals who were subjects of the Bourbons and of the Habsburgs formed an unquestionable majority in the Sacred College and ensured the absolute success of the allied schemes. A pro-Jesuit pope could not possibly be elected, for Choiseul had issued instructions to the various ambassadors in Rome to inform their compatriots that in the coming conclave no private sympathies were to be allowed to influence their suffrage and that they were to obey the French leader—Cardinal de Bernis—without question, or run the risk of drastic penalties. There was no doubt whatever that these threats would be rigorously enforced, as each country would make its allies responsible for any backsliding of their dependents, and of this the prelates were well aware. Consequently during the *novemdiale* the Jesuits' penitents dwindled to vanishing-point; their confessionals were deserted, the palaces of all foreign subjects closed against them, and obscure Dominican and Franciscan monks were promoted to the tending of consciences which needed no guiding hand to turn in the direction from which the sun shone brightest.

Of Ricci's followers there remained only the Roman prelates and a couple of Milanese who were already on such bad terms with the Austrian Government that they had nothing to lose by defying it. All the Catholic monarchs being in perfect agreement there could be no separate political parties, and many of the disabilities which in other circumstances might have gone against this candidate or the other, were now deemed of no importance. The only information sought concerning a would-be pope was: Is he for or against the Jesuits? On the answer to that one question rested his desirability or his exclusion. The conclave assembled on February 15th, 1769, the belligerents immediately taking up their respective positions on the battlefield. Skirmishing began at once; the Jesuit party put forward a couple of candidates to test the exact strength of their forces, and found them painfully inadequate. An unfortunate incident followed the defeat of these candidates. One of the Roman nunneries boasted of a prophetess, who had predicted that the future pope would occupy the cell bearing the number 17. It fell to the lot of Cardinal delle Lanze, who, being both credulous and conceited, never doubted the correctness and suitability of the conventual sybil's prognostication. His failure to impress his colleagues with his own belief in his high destiny so affected him that he actually lost his mental balance. He became convinced that he really was Pope, and he would wander about the passages distributing blessings and indulgences. Eventually his health gave way, and although he was perfectly harmless it was thought advisable to remove him from the Vatican.

Meanwhile the allied leaders, certain of the election of any candidate they favoured, were carefully studying the qualifications of the numerous potential popes before making a decisive and final selection. During this period, a dull one for the bulk of the suffragists, the inmates of the Vatican were provided with a unique and exciting diversion from the tedium of their inaction, by the unexpected appearance in their midst of Joseph II and his brother the Grand Duke of Tuscany. These two princes presented themselves arm-in-arm at the door of the conclave, the Emperor requesting leave to enter the forbidden premises. Such an occurrence had never been recorded in the annals of conclaves, and there being no precedent upon which to act, the custodians summoned the Dean, who, after holding a hasty consultation with the leading lights of the Sacred College, decided to break the seals and admit the exalted sightseers. As the Emperor stepped over the hallowed threshold he made a show of unbuckling his sword, but this the Dean would not permit. Having gained admittance as His Apostolic Majesty, Joseph now insisted on being treated as plain Count Falkenheim. It is on record that he wore the undress uniform of his regiment—a bright yellow waistcoat gold-braided, a brimless hat, and his hair gathered in a small queue.

In compliance with his wishes the cardinals on being presented to Joseph II respected his incognito in so far as they omitted to remove their skull caps, which they only did when addressing royalty. He was gracious and even familiar with them all, asking innumerable questions while with the Grand Duke he inspected everything minutely. The cubicles, the refectories, the chapel, the voting papers, the chalice, the stove—no detail was too insignificant to arouse his inquisitive interest. While their guests were thus occupied, their Eminences' servants had been hurriedly despatched to collect all available delicacies together with the choicest wines from their employers' reserves in the city, to provide adequate refreshment for the royal visitors. The Emperor professed himself delighted with his reception, excused himself most courteously for having interrupted the labours of the Sacred College, and the brothers took their depature with no more ceremony than had attended their arrival, Joseph wishing their Excellencies "the fulfilment of all their hearts' desires"!

This pleasing episode had an immediate reaction on the spirits of the recluses. The vast quantity of food and drink left over from the afternoon's entertainment had to be disposed of somehow; parties were organised, civilities exchanged from cell to cell, and flurried conclavists rushed about securing boards and trestles for the improvised banquets. Young Cardinal Albani sent out invitations to all the junior members of the Sacred College and treated them to the most delicious pasties and sweetmeats, washed down with priceless Tokay. The success of his party was such that the whole conclave caught hospitality fever and entertaining became the rage.

Had it not been for this excess of conviviality it is possible that Ganganelli would never have become Pope, for he himself kept modestly in the background, never attempting to attract attention or recruit adherents. He had attained a certain degree of notoriety a few years previously by the able and eloquent way in which he had addressed the consistory in favour of the canonisation of the Bishop of Palafox, a Spaniard, who had been an inveterate enemy of the Jesuits. Ganganelli had secured the beatification of his celestial client, which in view of the opposition of the Society of Jesus had not been a small triumph. He himself belonged to the Franciscan Order, was very popular with his colleagues, and those who knew him well had the highest opinion of his capacities and virtue, but none of the allied leaders, so far, seemed to have realised his undoubted qualifications to occupy the Holy See.

The Jesuit faction, it was rumoured, was preparing a surprise election, and a small incident which occurred at this juncture lent some colour to the report. One night when all the inmates of the conclave had long since retired to rest, the scrutiny bell suddenly clanged, and the panic-stricken cardinals rushed out of their cubicles, thinking the place was on fire. No trace of a conflagration having been discovered and there being nothing to account for the mysterious call, they all went back to bed. This ghostly summons, however, had made a disagreeable impression on the suffragists, who, leading such an abnormal, herded life, were easily upset and excessively prone to collective emotions. An atmosphere of nervous misgivings pervaded the assembly and at Albani's dinner-table the next evening the guests unanimously agreed on the necessity of a prompt election. As the evening wore on and the Tokay loosened their tongues, the prelates threw all caution to the winds and openly discussed the merits and demerits of the various *papabili* with vivacious candour.

Sala, the host's conclavist, who was considered the jester of the conclave, suddenly declared that he could give their Eminences the solution of the problem.

"Well, if you are on such good terms with the Holy Ghost," said one of the guests, "tell us what He wants us to do!"

"Certainly", replied Sala without hesitation; "elect Ganganelli—he pleaded so successfully for the Bishop of Palafox that he is quite capable of smuggling you all into Heaven!"

A storm of applause greeted this sally and Ganganelli's name was toasted to the echoes.

Several prelates attracted by the noise had congregated outside Albani's door, among them being Cardinal de Bernis, the French leader. Ganganelli's name caught his ear, and although it is probable that the advantages offered by the Franciscan's election had not altogether escaped him, yet it was undoubtedly the effervescence of Albani's guests which influenced him to take an immediate decision.

He settled the matter there and then in his mind, and as it was imperative that France should be the future pontiff's first patron, he sped swiftly to Ganganelli's cubicle and without so much as a preamble offered him the papal crown, informing him of Choiseul's conditions and pressing for an immediate answer. Ganganelli showed no emotion, and with great dignity replied that he had not sought the great honour which Bernis proposed to confer on him; that he was well aware that many popes had signed treaties before their election, but that without in any way blaming them for having done so he did not intend to follow their example. He categorically refused any territorial concessions whatever, but gave his word of honour that if he became Pontiff he would see justice done regarding the Jesuits and would abolish the Order if a free tribunal judged it expedient, and he himself was satisfied that such a measure should be taken in the interests of the Church. He agreed to give the secretary-ship of state to France's nominee, and Bernis was so impressed by his calm demeanour and unmistakable trustworthiness that he declared himself satisfied with Ganganelli's verbal promises. Anyway there was no time for more, as Albani and his exhilarated cohort were already clamouring for admittance. Bernis took the wind out of their sails by announcing that Ganganelli's election would take place the next morning and they dispersed more soberly to spread the great news.

Bernis interviewed the allied leaders, who issued orders to their factions to remain up in readiness for the final summons. By three o'clock the electors had all congregated in the Ducal Hall anxiously waiting for the first stroke of the chapel bell. At 3.30 Bernis gave the signal for it to be rung; the prelates rushed to Ganganelli's cell and an hour later he was proclaimed Pope under the name of Clement XIV. As the episcopal dignity had never been conferred on him, the Cardinal Dean immediately consecrated him as Bishop of Rome—for such was the formula employed to announce the Pope's accession to the diplomatic envoys and the world at large.

Clement XIV was sixty-three years of age, a man of magnificent physique and imposing presence, with a kindly, indulgent smile. He was mentally alert, sagacious and experienced in the ways of the world. The Jesuits had so far shown no animosity against him; as a Franciscan he had naturally had little intercourse with them; his advocacy of Palafox's merits had been conducted so tactfully that he had managed to keep off dangerous ground, and now the admirable catholicity with which he selected the members of the commission to sit in judgment on the Society was an added proof of his impartial frame of mind. During four years the tribunal sat weighing the conflicting evidence and debating on the advantages or disadvantages of suppressing the Jesuit Order. The Pontiff followed the case with the closest attention and firmly refused to be rushed into a decision which he considered so momentous, either by the Powers or the populace.

He was the soul of tolerance and moderation, and revived Benedict

XIV's policy of friendliness towards his fellow sovereigns irrespective of their religious beliefs. Although he himself lived in the Quirinal with the ascetism of a true Franciscan, he could display the greatest magnificence when it came to honouring distinguished guests. He entertained the Dukes of Gloucester and Cumberland with regal lavishness and charmed them so by his manner and conversation that Gloucester remarked that England would never have seceded from the Church of Rome had Clement XIV reigned in the days of Henry VIII. Conciliation was now the order of the day. An exchange of courtesies took place between the Holy See and Parma, Portugal, Spain and Naples; France evacuated Avignon and all was peace and neighbourly goodwill. The chroniclers report that "the Prince of Wales," who was a fervent partisan of the Jesuits, on hearing of Ganganelli's election, immediately left for Albano without illuminating his palace, and to this was ascribed the fact that Clement refused to address the Pretender as "Majesty". Such pettiness is unlike what one knows of the Pope's character, and his own explanation, that such empty blandishments could do the Pretender no good and would only make the position of Catholics in England more difficult, bears the hall-mark of his good sense.

Clement was the first ruler to insist on all medical practitioners being inscribed on a register, forbidding all quacks and charlatans from attending or receiving patients. He also attempted to abolish the custom of castrating boys to provide singers for the papal choirs. This effort, however, can only have had a temporary effect, for well into the second half of the XIXth century the admirable singing of the *castrati* in the Sixtine Chapel was one of Rome's great attractions. It is interesting in view of this fact to note the modern attitude of rigid dogmatism adopted by the Catholic Church towards the question of the sterilisation of the unfit. In his encyclical "Casti Connubii" Pope Pius XI, the present Pontiff, severely condemns those "who put eugenics before aims of a higher order," and adds that "Public magistrates have no direct power over the bodies of their subjects . . . and have no right to tamper with the integrity of the body either for the reason of eugenics *or for any other reason*".

Considering that for centuries successive popes countenanced the mutilation of numberless children for aims of no higher an order than the rendering of sacred or profane music by soprano instead of tenor or bass voices, the Church of Rome might, one cannot help feeling, make allowances for motives at least more altruistic, and be less categorical in its pronouncements on a subject which might not unreasonably be expected to cause it some slight embarrassment.

After mature deliberation the commission entrusted with the fate of the Society of Jesus concluded in favour of its suppression, unless its General would agree to a *radical* revision of the statutes, which Ricci stubbornly refused to do.

Clement was in complete agreement with the verdict, and on July 22nd, 1773, he issued the bull "Dominus ac Redemptor" in which he summed up in masterly fashion the causes and the motives which had guided the commission in taking its decision. The next day he signed the decree abolishing the Order founded by Ignatius Loyola 233 years before; which had covered itself both with glory and opprobrium, and whose members had proved themselves such incomparable servants and such deplorable masters. It is said that when Count Florida Blanca came to congratulate the Pope on the long-delayed execution, he smiled sadly, replying: "I have signed my death warrant, but I have obeyed my conscience". Notice was served on the General of the Jesuits on August 16th. He had had ample time to dispose of all compromising documents and to convey to a place of safety the large sums of money belonging to the Society. The scene in the gorgeous Church of the "Jesu" must have been deeply impressive when the Pope's bull was solemnly read to the assembled community. Ricci sat in his stall rigid as a statue, and when the echo of the last words, "The Society of Jesus has ceased to exist", died away in the oppressive silence, he rose slowly and in clear, steady tones exclaimed, "Et tertia die resurrexit!"

It may of course have been a mere coincidence, but a few months later the Pontiff, who up to then had enjoyed the most robust health and whose spirits had the buoyancy of youth, showed symptoms of a strange and unknown disease which completely baffled the court physicians. Clement was exceedingly abstemious and frugal; all his food was cooked by a Franciscan friar and could not possibly have been tampered with, so it is supposed that the poison—if poison there was—must have been introduced into some figs which the friar bought unsuspectingly one day from a street vendor. Be that as it may, the Pontiff gradually lost his voice while his tongue and throat became so inflamed that he was driven to keep his mouth perpetually agape in an attempt to obtain, through the freshness of the air, some relief from his sufferings. He, who had been so strong and untiring, became as weak as an infant; his limbs betrayed him and he could scarcely drag himself from chair to couch. Alternately he would be a prey to insomnia or fall into a stupor from which he could not be roused. His martyrdom was indescribable. He made heroic efforts to conceal his condition, fighting the complaint inch by inch with all the energy he could muster in his debilitated state. His gaiety flickered out; he became morose, irascible and suspicious; the virus after devastating his body attacked his mind. For hours this Pontiff, so wise and so diligent, would sit at his window pathetically intent on dazzling the passers-by with the reverberation of the sun's rays on a hand mirror. In his moments of lucidity he would express feelings of the most admirable fortitude and resignation. The physical and mental tortures he endured drew tears of compassion from those who served him.

"I knew", he is reported to have said, "that I would pay with my life for what I did; but I never anticipated such a long-drawn-out agony and such refinement of cruelty!"

There has been much controversy over the mysterious cause of Clement's death, which occurred on September 28th, 1774, but nothing has been definitely proved as to its nature. The autopsy would have been a difficult one at any period, as decomposition had actually preceded death, and in those days it was wellnigh impossible to cope with such conditions. The Pontiff himself was obviously obsessed with the conviction that he had been poisoned and it was the popular belief amongst his contemporaries. The details of his laying-out are horrifying. His remains had to be encased in plaster, and Cardinal Marefoschi, who according to the ceremonial should have placed a cloth over the dead Pope's face, feigned illness so as to escape the ordeal, the major-domo who had to take his place being so overcome that he closed his eyes and threw the veil in the direction of the bed without approaching it. A layer of plaster was hastily spread over the aperture where those features once so pleasing to look upon should have been exposed; and so was obliterated all trace of the brave, wise and virtuous Pope who had borne the name of Clement XIV.

PIUS VI
From a print in the British Museum

PIUS VI (BRASCHI)
1775-1799

❧

THERE were fifteen vacancies in the Sacred College at the time of the late Pontiff's death, and out of the remaining number of cardinals many were absent when the conclave assembled on October 5th. The Powers had again delegated full authority to Cardinal de Bernis; no political factions were to be countenanced, and the personality of the future pontiff only interested the allies in so far as he could be relied on to ratify Clement XIV's edict abolishing the Society of Jesus.

In France Louis XVI and Marie Antoinette had just come to the throne, and the Queen, who was the real ruler, was too intoxicated with her first taste of unrestricted freedom, and too engrossed in devising new amusements, masquerades, *fêtes champêtres* and theatricals, to take much interest in the remote intrigues of musty old cardinals. As to Joseph II, he had very determined views on religious and ecclesiastical matters and acted on his own initiative without any reference to the Holy See, whose approval or disapproval affected him not in the least. In fact, shocking the Ultramontanes seemed to be developing into his favourite sport.

Charles III of Spain was a monarch of the old school; an enlightened and respected ruler, whose word was law to the Bourbons of Italy. In a letter to his son, King Ferdinand of Naples, he writes:

As for me I have no other interest where the new Pope is concerned than that which is common to all Catholic monarchs— to wit: that we should be given a Pope both wise, and circumspect, who can distinguish what is due to God from what is due to Kings and who will not destroy his predecessors' good work.

In Charles' opinion the Jesuit danger was still as menacing as ever, and to his influence was principally due the fact that Bernis' instructions were so stringently narrowed down to the one condition of ratification to be obtained from the new pope. As the Zelanti had managed to erase from the inscription on Clement XIV's catafalque the reference to the abolition of the Jesuit Order, it was evident that its proscribed members could still boast of devoted supporters and that the Society did not consider itself irretrievably crushed.

There was no ambiguity about the situation, but unfortunately Bernis was now besotted with Princess Santa Croce and incapable of concentrating on anything but her charms. The first thing that claimed his attention after his entrance into the conclave was the devising of means for escaping from it. This problem was soon solved by knocking a hole in the wall of his cubicle, which was most fortunately situated at the end of a passage; the aperture being made sufficiently large to allow the prelate to crawl through it, provided a safe exit which could easily be concealed behind a hanging tapestry. Bernis made immediate and frequent use of this back-door to paradise, his escapades of course being no mystery to anybody; but as he was complete master of the situation and the acknowledged Pope-maker, he met with no open criticism.

In spite of the fact that the proceedings irked him almost beyond endurance, the French leader seemed quite incapable of taking any measures to bring matters to a conclusion by selecting and proposing an acceptable candidate. He simply could not spare the time to examine the qualifications of the thirty *papabili* who for four months attempted to court his notice. Try as they would, they could scarcely ever get a glimpse of him, as he was always either just adorning him-self preparatory to bolting through his hole or had just crawled back to recuperate.

The Sacred College, left to its own devices, amused itself as best it could. It was flooded with scurrilous pamphlets and caricatures throwing a lurid light on the questionable incidents in the past and present lives of most of the prelates. Even the memory of the late Pope was not respected and the tedium of their existence was such that they gloated over the most nauseating calumnies with prurient gratification.

Few of them escaped the attentions of the satirists; Braschi, the future Pope, was accused of sharing in the debauches of his valet and the man's mistress; Cornaro, who was supposed to be dominated by a woman called Anna Ciccaporci, was always alluded to as "Abbate Anna". Zelanda's name was inseparable from that of Princess Giustiniani, and as to Borghese the anecdotes about his hairdressers, page-boys, and the trick played upon him by a handsome young

Englishman called Banks, kept the cardinals in perfect convulsions of hilarity. But when Giraud and Zelanda were depicted in a cartoon as a couple of *soubrettes*, the one assisting Bernis to apply his cosmetics while the other tidied his underclothes, the measure overflowed. An order was issued for the burning of the picture by the public executioner and a reward of 500 crowns offered to whoever discovered the author. The Apostolic Chamber would not ratify this undertaking, declaring that it was not rich enough to pay such a sum, so Bernis and Giraud guaranteed the money between them. The culprit was found to be a Florentine called Setor, but as he had taken sanctuary in a monastery not much satisfaction was obtained by the French prelates for their outlay.

The ex-Jesuits, as we have seen, still had a group of partisans in the Sacred College, and Colonna, the leader of their party, moved heaven and earth to have Ricci set at liberty. The ex-General of the Society of Jesus had been incarcerated in S. Angelo for refusing to accept the late Pope's decree and thus challenging his authority. Most of the Roman prelates had kept in touch with the prisoner, as had also Rezzonico and the Cardinal of York; but too many members of the Sacred College had openly declared their animosity against the Jesuits to approve of a measure fraught with so much danger to themselves, and Ricci therefore remained in custody.

Reports of Bernis' scandalous neglect of his duties had not failed to reach Versailles, for it was now the end of December and the cardinals were losing patience. The elder Albani was even reported to have had words with the French leader on the subject of this inordinate delay. There seemed no reason why the conclave should not last as long as the Frenchman's infatuation. No doubt Bernis had many sympathisers at the gay Court of Versailles, but some move had to be made in the matter, and the Duc de Luynes was sent from Paris to reason with the lovelorn prelate and bring him to his senses. The news of the Duke's departure considerably affected Bernis' prestige, and Albani acting boldly on his own initiative started an energetic campaign on Braschi's behalf. When Luynes reached his destination he found Rome seething with excitement as the leading hairdresser in the city had just disclosed the fact that Braschi had sent him a lock of his hair and ordered a toupee to disguise his baldness. This was taken as proof positive that the candidate expected to wear the papal tiara! Luynes was not unfavourably impressed with Braschi's qualifications, and having been instructed to speed up the proceedings, was tempted to adopt the easiest means of doing so. But the Portuguese Minister, who hated Braschi, loudly proclaimed his belief in the accuracy of all the accusations of immorality brought against the candidate, adding that he was pompous, vulgar and had insufferable manners—that his grandfather had been condemned to the galleys for murder—that Braschi himself had a pecuniary interest in the money-lending business of a Jew called Ambram, and lastly that his relations were ambitious, grasping and unscrupulous.

This virulent attack caused Albani's protégé a momentary setback; but Luynes, after trying for a few weeks to discover a more suitable candidate, gave up the task as impossible and declared himself in favour of Braschi. A timely distribution of 12,000 crowns made among his most needy colleagues in Braschi's name also strengthened his following considerably. The sudden illness of Princess Santa Croce now clinched the matter. Bernis, who since his semi-disgrace had received many anonymous threats of exposure and no longer dared to make use of his emergency exit, had worked himself into a perfect frenzy of claustrophobia. On hearing of his lady-love's indisposition he decided to obtain his freedom at any cost. Braschi, he supposed, was as likely as any other of the *papabili* to make a satisfactory pontiff, and as Luynes seemed to think well of him the sooner the matter was settled the better it would be for all concerned. So Bernis made up his mind to interview the Pope-elect at once. Braschi accepted the condition imposed by the allies regarding the ratification of Clement XIV's bull suppressing the Society of Jesus, promised his friendship to the Bourbons and to the Habsburgs, and agreed to be guided by the allies in the distribution of State offices. The affair being concluded, Bernis on taking leave of his colleague kissed his hand, a sign of deference which a cardinal only gives to a pope. On February 15th Braschi was raised to the Holy See, and having hesitated a while between the names of Clement and Benedict, suddenly decided to call himself Pius, as there were fewer pontiffs bearing that name.

The Roman populace, who had at first shown some dismay at the announcement of Braschi's election, when once they had gazed on the handsome countenance, engaging smile and majestic figure of the new Pontiff towering above them in the *sedia gestatoria*, declared themselves delighted with their new Sovereign and applauded him enthusiastically. But alas! there was little besides his prepossessing appearance to recommend Pius VI to the love of his subjects. He was vain, weak, touchy and callous and he lacked judgment and mental stability. No coquette could have attached more importance than he did to the adornment of his person and the enhancing of his good looks. He spent an inordinate time at his dressing-table, which was covered with an amazing paraphernalia of unguents, lotions and perfumes. No affairs of State could have dragged him away from his mirror till he was made up to his entire satisfaction; he studied all his gestures with the application of an actor, and his poses while officiating at the altar were positively histrionic.

At the time of his accession Pius VI was fifty-eight years of age and his excellent constitution gave promise of a long pontificate. He belonged to a noble but impoverished family of Cesena and, being very proud of his birth, was much perturbed by the fact that his only sister had married a man of plebeian origin called Onesti. Such a *mésalliance* was bad enough in itself, but as Pius intended to raise his nephews to the highest rank and position he could dispose of, the absence of quarterings on the paternal side was a mortifying accident. He therefore commissioned a genealogist to make researches extending back to the dark ages if necessary, so as to discover in the Onesti pedigree some trace, however remote, of nobility or distinction. The task was a hard one; the Onesti's lineage seemed untraceable, and abandoning all attempts at grafting this unclassified cutting on to any aristocratic tree, the genealogist fell back on the notabilities of another and higher sphere, and trumped up a collateral relationship between the Onesti and St. Romualdo!

As no temporal privileges can be claimed through kinship with the canonised, the result of the investigation was considered very disappointing. The Pope solaced the wounded feelings of his family by creating his eldest nephew Duke of Braschi-Onesti, while the younger one was given the cardinal's hat. There followed a return to all the abuses of nepotism—but as it was no longer possible for the Sovereign Pontiff to dispose of land and property belonging to the Holy See for the endowment of his nephews, Pius undertook the draining of the Pontine marshes; inasmuch as land reclaimed became the property of the reclaimer, and so an apanage was formed for the new papal house.

Pius VI's popularity was short-lived; even had the people not seen through his affectations, the unblushing rapacity of his family would have earned for him a full measure of resentment. The Romans had nicknamed him the "Seccatore"—a name suggested by his desiccation of the Pontine marshes and the imposition of taxes which squeezed his subjects dry.

All the valuables and property confiscated from the Jesuits Pius bestowed on his relations. Yet these gifts did not satisfy them. A few former members of the Order had retained possession of a beautiful estate at Frascati, and as the newly married Duke Braschi-Onesti coveted this domain, the ex-Jesuits were lured out of it by a mean trick and it was handed over to him. But the Jesuits had proved themselves powerful and dangerous enemies, and fearful of the consequences incurred by his unscrupulous spoliation, the Pope sought some means of placating his victims. Providentially at this juncture the Empress of Russia approached the Holy See with a plea that the Society of Jesus should be allowed recognition in Russia. Catherine wished to have a few of its members as a rarity, saying that "she would preserve these exotic plants in her botanical gardens so as to supply seeds to those who applied for them!" Pius gave his gracious consent and trusted it would balance his account. But a margin on the credit side being always desirable, he openly affected great reluctance to canonise the famous Bishop of Palafox. Charles III, however, was not the monarch to stand any shilly-shallying, and Count Florida Blanca adopted such a threatening attitude that the Pope thought it wiser to give in at once.

Nor was there any friendliness or respect in the Grand Duke of Tuscany's attitude towards the Pontiff and it was soon evident that he was taking his cue from the Emperor. Pius wrote numerous letters to the latter complaining not only of his brother Leopold's behaviour, but hazarding fatherly rebukes to Joseph himself. The Emperor returned the Pope's letters with an annotation to the effect that they were improperly expressed, whereupon Pius rewrote them omitting all the censorious phraseology, for which he substituted terms of amity and deference. This effort at conciliation having failed to elicit any response, Pius, confident in the appeal of his prepossessing countenance, concluded that a personal interview could not fail to solve all difficulties and decided to visit the Emperor in Vienna.

Mindful of upholding the dignity of the Holy See, his journey was planned on the lines of a triumphal progress. He was accompanied by an innumerable retinue of officials and attendants; he took with him his most gorgeous robes and vestments, the richest of the triple crowns, ceremonial croziers studded with diamonds and the finest of the papal jewels. All the towns he stayed in vied with one another to entertain him with the greatest magnificence; but at Cesena, his native city, he himself acted as host to all his relations, giving a regal banquet in their honour. By short stages the Pontiff reached Göritz, where Cobentzel the Vice-Chancellor greeted him in Joseph's name. A squadron of the Emperor's Guards acted as escort, and all along his route to Vienna Pius was enthusiastically acclaimed by the population of the towns, villages and countryside. He reached the outskirts of the capital in a most elated and optimistic frame of mind, and here Joseph himself and his brother Maximilian were awaiting him. The Pontiff and the Emperor made a solemn State entry, driving slowly through the streets of the city while the guns boomed, the bells pealed and the crowd, shouting itself hoarse, fell reverently on its knees.

Pius was so moved by the ovation he received that he kept rising in the carriage to allow the faithful a better view of his person as he lifted his arms to bless them. Joseph sat silent and detached, a faintly contemptuous smile playing about his lips. He resented the presence of his self-invited guest, and the servile stupidity of his subjects irritated him considerably. During the entire month that the Pope remained in Vienna, the delirious fervour of the masses never abated. The Danube was so obstructed with the countless ships bringing pilgrims who wished to prostrate themselves before the Sovereign Pontiff that traffic came practically to a standstill. The streets all around the palace in which he resided were blocked by a compact mass of humanity clamouring for a glimpse of the Holy Father. Regularly five times a day Pius appeared on the balcony to bless the throng. Such streams of people begged for admittance to kiss his feet that, unable to cope with such a demand in person, the Pope had his slipper placed on a velvet cushion and exposed to the daily veneration of the multitude. Privileged devotees obtained the loan of such another hallowed object for a few hours in their own houses where they and their friends could give full rein to their devotion without being hurried and elbowed by the more plebeian element.

Joseph and his Chancellor Kaunitz watched these proceedings with sardonic amusement; the famous Braschi pulchritude had completely failed to propitiate them, and they made the fact abundantly clear to the surprised Pontiff. Pius soon discovered that he would need all the self-assurance and *savoir faire* he could muster to preserve appearances. He schooled himself to ignore the supercilious discourtesy of the Emperor, who never allowed him to broach any of the subjects he had travelled all the way from Rome to discuss. Joseph had not wanted to see him, was annoyed and bored by his visit, and made no mystery of the fact. As to Kaunitz, he had omitted to request an audience of the Sovereign Pontiff, which was an incredible breach of etiquette in itself. But when Pius, acting on his regal prerogatives, misguidedly insisted on an interview, the Chancellor's attitude became nothing short of insulting. Without even a pretence of ill-health he received the Pope wrapped in a dressing-gown, and when his august visitor offered him his hand to kiss, Kaunitz shook it with vigorous familiarity. He affected not to hear when Pius attempted to introduce political topics of conversation, and dragged him unceremoniously round his palace, forcing him to examine his collections, to handle his curios, talking incessantly meanwhile and never permitting the Pontiff a moment's rest or respite, till, baffled and almost hysterical with rage and mortification, he gave up the struggle and took his departure.

The time had now come to return to Italy and the sum-total of advantages gained for the Holy See by the ruinous and ill-advised journey Pius had undertaken consisted in a pectoral cross which Joseph had presented to his guest on taking leave of him, and in a patent of nobility for the Pope's nephew conferring on him the title of Prince of the Holy Roman Empire. With these somewhat tinselly tokens of regard Pius had perforce to be content. If inwardly he felt at all crestfallen, he certainly remained blissfully unaware of the fact that the Emperor had taken a violent personal dislike to him and was therefore more disposed than ever to thwart and defy the authority of the Holy See. Indeed, no sooner was Pius out of sight

than Joseph with renewed zest entered upon his system of ecclesiastical reforms which culminated in a scheme whereby the Pope
would be reduced to the mere status of Bishop of Rome. Bernis and
Azara managed to prevail on Joseph to abandon this plan, but only
after Pius himself, now thoroughly alarmed, had proposed certain
conditions which the Emperor considered sufficiently acceptable to
form the basis of a concordat, which was eventually signed by
both parties.

Pius VI has been accused of having led a futile and immoral life,
of having neglected his duties and of having been bad-tempered
and even brutal with his attendants. Allowance of course must be
made for enmity and exaggeration, but there can be no doubt that
the Pope resorted to low and crooked means of obtaining money,
both to meet the demands of his insatiable family and the cost of
his own extravagance. As a monarch he was isolated and ignored.
When the French Revolution broke out, the population of Avignon
and of the Comtat Venaissin turned out the papal officials and declared themselves French citizens. News of this event was received in
Paris with a great show of rejoicing and the Pope's effigy was publicly
burned in the gardens of the Palais Royal to the accompaniment of
ribald jokes and songs.

Pius immediately mustered a rabble army and sent it to reconquer
his lost territories. He then turned his attention to internal affairs
and ordered the arrest of all foreigners especially of French nationality
suspected of sympathising with the revolutionary movement. Italians
who showed any symptoms of liberal tendencies were not dealt
with more leniently, and as to freemasons they carried their lives in
their hands. Cagliostro, the famous necromancer, who had fled from
France after the scandalous affair of the Queen's necklace and taken
refuge in Rome, was convicted of affiliation to the dreaded brotherhood and condemned to death. This sentence was commuted by Pius
into one of life imprisonment; and so having escaped the Bastille,
from which he would have been liberated within a few weeks,
Cagliostro fell into the dungeons of S. Angelo, where he remained
till he died. For a clairvoyant of his repute such a shattering failure
to foresee where danger really lay must have added considerable
bitterness to his miserable fate.

The pontifical troops were easily routed by the French forces, and having no money with which to engage reliable mercenaries, Pius was now left with no weapons but anathemas. With these he bombarded the French Government, from which they elicited the following note:

> The Executive Council of the Republic to the Prince-Bishop of Rome.
>
> PONTIFF—
> You will immediately set at liberty the French citizens confined in your dungeons. If this demand is not complied with, you will learn to your cost that the Republic is too proud to brook an insult and too powerful to leave it unavenged!

On reading this message, so redolent of Roman scholasticism, Pius was amazed, outraged and infuriated; but his ministers having given his choler time to subside made it quite clear to him that the consequences of a hasty and comminatory retort would certainly prove disastrous, and he managed to control himself sufficiently to agree to the drafting of a peaceable reply. But he was not to be shaken in his resolve to order a general levy. The excited masses responded so heartily to his call that they set on the French residents then and there, murdering Basseville, a secretary of the French Embassy, and severely wounding several others.

France made immediate preparations to invade Italy, and now the frightened and demoralised Romans, making Pius responsible for their dangerous plight, attacked his nephew's residence, vociferous and threatening. Braschi, who apparently knew how to treat his uncle's subjects, had the doors of his palace thrown wide open and appeared on the threshold with a dog-whip in either hand. Lackeys carrying baskets full of gold now stepped forward, throwing handfuls of the coins to the snarling *canaille*. While they scrambled for the money the Prince-Duke strode through the grovellers, lashing at them right and left. He then returned to his palace and the doors were closed. The riot was over.

But the Holy See was not to escape retribution so cheaply. The Directoire, which had succeeded the Convention, entrusted Bonaparte with the mission of chastising the culprits, and at the head of his ragged, unshod army the young General swept all before him. Moving with deadly speed he defeated the Austrians and the Piedmontese, and the rapidity of his victorious onslaught found the

Pontiff quite unprepared for resistance. There was nothing for it but to sue for an armistice, thus paving the way for peace. Pius sent Azara to offer Bonaparte as reparation the legations of Bologna, Ferrara and the Romagna, besides a large sum of money and numerous works of art. These terms were accepted by the Directoire and a commission was sent to Rome to receive the Pope's pledges. Its members had orders to obtain from the Holy See a full retraction of his edicts against the *assermenté* clergy in France and to press in the name of humanity for the total abolition in Italy both of the Inquisition and of the degrading custom of castration. As fervent exponents of the *"droits de l'homme"* indeed they could do no less! Pius declared that he would have to call a consistory to examine these new conditions and so obtained a delay.

On hearing that Austria was preparing to take the offensive against France he immediately directed that an armed resistance should be organised in his dominions having the character of a crusade and entitling the combatants to the same spiritual benefits. Colonna enrolled most of the Roman aristocracy under the pontifical banners and the banker Torlonia supplied the sinews of war. This Torlonia, who was gifted with the most remarkable business acumen, had lately risen from the humblest origin to occupy a most important financial position in Rome, and by his timely offer of subsidies to the Holy See laid the foundations of yet another princely Roman house. The martial ardour of the lower classes equalled that of the nobility but with less restraint and a great deal more inclination to violence. The mob actually attempted to seize the French emissaries and would perhaps have succeeded in doing so had not the invaluable Azara given them protection in the Spanish Embassy.

Meanwhile a letter written by Pius to the Emperor Francis II was intercepted by Bonaparte's spies and forwarded to the General. It contained a detailed description of the means employed by the Pontiff to delay matters until such time as the Austrians should have routed the French, or his own troops be ready to take the field. Bonaparte, who was in Northern Italy, immediately swooped down on the Papal States without a word of warning. The training and preparations of Colonna's crusaders were far from complete, alas! and the defenceless Pope was constrained to accept the terms of the treaty dictated by Bonaparte and signed at Tolentino (1797). By this treaty Avignon, Bologna, Ravenna and Ferrara were handed over to France, who was also entitled to garrison Ancona. Amongst other clauses the Holy See was to pay an enormous war indemnity and deliver up many valuable works of art selected by French experts.

All these excitements so affected Pius VI that he fell seriously ill, and his court and family, thinking he was going to die, made the most of their opportunities, with the result that the large sums of money which had already been collected to meet the fine entirely vanished. The general belief was that the Braschi had appropriated them, and the fact that Pius, having recovered his health, did not take any steps to trace the delinquents certainly lent colour to the accusation. Means had to be found somehow of covering the deficit. The nobility had already been squeezed dry, the people had literally nothing to part with, the Jews had been bled so mercilessly that all those who had a shekel left had fled the country. There remained only the clergy from whom any contribution could possibly be obtained, but the clergy showed a decided disinclination to shoulder the burden. To add to the general state of tension Joseph Bonaparte now appeared accompanied by General Duphot to see that the conditions of the Treaty of Tolentino were rigorously observed. The Envoys had been instructed, in view of gaining popularity with the Pope's subjects, to press for the liberation of all Italian political prisoners, as well as for the abolition of the Inquisition.

No sooner were these proofs of Gallic fraternity made known than the wildest enthusiasm for all things French prevailed among the Roman citizens. The Envoys were now the heroes of the hour, revolutionary riots broke out in the Transtevere quarter and the French tricolour flag was carried in triumph through the streets. The Pontiff ordered his guards to fire on the insurgents, and Joseph Bonaparte and General Duphot, who had, it was later asserted, only just appeared to try and quell the disturbance, were caught in the *mêlée*, Duphot being killed outright. Azara again managed to dominate the situation and restore some sort of order. He urged the Pope to offer full apologies to Joseph Bonaparte, but failed to persuade him to do so.

Rome was a decidedly unhealthy resort for representatives of the French government, and Joseph Bonaparte went north; but the Pope's subjects, either because they feared reprisals or because they genuinely believed in "becoming a free People", offered no resistance whatever to the armies of the Republic when they marched through the Papal States under the command of Berthier, who had been sent to avenge the death of his comrade Duphot. The gates of Rome were thrown open, the mob acclaimed their "liberators" and a classical scene in the grand manner was enacted at the Capitol.

Pius VI, who had taken refuge in the Vatican, sent a delegation to treat with Berthier, but the French Commanding Officer refused to see them. The Roman citizens had already formed a provisional government which immediately decreed the deposition of the Pontiff and arraigned the Braschi-Onesti and several cardinals before a civil tribunal to answer charges of misappropriation of funds. These members of the Sacred College were imprisoned forthwith while others were banished, all their possessions and those of the Pope's nephews being confiscated. As to Pius himself he was unceremoniously bundled off to Tuscany accompanied by his doctor, his secretary and a few attendants. He first stayed in a convent at Siena, where he seemed resigned, almost content; he had only been there a few months, however, when a violent earthquake destroyed part of the town, and although the convent itself scarcely suffered, the shock so affected the Pontiff's nerves that it was deemed advisable to remove him to Florence; and for close on a year he lived in the Carthusian monastery so beautifully situated on the outskirts of the Tuscan city.

The fickle Romans having tired of their French liberators, now rose and clamoured for the Pope to be restored to his throne. With England's assistance the King of Sicily was making things very uncomfortable for the French in Southern Italy, and Pius not unnaturally did his best to aid and abet his former subjects in overthrowing the Power which had despoiled him. The French Government, alarmed at the precarious position of their Italian garrisons, decided to transfer the Pope to a safer distance from the field of activities and bring him to France where a keen watch could be kept on his movements and correspondence.

Pius was now an aged and very sick man, racked with pain and practically crippled. With needless cruelty the invalid was rushed over the Alps in the bitter cold weather and reached Valence, the place chosen for his detention, in a state of collapse. Adversity seems to have brought out all that was best in the Pontiff's nature. His fortitude was admirable. He grew kinder and more considerate towards those who served him. With how much more grandeur is the lonely, suffering figure invested when jolting and lurching along the broken roads in a battered conveyance on his way to exile, than is that of the resplendent, handsome and fêted Pontiff who a few years earlier had undertaken another journey made smooth and easy and accompanied by all the pomp and magnificence of regal state?

The tragedy of Pius VI's hapless end has earned for him the indulgence of posterity. He drained the cup of expiation. Neglected by his ungrateful relations, broken-hearted, suffering, isolated and homesick, the unfortunate Pontiff surrendered to his destiny and died on August 29th, 1799. So passed away for ever the old order of things pontifical: scandalous squandering of money, malversations, immorality, nepotism; these cankers disappeared with the XVIIIth century. In the new era which was just dawning ancient kingly prerogatives would serve unexpected purposes; for with subversive benefaction the rough hand of democracy was to cauterise the Pope's evil.

XIXth CENTURY

Pius VII · Leo XII · Pius VIII · Gregory XVI
Pius IX · Leo XIII

PIUS VII
From the painting by David in the Louvre Museum, Paris

PIUS VII (Chiaramonti)

1800–1823

✤

The Transalpine tornado which had swept over Italy uprooting thrones, tearing flags from their staffs, displacing boundaries and whirling the Sovereign Pontiff away from his capital, had also, but in more frolicsome mood, blown half a dozen cardinals' hats clean over the steeples, while the wearers of a couple more had only just had time to snatch them back by their tassels as they rose in flight.

What now remained of the Sacred College was scattered about Europe. Most of the French prelates had taken refuge in England, the Austrians had returned to Vienna, and the Sicilians to Naples, where they had been joined by the Cardinal of York. Albani, the Dean, resided in Venice as did several others of his colleagues, and it was therefore to Venice that the suffragists travelled to confer together and select the locality where the conclave should be held.

Venice was now an Austrian city. Bonaparte had dealt very leniently with the Habsburgs by the Treaty of Tolentino. They had been more than compensated for the loss of their northern provinces by the acquisition of Venetia; an exchange they would probably have been prepared to accept even had they been victorious, as it gave them an established hold on the Adriatic and welded their empire into one cohesive whole.

The Austrian star was decidedly in the ascendant, for as soon as Bonaparte had been recalled from Italy fortune had deserted the armies of the Republic. The Neapolitans, well supported by England, had chased the French out of Rome, while the Austrians routed them in Northern Italy and now occupied the territories which had formed the ephemeral Cisalpine Republic. It was only natural, no doubt, that they should wish to establish themselves permanently in these regions; but as most of the land had been wrested from the Holy See, such a pretension could have no solid basis but on the Treaty of Tolentino. Only if the surrender of these provinces made by Pius VI was accepted as definite by his successor could Austria be entitled to annex them. The new pope therefore must be willing to ratify the Treaty of Tolentino, for if he repudiated it, Austria would have either to restore the lands in question, or appear before Christendom as the spoliator of Peter's Patrimony.

This state of things constituted a serious objection to the holding of the conclave in Venice, as the likelihood of severe pressure being brought to bear by Austria either on the electors or the elected could not be overlooked. On the other hand the situation in Rome was scarcely more reassuring, for the Neapolitan Sovereigns now resided in the capital which was occupied by their troops, and in which they seemed to be rapidly taking root.

In the late autumn all the members of the Sacred College in a position to attend the conclave had assembled in Venice. Only one of the six secularised prelates had attempted to claim his electoral privilege, and he, needless to say, had been contemptuously ignored. After mature deliberation, and considering the dangers besetting it on all sides, the Sacred College decided to hold its sittings in Venice and entered the Benedictine monastery on the island of S. Giorgio on November 31st. Only thirty-four prelates settled into the monks' cells, and they took stock of their reduced numbers with undisguised misgivings. At first the Zelanti group kept strictly aloof from any political faction. It stood for the integral rights of the Holy See and its members glared impartially both at the Austrian party and at the "moderates", who though prepared to make all-round concessions were secretly inimical to Austria. Inevitably, however, the suffragists gravitated towards one or the other of these two factions; but they were both subdivided and so difficult to manœuvre that several weeks elapsed before either of their leaders—Hertzan for Austria and Albani for the moderates—dared take the risk of a serious scrutiny.

Meanwhile the Courts of Naples and Vienna were stalking one another round the still imposing ruins of the Papal Monarchy. They each professed their willingness to surrender to the Holy See any of its territories which they occupied, provided the other took the first step; but neither would do so without an exchange of guarantees. Apparently nor Francis nor Ferdinand set much store by a gentleman's agreement and no doubt they knew what they were about.

At the beginning of February, Hertzan considered the time had come for his party to produce a candidate. His choice of Mattei, one

of the prelates who had strongly advocated the signing of the
Tolentino treaty and was therefore bound to uphold it, though
sound enough in view of Austria's policy, was too defiant a challenge
to the opposition. It spurred its various components into closer co-
operation, with the result that Albani's party showed such a firm
and unbroken front that by the end of the month Mattei's candidature had foundered hopelessly. But it was one thing to combine in
defence against a common enemy and quite another to take the
offensive. Here the task was complicated not only by the divergent
aims sectioning the party, but also by the fact that it was not known
which of the candidates was to be excluded by the Austrian veto.

The situation seemed so inextricable that Albani suggested an
ingenious innovation which might help to solve the problem. Each
party was to select three candidates, and whichever side polled the
greatest number of votes would have the right to nominate one of
its three candidates to receive the papal crown. This infraction of all
canonical regulations was not approved by the majority, as the
election would in all probability have been contested by the defeated
faction, thus entailing disastrous consequences.

The only chance of a solution now lay in selecting a neutral
candidate and, as had often happened before, the Pope's election
was due to entirely fortuitous circumstances. Among the Neapolitan
prelates was one Cardinal Ruffo, belonging to a princely Sicilian
house and a devoted adherent of the Braschi. He it was who had
devised their misappropriation of the Jesuits' property at Frascati and
who had consistently aided and abetted his patrons in all their
schemes of enrichment. In consequence he had a great hold over the
late Cardinal-Nephew; but as his name had been associated with that
of the King and Queen of Naples and of Acton, the Prime Minister,
in connection with the anti-revolutionary campaign in Rome, the
liberal faction held him in execration. As to the Zelanti, Ruffo's unedifying life at the court of Queen Marie Caroline horrified them,
and they would have nothing whatever to do with him; being a
Sicilian he was naturally mistrusted by Austria, so that for one reason
or another most of his colleagues cold-shouldered him.

It happened that the occupier of the next cell to his was a French
cardinal called Maury, the representative of the exiled Louis XVIII
at the conclave; a man who cared nothing about local tittle-tattle

and who was a great fancier of good chocolate. As luck would have it, Marie Caroline had provided Ruffo with the most delicious brand of this delicacy, unobtainable by ordinary mortals, and the titillating aroma emanating from his neighbour's cubicle made Maury's mouth water. It was simple enough to make some civil overtures to Ruffo, who responded with an invitation to partake of the exquisite beverage; and so began a pleasant, and for the Sicilian a most profitable friendship, for he considered that he had discovered the ideal Pope and Maury was just the ally he needed to bring about a successful election. Ruffo was well aware that his open sponsoring of any candidate would be sufficient to ruin his chances with the majority of his colleagues, and that he himself would have to keep severely in the background if his efforts were to be crowned with success.

The man that Ruffo was so anxious to raise to the Apostolic See was Chiaramonti, a cardinal who, in spite of the general ostracism, had always treated Ruffo with the greatest courtesy. The two prelates often met in the monastery gardens and strolled or sat together discoursing on a variety of topics with mutual sympathy and understanding. Chiaramonti had always held himself carefully aloof from party politics and, when the French and Austrian forces had been fighting near his See of Imola, had shown equal kindness to the wounded of both armies. His ideas and tendencies were moderately liberal, while his virtues and the rectitude of his private life were such as to satisfy even the requirements of the Zelanti. At the time of the conclave Chiaramonti was fifty-eight years of age, the son of Count Chiaramonti of Cesena, whose family was related to that of the Braschi. When still very young he had joined the Benedictine Order and owed his successful career entirely to the patronage of Pius VI. Braschi's support would therefore be assured, and through him—Albani's. Now Maury's friendship would be a link with Consalvi, one of the most influential personalities in the conclave. Consalvi, the secretary of the conclave, was not a cardinal, therefore not himself a suffragist, but was acknowledged to be a coming man. He had held important offices under Pius VI, was remarkably clever and tactful, and an appeal to his natural ambitions, together with the undeniable qualifications of the candidate, could not fail to secure his adherence. Consalvi accepted the offer of the hat and of the secretaryship of state and the matter was concluded.

To him was delegated the difficult task of capturing the necessary number of Austrian votes. He undertook it willingly, for added to the advantages he was to reap from Chiaramonti's election, Consalvi, on becoming better acquainted with the future Pontiff, developed a deep personal attachment for him and joined his cause wholeheartedly. The candidate's age, which in other circumstances might have been a barrier to his election, would at this juncture be a distinct advantage; for the political horizon appeared so stormy that the Sacred College would welcome the probability of a long pontificate which might give Europe time to settle down and thus save the electors from the complications and dangers another conclave held in the near future might well expose them to.

Consalvi knew that Hertzan would be absolutely intractable on the subject of the ratification of the Tolentino treaty, so did not even attempt to parley with him, but by various means enticed away a few of his followers. The only danger now lay in the Austrian veto, but it was extremely unlikely that Chiaramonti had been singled out as its victim when there were so many others more likely to have attracted the Emperor's exclusion. Anyway the risk had to be taken. Chiaramonti's interests proved to be in capable hands; for Hertzan only realised what was happening the evening before the decisive scrutiny, and it was then too late for him to take any measures to prevent Chiaramonti's election. The veto which he held as leader of his party evidently did not bear this candidate's name, for on March 14th, 1800, he was proclaimed Pope under the name of Pius VII.

The new Pontiff was a simple, gentle soul beloved by those who served him; his behaviour had always been exemplary, his manner was invariably kindly and pleasant. His elevation to the Apostolic See was popular with all but the Emperor Francis, who immediately marked his displeasure by forbidding the ceremony of enthronement being solemnised in S. Marco as the Venetian municipality had planned, ordering instead that it should take place with as little pomp as possible in the island of S. Giorgio itself. For the first time for centuries the new Pontiff did not appear on the loggia of St. Peter's to bless the assembled multitude; nor were his subjects likely to become acquainted with their Sovereign yet awhile for Francis raised every conceivable objection to his going to Rome. He tried to induce Pius to come to Vienna, and having failed to do so, declared that the Pope was to remain in Venice until the question of the ratification of the Treaty of Tolentino was settled.

Bonaparte had now returned to Paris from Egypt; as First Consul he was free to act on his own judgment and initiative and it was clear to all but to the Emperor Francis that the future fate of Italy depended on him alone. Pius therefore refused to enter into profitless discussions and insisted on being given a pass to return to Rome; but all his attempts to leave Venice were frustrated by the cabinet of Vienna, and it was not until the captain of a Turkish frigate offered the marooned Pontiff a passage on board his boat that the Emperor was shamed into sending an Austrian battleship to transport him to Ancona.

Bonaparte was already on his way to reconquer Italy, and by June 14th had shattered, on the battlefield of Marengo, all the hopes and schemes founded by Austria on her evanescent conquests. Nowhere so arbitrarily as in Italy did Napoleon (to borrow a metaphor from Byron) compel destiny to change horses. After Marengo he completely transformed the map of Northern Italy. He constituted several departments which were annexed to France and created a couple of new principalities quite irrespective of the right to "self-determination" of the natives. Again in 1805 a new plan was drawn up whereby Italy became a united dominion to which Venice had been annexed. In 1806 Joseph Bonaparte was made King of Naples. In 1807 with one stroke of the pen Napoleon annihilated the Kingdom of Etruria which he had himself created, his troops occupied Rome, and in 1808 the Pope was deported to France and the whole of the Peninsula fell under the imperial sway.

But to return to 1800, when, after Marengo, Bonaparte was trying to reorganise France and to wrestle with the state of chaos produced by the Revolution, the advantage to be gained by re-establishing the Roman Catholic worship in the country could not fail to strike him. A free-thinker himself, he was always an advocate of religious beliefs for women and for the lower classes, and fully realised what an invaluable auxiliary a properly disciplined clergy would be to his Government. In fact he considered the prompt settlement of this question of such paramount importance that, in his anxiety to gain time, he agreed, by the concordat which he signed with Pius VII in

1801, to several clauses which he later regretted and attempted to evade.

At first all went well between the Consulate and the Holy See, but as Bonaparte's power developed and was consolidated, his attitude became insufferably dictatorial. After his proclamation as Emperor he requested the Pontiff's presence in Paris to enhance the glory of his coronation. Although the invitation was worded less in terms of a favour craved than of an imperious command, Pius thought it advisable to comply with Napoleon's wishes. He was escorted through France by a crowd of officials and courtiers sent from Paris to attend him, and was received in the capital with every mark of honour and respect.

The pageant of Napoleon's coronation surpassed in magnificence and brilliancy anything that Parisians could ever remember having seen. Not the least resplendent among the beplumed, dazzling and gorgeous personages who graced the occasion was Pius himself wearing a cope of cloth of gold profusely sewn with sparkling gems and a triple crown ablaze with diamonds. His figure was thrown into high relief by the scarlet robes of the cardinals who surrounded him, making a wonderful sustained note of colour among the variegated apparel of the courtiers. But the Pope was made to feel that, like all the other guests and officials at the ceremony, he was merely a unit in the constellation revolving round the central luminary; for having been solemnly installed on his throne in Notre Dame, he had to sit there patiently awaiting the Emperor's arrival, an unheard-of situation for a Sovereign Pontiff to find himself in. More mortifying still, when he had anointed the new Emperor and was preparing to place the crown of St. Louis on his brow, it was suddenly snatched out of his hands by this outrageously unconventional "most Christian Majesty" who, having firmly fitted it on his head, turned and crowned the Empress himself! This unrehearsed breach of ceremonial etiquette was no doubt intended to impress the onlookers as a symbol of the personal achievements which had put the insignia of sovereignty within Napoleon's reach. A less accommodating Pontiff who, having travelled all the way from Rome to perform the ceremony, was not allowed to proceed with it, might have shown some annoyance at being placed in such a ridiculous and embarrassing position; but Pius was too kindly and indulgent to resent Napoleon's impetuous behaviour and made no subsequent allusion to the scene.

He had naturally hoped that the tokens of goodwill he had given to the Emperor would have disposed him to grant certain concessions concerning both the spiritual and temporal powers of the Holy See which had been submitted to him. But Napoleon dismissed these questions without even a pretence of discussion and dashed off to Milan for yet another coronation, this time as King of Italy, while Pius, now thoroughly perturbed about the future, started on his return journey to Rome.

The first open rift between Napoleon and the Holy See occurred in connection with the annulment of Jerome Bonaparte's marriage to Elizabeth Patterson, which had taken place in 1803 in America, and which the Emperor, having more ambitious matrimonial views for his brother, wished dissolved. To Napoleon's surprise the mild and pliable Pontiff peremptorily refused his assent. Pius and his ministers had heard many rumours during their stay in France concerning Napoleon's intention of repudiating Josephine and were convinced that this first demand would eventually be followed by another and more portentous one. When the Empress, succumbing to a belated but highly opportune attack of scruples, had confessed to the Pope on the eve of the coronation that her union to Bonaparte had never been blessed by the Church, Pius had insisted on an immediate ceremony which he himself performed. This stroke of diplomacy on Josephine's part had caused the Emperor an irritation which he did not trouble to conceal. Although he would not of course let it stand in his way when the time came, it was bound to cause unnecessary complications, and the bridegroom plighted his troth with an ominous scowl on his countenance, a fact which had not escaped the Pontiff. Nothing more was said about the matter—a divorce was pronounced in Paris and Jerome married to a Princess of Würtemburg without further ado.

The Emperor now adopted the "Roi Soleil's" arrogant attitude towards the Holy See. The pretensions of the Gallican Church were revived and the ensuing disputes were nominally the cause of the investing of Ancona and Civita Vecchia by the French troops and of the annexation of Benevento and Pontecorvo to Joseph Bonaparte's Kingdom of Naples. The real motives of this military display, however, were given in the following *communiqué* to the French press:

"Considering that the Sovereign of Rome has constantly refused to make war on the English and to join the coalition for the defence of the Peninsula, etc." Pius had in fact refused to do these things, arguing that his high office stood for peace, that he was the Father of all Christians, and that strife was not his rightful field of action. He remained on excellent terms with the English Government, so much so that the Prince Regent sent him his portrait as a token of personal friendship. As Pius was not to be moved from his attitude of peaceable neutrality, Napoleon ordered his generals to occupy Rome, and the Pope was removed to Savona.

When in 1810 the Emperor divorced Josephine and married Marie Louise, Pius forbade the French cardinals to attend the wedding ceremonies, and the Emperor retaliated with a threat to depose him. As Louis XIV had done, Napoleon called a meeting of bishops to examine the questions upon which he was at variance with the Holy See, and was dumbfounded to discover that unlike the Bourbon King he lacked the prestige and influence over his subjects which had made the clergy of the Gallican Church stand by their Sovereign to a man. The majority of the bishops openly sided with Rome. The meeting was immediately broken up, the ringleaders imprisoned and the remaining members of the conference ordered back to their sees. In June 1812 Pius was brought from Savona to Fontainebleau, where rooms had been prepared for him in the palace, and there he remained a closely guarded prisoner for over three years.

He was deprived of his own attendants and Court functionaries and only allowed to receive the visits of those cardinals resident in Paris who had disobeyed his injunctions and been present at Napoleon's marriage to Marie Louise. The Emperor was absent during most of the Pope's captivity but he left his victim in good hands. Perpetually badgered and browbeaten, the isolated prisoner, whose disposition was yielding to the point of weakness, was allowed to hold no communication whatever with his ministers and usual advisers. All political news was kept from him and pressure never relaxed. At last he succumbed and signed a concordat by which he bound the Holy See to clauses absolutely disastrous to its spiritual supremacy, also renouncing temporal sovereignty, and agreeing to transfer his residence to France.

This ignominious capitulation was announced in Paris with a

tremendous flourish of trumpets in January 1813, and a public ceremony took place in the course of which the Emperor and the Pope exchanged fraternal embraces amid the acclamations of the multitude. After this affecting scene Pius was given his liberty, and Consalvi, the Secretary of State, and Pacca, the Camerlingo, received permission to attend on His Holiness. The poor Pontiff had fully realised by now how disastrous his surrender had been. He was covered with shame and confusion and quite prepared for the advice his Ministers gave him of disowning with solemn publicity the pact by which he had signed away Peter's Patrimony. This he did at once in an autograph letter to the Emperor, annulling the concordat of Fontainebleau.

In the meantime other and greater problems had beset Napoleon, problems far more vital to him than any religious issues could be; and wishing to rid the country of an additional source of trouble he surlily gave Pius leave to return to Rome. Events now crowded on one another so fast that it was difficult to keep up with them. The Emperor's fall; Louis XVIII's accession; the Congress of Vienna; and, just as the Papal States were being pieced together again, Napoleon's return from Elba! Pius took refuge in Genoa and Louis XVIII in Ghent—the Congress was suspended while Europe flew to arms—Waterloo—the caging of the eagle—the Bourbons handed up once more on to their several thrones—the Pope's return to the Quirinal—peace.

In Vienna the Congress resumed its sittings, old maps of Europe were exhumed, and the Holy See regained possession of all its former territories with the exception of Avignon and the Comtat Venaissin, which remained French. There is a certain piquancy in the fact that it fell to Talleyrand's lot to draft the document of restitution whereby his own principality of Benevento, bestowed on him by Napoleon, was restored to the Holy See. Louis XVIII also returned most of the works of art which had been included in the reparations imposed on Pius VI by the Treaty of Tolentino, in acknowledgment of which courtesy Pius VII made a personal gift to the King of the curiosity known as the porphyry chair.

Now would have been the time to reorganise the whole system of administration in the Pontifical States; to start afresh on more modern and more liberal lines; and that is what Consalvi attempted to do.

Pius VII had been so shaken by his failure to withstand the test of persecution that he had developed a positive inferiority complex and was less inclined than ever to take any personal initiative in matters of State. Consalvi on the contrary considered himself quite capable of piloting Peter's barque, and had he been free to act according to his own views and judgment he would probably have given the temporal power a new lease of life. But he was not only hampered by the restrictions imposed on the Holy See by Metternich, upon which the restoration of the temporal power had been made conditional, but he also encountered in the College of Cardinals the most stubborn and disheartening resistance. He was in open conflict with Pacca; and all those officials and their sycophants, who feared to lose their lucrative sinecures under a new régime, banded together to defeat him.

The finances of the Holy See were in an alarming state of confusion. Loans had to be raised repeatedly from Torlonia, now a duke, or from Madame Letitia, Napoleon's mother, who had retired to Rome and had a remarkable flair for lucrative transactions; from this stoical and business-like matron money could be obtained at a slightly less exorbitant rate of interest than from the banker.

Although Pius stood staunchly by his Secretary of State, it was impossible for Consalvi, unsupported by the majority of his colleagues, to stem the tide of reaction which was in full swing. The State offices which had been in civilian hands during the French occupation were now again held by churchmen. All the antiquated traditions came once more into their own and the obsolete legislation of bygone days ousted the "Code Napoleon" by which Italians had been judged for fifteen years. The abolition of civil tribunals caused the greatest discontent to the Pope's subjects, who objected strenuously to ecclesiastical jurisdiction. The general upheaval had shaken the very foundations of the Pope's sovereignty; the new ideas imported into Italy by the French armies could not but have a repercussion through every social stratum. From the time of the Pope's return to Rome till the fall of the temporal power there was to be a perpetual struggle between the ultramontanes and the liberals, with the object on the one side of preserving established customs—which really meant the maintenance of purely honorific sinecures and out-of-date prerogatives; on the other, of introducing urgent reforms and rejuvenating the entire governmental system. It was an unequal contest of course, for there were so many who had something to lose by the change and the ultramontanes won easily enough.

No return to better times could be complete without the reappearance of the Society of Jesus, which under various disguises had never really ceased to exist. Pius VII therefore reinstated the Order; and no sooner had he done so than hundreds of full-blown Jesuits appeared overnight, so well provided with funds that both in France and in Italy they started immediately to buy properties destined for colleges and seminaries. They found their way back to the palaces of the mighty, resumed their nursing of aristocratic consciences, and sat once more in their baroque confessionals in readiness for out-patients.

A new and entirely satisfactory concordat was signed with France and a veil drawn over the painful episode of Fontainebleau. But there were many among the Pontiff's *entourage* who were convinced that he himself had never forgotten it, and that he brooded incessantly over what he considered a shameful betrayal of his great trust. In the early summer of 1823 Pius had a fall which at his advanced age was almost bound to prove fatal, and on August 20th he passed peacefully away.

Thus ended one of the longest and most troubled pontificates the Apostolic See had ever known.

LEO XII (DELLA GENGA)
1823–1829

❧

PIUS VII had dispensed with a cardinal-nephew, and Consalvi as Secretary of State was naturally the leader of the late Pontiff's creatures; but his unpopularity in the Sacred College undermined the influence he should have had over them. His colleagues could not forgive him either for having centralised and absorbed so many branches of government of which they had so far enjoyed the benefits without hindrance or supervision, or for having shackled their authority at every turn as he had done. The system of progressive evolution which he had striven to establish had roused the bitterest resentment among the ultramontanes. He had also antagonised the Austrian Government by his energetic opposition to its hectoring policy towards the Holy See, and by his persistent struggle to free Italy from the stranglehold Austria was gradually acquiring over the entire Peninsula; therefore in that quarter he had nothing to expect but systematic hindrance. To make matters even worse, Consalvi was in a most precarious state of health and in constant physical pain; but undaunted and mettlesome he fought the losing battle which he knew must be his last, without yielding an inch and without showing the slightest sign of discouragement or lassitude. His life's work was in the balance. Would the more enlightened system of government he had inaugurated survive or be abolished? The odds against him were formidable, for he was beset with enemies, and the Powers, who having no cause for hostility against him might have given him their support, were at this juncture but broken reeds owing to the notorious incapacity of their representatives in Rome.

Never had the diplomatic corps presented such a lamentable collection of incompetent figureheads. Owing to the fact that since the restoration of the temporal power the Holy See was known to be in Austrian leading-strings, Rome was considered by the various European Courts to be a post of secondary importance. They had therefore been sending ambassadors or ministers either too old or too stupid to be employed elsewhere, or favourites who wished for a temporary diplomatic appointment, or even officials who had failed in other capacities but for one reason or another could not well be dismissed. Even the French Ambassador, the Duc de Laval, though a charming and cultured man of the world, was so flighty and unreliable that he could not be given any responsible office and there was nothing whatever to be hoped from his co-operation.

Such was the situation when the forty-nine suffragists, who were to elect the new pope, met in conclave on September 2nd, immediately taking up their respective positions as Consalvists or anti-Consalvists. The troublous times had left their mark on the Sacred College. It was no longer the exclusively aristocratic body it had been during the XVIIth and XVIIIth centuries. There was a distinct infiltration of the plebeian element and consequently less formalism and less ostentation. It seemed at first as if a happy solution had been found in the candidature of Severoli, who, though a member of the Zelanti, had friends in all groups, but at the last minute his chances were shattered by the Austrian veto. The explosion of this bombshell was due to Severoli having refused to attend the marriage of Napoleon and Marie Louise which had taken place during his nunciature in Vienna.

Castiglioni also came very near to securing the necessary majority; he was the Bourbons' nominee chosen by them as a result of the persecution he had endured at Napoleon's hands. He had been a great favourite with Pius VII, who always referred to him as Pius VIII, and he was secretly supported by Consalvi. Unfortunately at one of the scrutinies Cardinal Pallotta, who happened to be a scrutator, recognised Consalvi's writing on a ballot paper bearing Castiglioni's name. He immediately gave the alarm and the candidate lost all the votes of the Zelanti party without which his election was impossible.

Cardinal della Somaglia, one of the two prelates who had been within an ace of renouncing his ecclesiastical dignities during the French occupation, now came forward as a potential pope, but the fact that during the regrettable period of his temporary aberration he had signed his letters "Citizen Somaglia" made his elevation to the Apostolic See unthinkable to the majority of the suffragists.

Austria had shot her bolt, and that complication at least could be discounted; but the contest would probably have lasted a few weeks longer had not the most disquieting news reached the Sacred College regarding the activities of the secret societies which honeycombed the country. Emboldened by the judicial coma consequent on the vacancy of the Holy See, they were raising their heads above ground and openly spreading their poisonous doctrines. These alarming reports drew the reactionary party more firmly together and frightened many of the liberals into joining their opponents. It was generally felt that a prolonged conclave might endanger the security of the Holy See, and the outcome of the scare was the immediate proposal of Cardinal della Genga as candidate by the Zelanti-anti-Consalvist party, his election being rushed through before the French leader could secure a veto from the King. Della Genga had pleaded ill-health, and to discourage his adherents from pressing the burden of Papacy upon him had lifted his robes and displayed a pair of shockingly swollen and ulcerated legs. But the only effect of this distressing exhibition had been to make his followers all the more eager to confer the papal dignity upon him, and this they accomplished on September 28th, 1823, on which day he was proclaimed Pope under the name of Leo XII.

The new Pontiff was only sixty-three years of age, but a prey to so many infirmities that a short pontificate could reasonably be anticipated. He was a tall, thin, ascetic-looking man with a forbidding and melancholy countenance. He ate practically nothing; in fact he was reported to live on one plate of *polenta* a day, even that meagre portion being shared by him with his favourite cat. He fell so ill shortly after his enthronement that his life was despaired of, but to the dismay of some and the surprise of all he rallied and was soon struggling up to attend to his duties. He had no desire to live and watched himself wasting away with a serenity akin to relief. Several times he was at death's door, but for six years managed to survive the most exhausting attacks of sickness and the excruciating treatment inflicted on him by the most ignorant and clumsy of medical attendants.

Leo XII was a typical martinet who never showed a trace of affection or cordiality for anyone. He never spared himself, was a slave to duty and attended to business both spiritual and temporal with methodical punctuality. He was simple, even austere in his apparel and mode of life. He had been rather wild in his youth, and his passion for shooting had caused him, so it was said, to have killed a peasant with whom he had quarrelled about certain sporting rights. Needing auxiliaries to help him in his fight with the revolutionary secret societies, he employed the Jesuits. In compensation for the loss of such properties as his predecessors had confiscated, he bestowed on the Order important donations and several fine buildings in Rome, among others the Roman College and the Church of S. Ignatius. He also gave them every encouragement and facility to pursue their educational schemes; in fact over the entire Papal States the Jesuits enjoyed a virtual monopoly of tuition.

In France things had not been made so easy for the Society of Jesus. Charles X, minus the Pope's unflinching strength of purpose, represented on the throne of St. Louis the aims and ideals that Leo embodied on the throne of St. Peter. Both Sovereigns longed to turn back the clock to the good old days before the Revolution, and both did their utmost to re-establish an order of things which had disappeared for ever. The Paris University put up a vehement defence for its educational prerogatives, and Count Frayssinous, the Minister of Public Instruction, called on the Chamber of Deputies to prohibit the Jesuits from introducing into France their own methods of schooling. A law was passed imposing on all colleges the curriculum of the University, and subjecting them to severe governmental supervision.

As Pius V had done, Leo XII made himself intensely unpopular with his subjects by constraining them to observe endless rules and regulations concerning private as well as public matters. Not only did he prohibit vaccination, he also renewed all sorts of obsolete privileges such as that of sanctuary, and decreed that any dressmaker who sold low or transparent dresses would be *ipso facto* excommunicated. To ensure against any possible disregard of this spiritual chastisement, the penalties for wearing the offending garments were made tangible and immediate, so it is unlikely that the sempstresses' pious allegiance was often put to the test. But if the ladies had cause for complaint, the Jews fared even worse. The Pontiff denied them the right to possess property, allowing them only the shortest possible time in which to sell what they owned. He exhumed laws of the Middle Ages regarding their segregation and the marks of infamy they should wear on their clothing, and finally placed them under the power of the Inquisition. It was only logical of course that this hideous institution should have been restored, and delation not only encouraged but made compulsory. This system of anonymous denunciation was welcomed by those who, being unhampered by scruples and having a score to wipe off, were enabled thus to do so with absolute impunity; nor did the advantages which might accrue to the cunning escape the blackmailers, as can readily be imagined.

In Spain the Cortes had abolished the Inquisition in 1820, and Ferdinand VII, much as he would have liked to follow the Pontiff's lead, did not find himself in a position to do so openly; the Holy Office was revived, however, under the name of *juntas da fé* and in 1826 in Valencia a poor schoolmaster called Rizaffa who was convicted of deism was condemned to be hanged and burnt at the stake. The first part of the sentence was duly carried out on July 26th; but as an unwilling concession to the new spirit of tolerance and humanity pervading the world, symbolism was substituted for reality where the burning was concerned, flames being painted as vividly as could be contrived on the old barrel in which the body was thrust into unconsecrated ground.

The religious principles and the morality of ambassadors accredited to the Holy See by the Catholic Powers were also the object of most searching enquiries, as the Pontiff would accept none who did not conform to his high standards of orthodoxy and domestic virtues; which naturally reduced the choice very considerably and caused much embarrassment to the various European Ministers for Foreign Affairs. The Vicomte de Châteaubriand, the famous French writer, had to undergo a severe cross-examination by the Papal Nuncio in Paris before he could be given his credentials. He was compelled to make an official declaration of such stringent ultramontanism that the Duc de Blacas jokingly said that "Châteaubriand had founded a sect to which he did not belong!" Leo received the new Ambassador with stiff formality, as was his wont. The Pontiff's well-known detestation and mistrust of all things French was difficult to circumvent; but the eloquent Vicomte must have managed to do so, as Leo left him one of his favourite cats in his will—a signal mark of esteem.

With Austria the Pope was continually at loggerheads, but considering the overbearing attitude of the Court of Vienna this could scarcely have been otherwise. When the announcement of an "Anno

Santo" was made from Rome and widely advertised all over Christendom, the Austrian government refused to grant its subjects the necessary passports to attend the ceremonies, thus depriving the would-be pilgrims of inestimable spiritual benefits and the Holy See of considerable material ones.

Leo XII's death, which had been so often anticipated, took place on February 11th, 1829. Few mourned the anachronistic, pallid evocation of the great and terrifying popes of yore; the Pontiff who had floated above the realities of the XIXth century on a bank of artificial clouds which hid them from view; a flimsy fastness which was bound to disperse at the first gust of the coming revolutionary storm.

PIUS VIII (CASTIGLIONE)

1829–1830

❧

CONSALVI had died very shortly after Leo XII's accession, and his party, now called the "Progressists", was even weaker and less united than it had been in his lifetime. The Zelanti on the contrary were a compact solid phalanx knowing exactly what they wanted and why they wanted it. To guard against the remotest danger of backsliding, their leaders had exacted a solemn oath from the members of the faction never to leave their cells so long as the conclave lasted except to go to the chapel. They were to receive no visitors but those who could give the secret password, and a large white cross was to mark their doors.

For various reasons the Catholic Powers mistrusted these Knights of the White Cross, Austria because she feared that a fanatical pope would attempt to shake off her thraldom, and France because, in spite of her reactionary King, the country was tending more and more towards liberalism and the country's wishes could no longer be disregarded. Metternich attempted to form a League of the Powers to oppose the Zelanti, but the interests of the various countries were too much at variance to make it efficacious. Moreover, the diplomatic corps, except for Châteaubriand, was as incompetent as ever. Count Lützow, the Austrian Ambassador, was pleasant and civil, but his chief claim to distinction seems to have been based on his wife's fine soprano voice, though Châteaubriand complained that she always sang the same tune. Baron de Bunsen, the Prussian Minister, was absorbed in scientific research, an occupation far more congenial to him than dabbling in electoral intrigues. Prince Gagarin, the Russian representative, lived entirely on memories of his prowesses in the field of gallantry, no other subject being of the slightest interest to him. The Marquis de Labrador, the Spanish Ambassador, was a taciturn, solemn diplomat, who shunned society, went for long solitary walks, and his French colleague confessed to having failed to discover whether his thoughts were too deep to be expressed in words or whether his mind was a complete blank. Fuscaldo, the Sicilian Minister, "represented Naples as winter would represent the spring", for he was sombre and suspicious, for ever obsessed by his terror of the *carbonari*, the Sicilian brotherhood of death which had threatened his life. Funchal, the Portuguese Minister, described as being as ugly as a monkey, had an overwhelming passion for music and would have given all the conclaves which had ever been held for an aria of Mozart's.

Among these men who, whatever their specialised talents may have been, could scarcely lay claim to being distinguished diplomatists, Châteaubriand naturally stood out as the most prominent personality. He made up in supreme self-confidence for whatever he may have lacked in electoral experience and always remained convinced that he had personally managed the conclave, and had done so with remarkable skill. It was customary for the ambassadors of the great Catholic Powers to address a few words to the Sacred College before leaving the precincts of the conclave; but Châteaubriand, as the greatest French writer of his day, considered himself entitled to more than a short speech. He was not disposed to let such an opportunity escape him of displaying his gifts of eloquence, to which his perfect elocution did full justice. So for over an hour he flooded the unfortunate prelates, most of whom could scarcely understand a word of French, with torrents of the most admirable rhetoric and faultless classical periods. His sublime flights of imagination soared ever higher in the spheres of hyperbole, reaching at last a climax irreproachable, both in its logical sequence and perfection of language, but completely wasted on the bored and sleepy or exasperated cardinals who had but the vaguest glimmering of what it was all about!

The conclave set to work as soon as the preliminary ceremonies were over, and by the middle of March the French faction proposed Gregorio, whose candidature appeared promising enough. He was eighty years old and belonged to the moderate Zelanti party, not to that of the grim wearers of the white cross. He was clever, still very active and his morality was above suspicion; but he was known to be hostile to the Jesuits, and the Society would strenuously oppose his elevation to power. Albani also would be anxious to defeat any French candidate, as Châteaubriand had been so ill-advised as to let it be known that he held the veto against him. Unable to take a personal revenge on the Ambassador, the prelate was determined to work it off on his nominee and did not hesitate to spread a rumour that Gregorio, who was a Sicilian, had at one time been affiliated to the *carbonari*. Nothing could have been more absurd than such an accusation, yet it took effect on several of the most credulous suffragists and resulted in a distinct dwindling in the number of Gregorio's followers. The libel was all the more ridiculous as Gregorio was known to be a son of Charles IV of Spain, was proud of his royal parentage and held all revolutionary ideas in abhorrence. He had approached the Catholic ambassadors with a plea for support on the grounds that, being of Bourbon blood, he hoped their respective Sovereigns would favour his elevation to the Apostolic See. His exalted relatives, however, were less impressed by his claims to kinship than by his avowed enmity towards the Society of Jesus, and Charles X, behind the back of his Ambassador in Rome, was actively working to defeat him.

Châteaubriand was in despair; he could not understand why his candidate was losing ground and came to the conclusion that it must be a question of money. His despatches to Portalis bear repeated reference to the subject; a few millions, he keeps writing, would make success a certainty. But where were these few millions to come from? French finances were at a distressingly low ebb, and the Ambassador was finding it increasingly difficult to obtain occasional drafts on what was due to him personally by the Treasury. However ardent his zeal in Gregorio's cause might be, as time wore on, Châteaubriand, with an eye on the ever-increasing sum of his arrears of pay, ceased referring to the subject of electoral subsidies, while his candidate's name gradually faded away from the scrutinies.

Albani's ambition was not, as Châteaubriand imagined, to become Pope, but to secure for himself the office of Secretary of State, a far safer and more remunerative one at this juncture than the pontificate itself. While he was still searching among his colleagues for the man most likely to answer his purpose, various names, to none of which any importance was attached, appeared on the ballot papers, one of them giving rise to a somewhat unedifying incident in the chapel itself. A certain Cardinal Vidoni, who had led the most shockingly immoral life and fully realised his own unworthiness, was amazed one day to hear his name read out by the scrutator: "Is the Holy Ghost drunk?" he bluntly exclaimed! Then addressing his colleagues, he requested in most unparliamentary terms to be told "who the —— might be who was trying to make a fool of him"! His expression of puzzled irritation was so comical, and the word he had used so incongruous in such surroundings, that practically the whole assembly burst out laughing, only a few of the wearers of the white cross managing to compose their features to an expression of disgusted reprobation.

The only *papabile* Albani could find who was likely to suit his requirements was Castiglione, who had come so near to being elected in the last conclave and indeed would have been had he consented openly to disavow Consalvi's patronage. He was old and such a physical wreck that he would certainly be incapable of taking any active part in the government of his realm, and be only too relieved to hand the reins over to Albani. The undoubted influence Albani exerted over the Sacred College was due partly to his great wealth and position, and partly to his own strange forceful personality. He was not a lovable person; miserly, cynical and so dirty and ill-kempt that he was commonly known as "the pig". But this unflattering nickname, of which he was well aware, troubled him so little that he often used it when referring to himself.

Having selected his candidate and being assured of the necessary majority of votes, he now drew up an agreement by which he secured the appointment of Secretary of State, which had all along been his objective, and in addition inserted a clause by which he would have the monopoly of advancing money to the Holy See, a financial transaction which was certain to prove most advantageous to himself. Castiglione signed the treaty without demur and on March 31st became Pope Pius VIII.

Châteaubriand, under pretext that he had patronised Castiglione at the last election, claimed his share of kudos in Albani's victory and wrote to Paris in most optimistic vein, especially as he took Gregorio's nomination to the office of Grand Penitentiary as a personal act of courtesy to himself! Belatedly Pius VII's prophecy had come true; but very belatedly indeed, for the new Pontiff had only a few months to live and was not in a condition to enjoy the advantages of his high dignity. He had an excellent record: as Bishop of Cesena in

1808, acting under the Pope's orders, he had refused to take the oath of allegiance to Napoleon as King of Italy—the result being his incarceration in the Castle of Mantua, from which prison he was later transferred to another in the South of France. Freed in 1816, he had taken up his residence in Rome at the time when Pius himself had just returned from Genoa, and the similarity of their tribulations had laid the foundations of a genuine friendship between the two Napoleonic victims. The Pontiff bestowed the hat on Castiglione, and always treated him with affectionate familiarity.

As a cardinal, Castiglione had continued to live modestly, made no enemies, and although his own private life had always been irreproachable, he had shown no signs of censoriousness where others were concerned. He suffered from a very painful and distressing complaint, having perpetually suppurating sores on his neck and body, and was far too ill and feeble to do more than sign the documents presented to him by Albani, who ruled the Papal States as autocratically as though he had himself worn the triple crown. Albani allowed the reactionary impetus given to the internal policy of the Government under Leo XII to run its course, but his foreign policy was frankly pro-Austrian. He was generally feared and distrusted, and there was a violent and mutual antipathy between him and Châteaubriand. When the French Ambassador paid him his first official visit after Pius's enthronement, Albani, having pointedly and at length surveyed his caller's elegant attire and impeccable appearance, remarked: "Well, well . . . and so you have come to see the pig!" To which unconventional words of welcome the punctilious diplomat could find no adequate rejoinder!

The July revolution of 1830 in Paris, which cost Charles X his throne, reverberated all over Europe. Numerous risings occurred in the Papal States, but the insurrectionary movement was badly organised, the leaders differing as to their aims and the means of attaining them. Some wanted one prince, some another, while a third party insisted on a Republic; but they all rallied to the battle-cry of "Down with ecclesiastical tyranny!" Albani turned to Austria for assistance to subdue the Pope's rebellious subjects, and in the midst of all the turmoil, on November 30th, Pius VIII died and Albani ceased to reign.

GREGORY XVI
From a print in the British Museum after a drawing by Delaroche

GREGORY XVI (CAPPELLARI)
1831–1846

❦

AUSTRIA's suzerainty over Italy, though gratifying to her national pride, had not proved an unmixed blessing, and the Papal States in particular caused Metternich endless anxiety. At each new conclave a hostile or unreliable pontiff might be elected who would refuse to consider, or fail to grasp, the vital importance of solidarity between the Papal States and the Lombardo-Venetian realm.

So far Metternich had kept the situation well in hand, neither Consalvi nor Leo XII's Government being in a position to defy him, and Albani acting for Pius VIII having proved absolutely dependable. But in the restive and unsettled condition of the Italian Peninsula, where revolutionary ideas were daily gaining ground, the new pontiff's personality might either precipitate a catastrophe or help to maintain the *status quo*. Austria seemed to have little interference to anticipate from the other Catholic Powers at this juncture, as they did not appear to be taking any active interest in the coming election. In his allocution to the Sacred College, the Marquis de Latour-Maubourg, representing the democratic Louis Philippe, informed their Eminences that France did not intend to make use of her right of veto in this circumstance and politely expressed the conviction that only a wise and virtuous pontiff could be elected by such a wise and virtuous assembly.

During the *novemdiale*, Albani, having singled out a Camaldulian monk called Cappellari as the best qualified candidate to fulfil Austria's purpose, had convened him to a secret interview at the Villa Albani to discuss the conditions of his elevation to the Holy See. Cappellari was an Austrian subject, had always shown great deference to Albani, and there was every reason to think he would be amenable to Austrian influence. The monk was not quite as simple, though, as Albani imagined, and having supporters in other parties was determined not to bind himself to any definite undertaking with the late and would-be future Secretary of State. He agreed verbally to all

317

Albani's stipulations but stubbornly refused to commit himself to anything in writing. This self-assertive attitude struck Albani as suspicious and he broke off negotiations, immediately casting about him for a more tractable candidate.

During his twenty months of power, Albani had made himself generally unpopular and lost ground considerably with his followers. His Italian colleagues resented his unblushing servility towards Austria, and all the Bourbons had been outraged at the precipitancy with which he had recognised Louis Philippe as King of the French after the fall of Charles X. He had certainly served Metternich with exemplary fidelity, but was hated by the Austrian cardinals—as Gaisrück, their dean, bitterly resented the fact that Metternich had entrusted Albani instead of himself with the leadership of his party in the conclave, a resentment which was shared by all his compatriots. Furthermore he had quarrelled with Lützow, the Austrian Ambassador, so that outside as well as within the conclave he would find latent enmity and ill-will.

Forty-five members of the Sacred College entered the Quirinal on December 10th, forming two opposing factions, one led by Albani, the other by Bernetti, both antagonists aiming at the secretary-ship of state as personal objective. Bernetti was younger than his rival, and having been in office under Leo XII had therefore had his share of political experience. He foresaw the coming death struggle between democracy and absolutism and had even been known to speak of the fall of the temporal power in a more or less distant future as practically inevitable. His was certainly the stronger party of the two, especially as it stood for a change of régime always so welcome to the suffragists.

Albani had now decided on a prelate called Giustiniani to take the place of the disappointing Cappellari, and he sent one of his conclavists in the dead of night to inform his followers of the fact and give them orders for the next morning's scrutiny. So as to ensure his passing unnoticed Albani had forbidden the messenger to carry a light, with the result that he crept by mistake into the cubicle of one of the Spanish cardinals, who, having realised the portent of the whispered message, rushed to his leader with the news. No candidate of Albani's could be welcome to Spain, and the Spanish veto having been cautiously left in blank to be made use of at the leader's discretion, he hastily filled in Giustiniani's name and presented it to the Dean of the Sacred College just before the morning scrutiny. The routed candidate made an impassioned protest against the arbitrary interference of the Powers and, refusing to be pacified, insisted on leaving the Quirinal.

Albani had rashly discounted the danger of any veto being produced in this conclave, but Spain did not intend to let her prerogative lapse, and used it much in the same spirit as a right-of-way is closed to traffic once a year to assert its legal ownership.

Meanwhile the weeks were slipping by and the Court of Vienna, which was waiting for a dispensation to proceed with the marriage preliminaries pending between one of the Archdukes and a Princess of Naples, remonstrated with the Sacred College on their procrastination. The Roman people also showed signs of impatience, which they expressed by perpetually exploding squibs round the Quirinal, which frightened the old cardinals out of their wits, much to the amusement of their younger colleagues. The *dénouement*, however, notwithstanding all obstacles, was not far distant, as Cappellari had by now managed to enlist Bernetti's support, and his election was only a matter of days. But Albani did not consider himself beaten yet, and when a thieving conclavist sold him a letter written by Bernetti to Cappellari giving him last-moment instructions and thus exposing their plans, he made a supreme effort to defeat them. Seeing no other means of averting the danger he decided that the only solution consisted in becoming Pope himself. He therefore called on all his adherents to attend a secret meeting which would enable him to ascertain what his chances of success really were.

The Quirinal being riddled with spies, Lützow, as might be expected, was informed within a few hours of Albani's new scheme. Now not only was the Austrian Ambassador a personal enemy of Albani's, but he also knew that Metternich, much as he valued the late Secretary of State's services and much as he desired him to retain the post under the future Pontiff, would certainly disapprove of his own elevation to the Apostolic See. Metternich had no illusions as to Albani's reliability where his own interests were not concerned, and as Sovereign Pontiff he might adopt quite a different policy. Lützow therefore took it upon himself to write a note to Albani threatening him with Austria's disavowal if he persisted in his project. Albani was

not powerful enough to take such a risk and fell back on the candidature of Pacca, a prelate as old and decrepit as Pius VIII had been,
and the battle now entered on its last and decisive phase. The victory
would be not so much with the candidate who carried off the papal
crown as with the one who secured the secretaryship of state.

There was, as we have seen, no loyalty to Albani in the Austrian
faction and from that quarter came the blow which finally destroyed
him. Gaisrück and Lützow between them, unaware that Cappellari
was Bernetti's nominee and that they had been prompted to do so by
one of his confederates, persuaded Metternich to give the wily monk
his covert support. Betrayed by his own followers, Albani naturally
failed to secure the necessary majority for Pacca, and on February
1st, 1831, Cappellari was elected Pope, choosing the name of
Gregory XVI.

The new Pontiff was tall and lusty, with a coarse rubicund countenance; the typical gormandising, bibulous, hoydenish monk of the
irreverent French novelist come to life in the XIXth century. He
lacked both poise and dignity, and his favourite recreation consisted
in playing blind-man's-buff with the least aged of the cardinals. So
roughly did he treat his unfortunate playfellows that in his exuberance
he knocked down Cardinal Soglia one fine day, the shock being so
violent that the victim almost died of it. In another mood he would
order all the palace servants to be assembled in the courtyard and
from a window would throw down handfuls of money to them,
laughing till his sides ached to watch the ensuing scrum. The only
person he showed any affection for was his barber Morrone, who was
his most trusted adviser and confidant. This man and his wife lived
in the Quirinal, where the couple occupied a luxurious apartment,
and the christenings of their numerous progeny were made occasions
of important Court functions to which the Sacred College and the
diplomatic corps were solemnly bidden. The Romans of course made
the Pope's predilection for his barber's offspring the subject of endless jokes and pasquinades of the usual disrespectful nature.

Bernetti did not remain long in office—Austria disapproved of his
liberal tendencies and Gregory, having neither the strength of mind
nor the loyalty to resist the pressure put upon him by Metternich,
asked Bernetti to resign his post. The indignant Secretary of
State flatly refused to comply with this demand, which he denounced

as violating a contract to which, in honour, the ungrateful Pontiff stood committed. Gregory said no more, as indeed there was nothing much he could say, but as soon as Bernetti had left the presence His Holiness wrote him a letter officially accepting his resignation. This he sent by the Dean of the Sacred College, who was also entrusted with another to Cardinal Lambruschini notifying him of his appointment to the secretaryship of state. Bernetti had perforce to accept his dismissal, his resentment at such a flagrant breach of faith being perhaps tempered by the knowledge that Gregory had given himself the most rigid and tyrannical of monitors.

Lambruschini's appearance was in perfect conformity with his disposition. His tall gaunt frame never relaxed, his haughtiness never unbent. He was gifted with a clear perceptive intellect and his nature was determined and steely. His diplomatic calling had taken him to many Courts, he knew the world and despised it. His policy was ultra-conservative with an avowed hatred for France, whence had come the epidemic of sedition, and his attitude was that of an inexorable disciplinarian.

No doubt Austria had imposed him on Gregory, for it seems incredible that the Pope should himself have selected this prelate whose aims, tastes and character were so diametrically opposed to his own, as the holder of an office which brought them into perpetual contact. On the other hand Gregory may have been personally impressed by those very characteristics which he himself lacked so utterly and have acted on an impulse of genuine esteem and admiration. Whatever the reasons which had prompted his nomination, Lambruschini soon gained complete ascendancy over his incompetent Sovereign, who was so overawed by his formidable Minister that he agreed to all his suggestions before the words were well out of his mouth, and hastened to sign all documents put before him, scarcely daring to read them. If he had had too much to drink, which was not a rare occurrence, the mere sight of Lambruschini's red robe would sober him in an instant.

And yet Gregory XVI was not unprincipled nor was he a nonentity. He had the reputation of being an able theologian and had written several scholarly works on the subject; but he had no talent for statecraft and not a trace of political acumen. He was feckless, too easily influenced by his familiar and vulgar associates, and more than willing to let another shoulder the responsibilities and cares of government. So Lambruschini ruled and time hung heavily on the Pontiff's hands.

Morrone, the barber, searching for some means of amusing and occupying his master, now had an inspiration. Why should not the Holy Father take a trip through the Papal States? He could worship at miraculous shrines, visit many places of interest under pleasant and favourable circumstances, and his travels would bring him into direct contact with his people. The Pope was so delighted with the notion that he actually defied Lambruschini, who disapproved of the plan, and triumphantly asserted his determination to please himself in the matter. The Secretary of State of course had to remain at his post, and the Pontiff, like a truant schoolboy, freed from censorious and oppressive supervision, enjoyed himself whole-heartedly. His peregrinations lasted six weeks and cost the Treasury 400,000 crowns, which fact did not deter him from renewing the experience in 1843 with equal satisfaction and at no less an expenditure.

He welcomed every opportunity of getting away from Rome and would prolong his residence at Castel Gandolfo far beyond the customary limits. He grew yearly less in touch with State matters and more absorbed by the material satisfactions in which circumstances allowed him to indulge. Epicurean gratifications assumed tremendous importance in his life, and he would travel miles to taste a celebrated local dish or to enjoy one of the famous *maigre* dinners cooked by Capuchin monks, especially by those of the Genzano monastery. All his princely neighbours in the country, such as the Torlonia, Barberini and Orsini, were expected to provide at least one banquet a season for him, and as the expense of entertaining His Holiness and his entire retinue was stupendous, the Sovereign's condescension in gracing their boards was, one presumes, only moderately prized by his subjects.

Meanwhile Lambruschini governed with an iron hand, and conspiracies, risings and general discontent were the result. The insurrections at Viterbo in 1836, in various parts of the Legations in 1840, at Ravenna in 1843 and Rimini in 1845, were followed by wholesale executions and severe sentences to the hulks, hard labour or exile, but still the country seethed with unrest.

On June 1st, 1846, Gregory died after a very short illness. His end was peaceful and edifying. Under different circumstances he might have been a good Pontiff but the times in which he was called to his high dignity were times of transition and ferment that he had not the breadth of mind or ability to cope with. Nothing in his upbringing or past experience had fitted him to assume the crushing responsibilities, or to face the problems, which beset the papal government at such a crucial period of Italian history. He did not attempt a task of which he knew himself incapable, and, thus reduced to the status of a figurehead, with a figurehead's empty hours of leisure, and encouraged thereunto by his vulgar and sycophantic *entourage*, he allowed his coarser instincts free play. But it must be borne in mind that the conventual code of propriety, in his days, dealt very indulgently with gastronomical excesses and looked upon such transgressions as mere peccadilloes, the penalty for which rested more appropriately with outraged Nature than with a higher tribunal.

PIUS IX
From a print in the British Museum

🐚

By his arbitrary remapping of the Italian Peninsula Napoleon doubt-less laid the foundations of United Italy. Without any apparent difficulty age-old republics were transformed overnight into king-doms, principalities into republics, and the ecclesiastical government of the Papal States was taken over by civilian officials. Yet these amazing changes seemed scarcely to affect the even tenor of life, which con-tinued to flow as regularly and in some cases even more easily than it had done before. Neighbouring States which had been hereditary foes discovered to their surprise that they could live together on terms of peace and even of amity under a common rule. Moreover, con-scription, introduced into Italy by Napoleon, brought the natives of various provinces into fraternal contact through a community of hardships, danger and glory; it freed them from parochial prejudices and to a great extent from the domination of the priests. It improved their physical powers of endurance and broadened their outlook. They were now capable of focussing on a more distant horizon, and of realising the immense advantages to be derived from the formation of a great and united nation, which would give the lie to Metter-nich's aphorism that Italy was merely a geographical expression.

The tone adopted by the various ephemeral régimes imposed on the Peninsula since the beginning of the XIXth century also played an important part in the development of these nationalistic ten-dencies, as the intruders invariably courted popularity by appealing to the patriotism of the native populations. The following proclama-tion issued by Murat is typical of them all: "Italians! Providence has at last enabled you to become a free nation. Henceforward from the Alps to the straits of Scylla only one cry should be heard: Independent Italy!"

The cry was indeed heard, and to some purpose; for it produced such patriots as Manin, Mazzini and Garibaldi, albeit they gave to the clarion call a very different interpretation from the one Murat himself had in view. These men wanted no sovereigns either human or divine, and above all they wanted no foreign rulers not excepting French heroes; but equality, freedom and justice for all under a republican system of government. These Utopian aspirations had been exasperated by the violent reaction following on the restoration of the various ruling houses and of the temporal power of the Holy See, after the Congress of Vienna. Petrucelli asserts that between 1821 and 1846, 200,000 people suffered punishment for political offences either by death or by life sentences of imprisonment, and that over one million and a half were subject to constant police supervision.

Under Austrian sway in Italy, schooling was reduced to a minimum on the principle enunciated by the Emperor that faithful and not scholarly subjects were what a monarch needed. Militarism of course was promptly suppressed. Italians were no longer allowed to shoulder a musket, but they were encouraged to become *sbirri* (policemen) and especially to join the spying service. The armed forces were composed exclusively of Austrians and Swiss. Newspapers were virtually abolished and the censorship of books was so severe that few escaped the ban. Special tribunals sat permanently to try political offenders and the gallows were never removed from the main piazza in all Italian towns during this reign of terror. It was difficult enough for the accused to get a hearing anywhere in Italy; but in the Papal States vindication was a practical impossibility, as Leo XII decreed that only the Latin language should be used and spoken in the law courts, which debarred the great majority even from following the course of the prosecution.

As no meetings of any kind were tolerated, the masses were naturally driven to join the secret societies, which they did by the thousands, their legitimate yearning for freedom soon degenerating into a fierce hatred of all authority. The intellectuals, who cared little for political liberty as the republicans understood it, had yet an equally forcible longing for independence of thought and religious emancipation. Poets were never more numerous or poetry more popular in Italy than at this time. Bards sang everywhere in rousing rhythm of liberty, glory, laurels and blood; or striking the lyrical chord, they wept over the desecrated soil of the Fatherland or mourned the heroes who died for it. They kindled the flame of patriotism in the young and fanned it into a conflagration. Poems written in the dialects of the various provinces reached the most remote villages, bringing them into touch with the new nationalistic spirit, and in the Papal States, where the Austrian troops were always called upon to repress popular risings, the Holy See and the foreign oppressors were linked together in the minds of the people, who held them both in equal abhorrence.

The members of the Sacred College knew exactly how matters stood and the greater number of them fully recognised the necessity of the Holy See steering a more liberal course to conciliate the lower orders and reinforce the defences of the now tottering temporal power. But the European Governments, viewing the matter each one from its own particular standpoint, saw no object in any immediate change of policy: Guizot, addressing the Chambre des Pairs, declaring that no modifications beyond the Alps either political or territorial would be advantageous to France; and Lord Palmerston sending a message to Metternich to the effect that Her Majesty's Government was of opinion that the conventions of the Congress of Vienna should be adhered to in Italy as well as in other European countries, and that no alterations should be made in the boundaries agreed to in that treaty without the sanction of the signatory Powers.

This determination of the European Cabinets to preserve the existing order of things having become known to the suffragists, influenced many of them to take a more optimistic view of the situation. Nevertheless a number of reforms were absolutely indispensable and there was no reason to think the Powers would be averse to their adoption, even Metternich admitting the necessity of certain concessions being made to modernism. The voice of the country was anyhow too clamorous to be altogether ignored. From every city in the Papal States petitions were reaching the College of Cardinals pleading for urgent judicial and other reforms and for a general amnesty.

Elaborate precautions were taken to preserve order during the coming conclave. Austrian troops occupied various strategic points and four Austrian battleships in the port of Ancona brought their broadsides to bear menacingly on the town; while reliable and determined churchmen were entrusted with the provisional government of the provinces pending the Cardinal Legates' absence in Rome.

On June 14th, after various *contretemps* had delayed their departure, the assembled suffragists filed out of the church of S. Silvester on Monte Cavallo to enter the Quirinal. Rain was falling heavily and the older cardinals, fearful of catching cold, gathered up their robes and hurried along, jostling their colleagues, and being in turn jostled by the crowd as they broke the ranks, quickening their pace to a run. The younger prelates naturally followed their elders' lead and the procession, which should have been so stately and imposing, degenerated into a most undignified scramble. Cardinals, conclavists and onlookers, all equally drenched and bedraggled, raced along higgledy-piggledy, stumbling into puddles, hopping over gutters; the cardinals doggedly panting out the "Veni Creator" while their unwelcome retinue, composed largely of the Roman scum, vociferated threats, witticisms and abuse at them as they ran.

The Sacred College, now immured within the Quirinal, formed itself immediately into three groups. Lambruschini and Bernetti, the two late Secretaries of State, each led an opposing faction, and between the two hovered the "moderates" who would inevitably be swayed sooner or later in the one or the other direction. Lambruschini was himself Austria's nominee and Bernetti's candidate was Mastai, a prelate belonging to the moderate party. Diplomats played a very secondary part in this conclave, which only lasted forty-eight hours, the French Ambassador, Count Rossi, being the only one to take any active interest in the proceedings. He was anxious to secure the election of Cardinal Gizzi, who was both hostile to Austria and to the Jesuits, this latter idiosyncrasy appealing to him very specially, there being just then in France a general anxiety to rid the country once more of the intriguing fraternity. Rossi worked so hard in Gizzi's cause that he was nicknamed by his colleagues the "Count of the Holy Ghost"; albeit his efforts were all in vain, for it was obvious at the very first scrutiny that the contest would be a straightforward one between Lambruschini and Mastai.

Bernetti having been informed that Gaisrück was on his way from Vienna bearing the Austrian veto against Mastai, fully realised that he would have to obtain the necessary majority for his candidate within a few hours or resign himself to Lambruschini's elevation to the Holy See. With incredible energy and notwithstanding the fact that he was a dying man, Bernetti managed within the short space of time at his disposal to overcome all difficulties. This success was due entirely to his personal efforts, as Mastai himself made no attempt to recruit any adherents, gave no promises and maintained an attitude of serene aloofness.

In his heart, however, Mastai was not as indifferent as he wished to appear. At the decisive ballot he happened to be one of the scrutators, and his emotion was such that his voice failed him while reading out the result of the votes. He even begged to be relieved of the task; but as such a step would have invalidated the election, he was prevailed upon to remain at his post, and so enjoyed the rare experience of announcing his own election to the Sacred College.

When Pope Pius IX, as Mastai was in future to be known, appeared on the loggia of the Quirinal to bless the waiting throng, he was received without much enthusiasm by the Romans, who knew little about him and had hoped for the election of Cardinal Micara, a special favourite of the people. That first coldness, however, soon wore off; it was rumoured that Pius was liberal-minded, generous and anxious to promote the welfare of his subjects. Prompted it is said by Mazzini's confederates, who had made it their business to discover the vulnerable chink in the pontifical armour, the Romans now uproariously acclaimed and applauded the Sovereign Pontiff on every possible occasion, continually clamouring for his appearance on the loggia of the palace, where he showed himself willingly enough to distribute smiles and blessings. He was genuinely solicitous of his people's happiness but their ovations turned his head, as they were meant to do. He found it an irresistible temptation to raise storms of enthusiasm by granting a concession here and there; for the Pontiff's weakness, a weakness, alas! which was to deliver him bound hand and foot to his enemies, was an inordinate thirst for approbation and popularity.

Petitions now rained at the Quirinal and bit by bit Pius yielded to all the mob's demands, being cheered to the echo in consequence. After the demolition of the ghetto and such-like minor requests had been conceded, came a persistent cry for a general amnesty and later for the expulsion of the Jesuits, which went sorely against the grain but which Pius dared not refuse. He became the idol of his people; they surged round his carriage whenever he left the Quirinal, occasionally, such as after the granting of the general amnesty, unharnessing the horses to drag the lumbering coach themselves. They yelled themselves hoarse with *vivas* while the ultramontane party looked on with grim disapprobation.

Pius IX's early career had been more chequered than that of most pontiffs. His ambitions as a young man had been centred on a military career. Born at Sinigaglia in 1792, the son of Count Mastai-Ferretti, he had grown up during the Napoleonic era when the youth of Italy had been stirred by martial enthusiasm and patriotic ardour. His elder brothers were in the army and Giovanni Mastai hoped to follow in their footsteps. Owing to his delicate health his early education had been very neglected. As a young man he learnt to fence and to ride, and added to a smattering of the gentler arts of music and poetry these superficial accomplishments made up the sum-total of his proficiency.

He was a fine handsome lad with a craving for admiration. To attract notice he had adopted a peculiar style of dress, wearing a grey frock-coat, pantaloons with broad stripes, spurs and an open collar *à la* Byron with a fly-away scarlet cravat. He always sported a flower in his buttonhole, and in this get-up would swagger past the Sinigaglia cafés smoking a huge cigar; the women adored him and he was accounted the local Don Juan.

But Giovanni's chances of a brilliant future were not as promising as might at first appear, inasmuch as he had from infancy been subject to epileptic fits so there could be no question of his joining the regular army and covering himself with glory on the field of battle. The best he could hope for was to obtain a commission in the Pope's Noble Guards, and with this object in view he set out for Rome. His family being distantly connected with that of Pius VII he would probably have secured the coveted appointment and history would never have recorded his name, had he not had a sudden seizure in the street, probably brought on by the unwonted excitement. The unfortunate occurrence having reached the ears of the Commandant of the Pope's Guards, that officer decided that it was inadvisable to admit him to the corps in question.

Mastai's despair at having his hopes thus dashed was so bitter that he had, it was rumoured, contemplated drowning himself in the Tiber, only being saved from such an untimely end by a most opportune meeting with a friend of his father's, who pointed out to him with great good sense that if military glory had been his objective he had nothing to regret on that score, as patrolling the Vatican or escorting the pontifical carriage could scarcely be accounted deeds of valour. As for the showy and attractive uniform which the young man in his childish vanity had probably fancied himself as wearing so proudly, surely he could in those days of sartorial licence have contrived an individual touch here and there about his person reminiscent of the brilliant raiment he had so narrowly missed wearing. Mastai's intense despondency can easily be explained by the humiliating publicity of his accident and of his failure, and by the dread he must naturally have felt that his terrible complaint would preclude him from ever making his mark in the world, and would restrict the field of his activities, whatever they were to be, within the diminutive confines of his native town.

But this life sentence of Sinigaglia was not to be passed on him after all, for Pius VII, who was kindness itself, having been informed of his young relative's distress, offered to grant him the necessary dispensations if he chose to become a priest. Considering circumstances, this certainly seemed not only a wise course to adopt but even an un-hoped-for opportunity, so on December 18th, 1818, Giovanni Mastai took Holy Orders. It was concordant with his ardent temperament that he should throw himself heart and soul into his new avocation. He resolutely exchanged the gaudy forage-cap for the black shovel hat, and discharged his ecclesiastical duties with thoroughness and genuine religious zeal. Being gifted with a powerful and musical speaking voice and a natural fluency of speech, he soon acquired a reputation of eloquence which drew large crowds to his sermons. An adept at obtaining the best possible effects from circumambient conditions, he would preach preferably in the evening, when the shadows gathered about the church and a carefully contrived shaft of light threw his prepossessing features into high relief against the sombre background. Nor did he hesitate to resort to melodramatic means of impressing his audience, such as setting a skull with a lighted candle in it beside him in the pulpit while all the church remained in dark-ness, his own pale, handsome countenance alone being visible as he addressed the gleaming death's head.

His career was a successful one, honours following in easy suc-cession. His attitude to the world in general at this time of his life was one of effusive goodwill. That his friendly protestations were often mere empty words some had already discovered, but the majority accepted him at his face valuation and he was generally popular and universally respected. If Mastai was a *faux bonhomme* there could, however, be no doubt as to the sincerity of his beliefs. His faith was of the quality which moves mountains. It was the simple, blind, uncritical faith of the uneducated. His credulity regarding miracles was astounding. He accepted the most outrageous, grotesque hoaxes unquestioningly as divine manifestations; as for instance when, as Pope Pius IX, he approved of the publication of a document giving the contents of "A true letter of Jesus Christ sent by the hand of a Guardian Angel to a girl called Bridget, printed in letters of gold and found at the foot of a crucifix", etc., and proceeding to describe the miracles which it had accomplished!

The Pontiff's lack of discrimination is to be deplored, but it was the outcome of his intrinsic piety untempered by natural discernment. His mental capacities were distinctly limited; he never read a book and his intellectual activities were restricted to the writing of diffuse and sometimes scarcely intelligible encyclicals such as the one defining the dogma of the Virgin's Immaculate Conception. Had his judgment been as good as his intentions he might have done great things; but like those people who make pets of tiger cubs and are under the delusion that they have domesticated the pretty little creatures, Pius imagined he had tamed the monster of sedition because it licked his feet and fawned on him when he had fed it. But the time came when, sure of its strength and prompted by its predatory instincts, it behaved exactly as playful tiger cubs do when they grow up, and suddenly turned on its keeper.

Pius IX had been living for two years in this fool's paradise when in 1848 Europe burst into revolutionary flames. Louis Philippe fled from Paris, Metternich from Vienna, and Italy leapt at the chance of throwing off the Austrian yoke. Charles Albert of Savoy, supported by the copious good wishes and very small reinforcements sent to him by his fellow rulers in the Peninsula, attacked the Austrian forces, scoring a couple of victories at the outset of the campaign. But Radetzky, having been given command of the Austrian army, turned the tables on the Italians, inflicting a crushing defeat on them at Custozza.

Meanwhile the Pope, finding his subjects thoroughly out of hand, called on Count Rossi, the erstwhile French Ambassador who had now been naturalised a Roman, to undertake the secretaryship of state. Rossi was clever and enlightened, with a sound knowledge of Italian politics, but he was never given a chance to display his ability as the people, disapproving of his nomination, simply murdered him on the steps of the Quirinal. From his windows Pius could see the mob which had acclaimed him so deliriously and which he had taken for a lot of boisterous but good-hearted and loving children, surging this way and that waving banners inscribed with threatening demands, while their mutinous cries and imprecations swelled to an angry roar. The Holy Father was utterly taken aback at such unmistakable symptoms of ill-will, and unable to come to any decision as to the best course to adopt under such critical circumstances. Should he face the monster or more cautiously give it the slip? He hesitated, debated the question with his household, conferred with those diplomats who had managed to gain access to the Quirinal, and finally decided on flight. He managed to leave the palace undetected, disguised as a servant, and joined the Countess Spaur, the wife of the Bavarian minister, who was waiting for him with her family just outside Rome, and who smuggled him safely over the Neapolitan frontier.

As soon as his escape became known, the Romans declared the Pontiff-King deposed and proclaimed a Republic. For a year Pius remained the King of Sicily's guest at Gaeta, when France, wishing for political reasons to restore him to his throne, sent an expeditionary force to escort him back to his capital.

It was a very sobered and disgruntled Pope who returned to the Quirinal in 1849; gone was his popularity and with it his illusions and his liberalism. His subjects made it plain that they now detested him, and the rumour having spread that he had the evil eye they kept well out of his way, which, all things considered, was distinctly to the Pontiff's advantage. Pius, disgusted at so much ingratitude, handed over practically the entire responsibility of the temporal government to his new minister Antonelli, throwing all his energies into the spiritual guidance of his flock.

Evidence of his industry was soon forthcoming. In 1854 he promulgated the doctrine of the Immaculate Conception; in 1864 appeared the Syllabus, and in 1869 he assembled the Oecumenical Council to declare the dogma of Papal Infallibility. Many members of the Council were opposed to this new tenet, but after they had been browbeaten into either acquiescing or taking their departure, this portentous article of faith was triumphantly proclaimed to the world at large, causing several spectacular secessions from the Church of Rome and other no less spectacular submissions. This satisfactory conclusion was reached not a minute too soon, for war now broke out between France and Germany and the council was adjourned *sine die*.

The French troops were hastily recalled from Rome and the Pope's lieges rolled up their sleeves and were preparing to deal with their Sovereign, when King Victor Emmanuel of Piedmont, now promoted King of Italy, entered Pius IX's capital, so soon to be declared his own. The Pontiff shut himself up in the Vatican, where he remained unmolested, the Italian Government treating him with far more deference and consideration than he would have been likely to receive at the hands of his own people. The King's ministers did everything in their power to conciliate the fallen monarch, and consistently adhered to Cavour's principle of a Free Church in a Free State. The diplomats accredited to the Holy See continued to transact business with the Vatican and orders were issued by Victor Emmanuel that on all occasions Pius should receive the honours due to a monarch. The Government offered to provide largely for the Pope's material welfare, and he was given the free use of the Vatican, the Lateran, and the papal villa of Castel Gandolfo.

That, smarting under the loss of his Kingdom, Pius should have refused these proposals, was only to be expected. As regarded a civil list there was no need for him to put himself under any obligation to the enemy, as Peter's Pence would certainly make him independent of any State subsidy; the "captivity" of the Holy Father, properly exploited by the clergy all over the world, constituting a sound capital producing a splendid rent-roll. The more distant and gullible faithful imagined the Sovereign Pontiff as confined in a dungeon loaded with chains, and naturally wished to relieve his distress. The Republics of South America especially contributed enormous sums towards the fund, Ecuador even decreeing that half the State revenues should be devoted to the Pope's maintenance.

Poor Victor Emmanuel came in for endless abuse which he felt very keenly; he always hated having to play the part of spoliator but could not well help himself. It is a notorious fact that since the restoration of the temporal power in 1816, it was only maintained at the point of foreign bayonets; by the Austrians at first and the French later. The real temporal power had not survived the French occupation and the semblance of it, bolstered up by Metternich, could not endure for long. As to Napoleon III, he was merely, under the cloak of reverence for the Vicar of Christ, attempting to postpone the unification of Italy, which did not suit his views. All Italians were strenuously opposed to ecclesiastical rule and its ultimate collapse was inevitable.

Deep in his heart Pius must have felt some regard for Victor Emmanuel's individuality as is evidenced by several instances which occurred at the time of the King's death; but towards the Italian Monarchy he never disarmed; anathemas, complaints, indignant appeals to the faithful flooded the Catholic press; its readers never being allowed to forget the "Roman Question" and the duties it imposed on them. In Italy it only existed for a restricted set of the Roman aristocracy whose position or offices were so closely bound up with the Holy See that their solidarity was inevitable. As to the people and the great majority of the upper classes, they rallied enthusiastically round the flag of United Italy and were loyal to the King who had brought it into being.

If his late subjects harboured such vindictiveness against Pius IX as reports freely circulated abroad would have had the public believe, it in no way reflected on the new Government. It could have had no imaginable object in encouraging any hostile manifestations which could only bring onus and discredit on itself. The Italian Government was prepared to put a military escort at the Pope's disposal to ensure his safety at any time he might wish to leave the Vatican, but he stubbornly ignored the offer. And just as a few decades later martyrs to other causes refused nourishment while the outer world jeered or prayed, so did Pius IX refuse the freedom which, unlike food, could not be forcibly administered to him.

One cannot help nevertheless feeling great compassion for Pius IX during those last sad years of his pontificate. Considering how passionately he loved the limelight and how much he had revelled in his pseudo-popularity he must have drained the cup of bitterness when, from his Vatican fastness, ignored and almost forgotten by the masses, he heard the burst of acclamations which always greeted the appearance of the man who now reigned in his stead. On occasions of special public rejoicings such as the opening of the first Parliament; when the guns of S. Angelo boomed, the church bells pealed and a roar of cheering rose and fell, marking the progress of the King through the streets of his capital, the echoes of these demonstrations of loyalty to the new régime must have roused in the aged Pontiff unbearably sad memories of more fortunate days.

He settled down to his life of voluntary reclusion, however, without much apparent difficulty. His days were fully occupied with his religious duties, the granting of audiences, and the writing of numerous encyclicals. He had occasional moods of irritability and depression, but was usually cheerful and much addicted to the making of utterly childish puns. His disposition was essentially sociable, he could not bear solitude and was at his best when receiving the pilgrims who came in droves to kiss his feet and who never failed to succumb to his undeniable charm of manner. He was benevolent, impulsive and in a manner shrewd. His affections and sensibility, which had never been deep-rooted, wore very thin indeed as he advanced in age. The death of his minister Antonelli, who had been his constant companion for years, left him apparently quite unmoved, to the surprise and relief of his attendants, who had dreaded the ill-effects such a shock might have on his enfeebled constitution.

Pius IX and Victor Emmanuel I died within three weeks of one another early in 1878. The ceremonies of the King's funeral were scarcely over and the royal guests, whom the Pope had peremptorily refused to receive, had only just left Rome, when Pius followed his "sacrilegious despoiler" to the grave; the Pontiff's obsequies being attended with all the splendour and pageantry compatible with altered circumstances. And so were linked in death, as they must always be in history, the names of the first Sovereign of United Italy and the last Pope-King of Rome.

LEO XIII
From the painting by Lenbach, Pinakothek, Munich

CONCLUDING CHAPTER

LEO XIII AND HIS SUCCESSORS

✥

SINCE the conclave which raised Pius VI to the Holy See in 1775 no papal election had taken place in the Vatican. All the paraphernalia employed for the erection of the cubicles had remained stored away in the attics of the Quirinal, nor would it really have been possible to make use of it in the older building, where the cells had to be contrived on quite different lines. Five hundred workmen—masons, carpenters, joiners and upholsterers—under the supervision of an architect, worked feverishly night and day to have everything in readiness by February 18th, on which date the Sacred College was due to enter the conclave. The innumerable parasitic idlers who nested in the Vatican were pressed into service, being made to hold the workmen's lanterns, to shift furniture and run errands. The venerable edifice echoed with the sound of sawing, hammering, knocking and shouting, the hustle and pandemonium increasing in intensity as the final day drew near.

Meanwhile the busybodies shook their heads and hinted at mysterious dangers likely to encompass the assembly if it held its sittings in Rome. Various places of safety were suggested in Austria, France or Spain, and Cardinal Manning, who considered himself the leader of the ultramontanes, urged his colleagues to migrate to Malta, where they would be under the protection of the British flag. At first the majority of the suffragists, influenced by the genuine or assumed pessimism of the wiseacres, were in favour of setting out at once for foreign parts; but as time slipped by and no official invitations reached the Sacred College from any of the European Powers, the cardinals began to doubt the wisdom and even the feasibility of the plan. The Catholic monarchs on whose hospitality they had counted as a matter of course not only evinced no desire whatever to welcome them within their dominions, but went so far as to advise them strongly to remain in Rome. Most of the European cabinets had urgent problems

337

to deal with just then in various parts of the world and were only mildly concerned with the papal election. Moreover, being on good terms with the Italian Government, they were naturally disinclined to meddle in the matter. So strongly did the British Government feel on the subject that Sir Augustus Paget, the English Ambassador to the Quirinal, was instructed to inform the Italian Foreign Secretary that Cardinal Manning's proposal to hold the conclave in Malta had been made entirely on that prelate's own initiative.

In view of the ostensible aloofness of the Powers and of the difficulty experienced in selecting a suitable locality abroad, the cardinals at last decided to hold the conclave in Rome. This determination had not been arrived at without endless arguments and deliberations during which such absurd suggestions were put forward that Cardinal Ferrieri, losing patience one day, exclaimed sarcastically: "Why not in a balloon, then?" The dread of the older prelates for the trials and hardships of a long journey had proved a great deterrent, and the enormous expenditure such a move would have entailed also weighed heavily in the balance. On the other hand, the Italian Government had guaranteed the security of the conclavists, and their complete immunity from any form of interference, so it was becoming increasingly difficult to keep up the fiction of the perils which beset them. The Sacred College therefore adopted the only sensible course open to it, and thus the strenuous labours of the Roman workmen were not wasted.

When the prelates entered the Vatican on February 19th, 1878, everything was in readiness for their reception. No trouble or expense had been spared to minimise the discomforts of their claustration. A profusion of gas-jets sizzled round every corner dispelling the winter gloom, electric bells had been installed in all the cubicles, and the cubicles themselves been considerably enlarged. They were no longer the box-like contraptions of yore but real rooms in many cases, and where that had not been possible decent-sized cells had been contrived. Communal kitchens established within the precincts of the conclave itself precluded the necessity of the cardinals' meals being brought from their residences, thus obviating the confusion and disturbance at the wickets inevitable under the old system. All their Eminences had agreed to this arrangement with the exception of Cardinal Hohenlohe, who detested macaroni, and being something of a gourmet insisted on being supplied with food cooked in his own palace.

Owing to the increased facilities for locomotion sixty-two prelates, almost the largest number ever gathered together for a papal election, answered the Camerlingo's summons to Rome. Under Pius IX's long pontificate the Sacred College had been virtually renewed, only four of the cardinals having ever attended a conclave before; and in spite of the improvements made in the accommodation, many of the inmates complained bitterly of the discomfort of their quarters. Cardinal de Falloux declared that the smell in his room was intolerable and that he would sleep in the passage as long as the conclave lasted. If he did so, it was only for a couple of nights, as the whole proceedings were over in thirty-six hours; in fact, had it not been for the inexperience of the suffragists, the business would have been concluded even sooner, but they invalidated the first scrutinies by committing every sort of blunder imaginable.

The loss of the temporal power, and the pose of voluntary captivity bequeathed to his successor by Pius IX, had considerably reduced the number of aspirants to the Sovereign Pontificate, and several openly declared their unwillingness to shoulder a burden for which there were now no material compensations. The total absence of simony and of political intrigues resulted in the suffragists arriving at a rapid and satisfactory conclusion, there being now no obstacle to their choosing and electing the man they considered the most worthy to wear the triple crown.

Practically all the cardinals entered the conclave with their minds already made up as to whom they would give their votes. The majority were in favour of Pecci, the Camerlingo, who had shown so much competence and decision during his short period of administration. He was generally credited with possessing the very qualities needed at this juncture to make the perfect Pope. His morality, godliness, rectitude and ability were unquestioned. A long and successful diplomatic career had particularly fitted him for the task of establishing friendly relations with the foreign Powers, some of which had been on distinctly bad terms with Pius IX. Pecci was in every way the exact antithesis of the late Pontiff, being as quiet and reserved as Pius had been impulsive and exuberant; as studious, erudite and witty as the other had been shallow, uncultured and jocular. Physically also he contrasted strikingly with the late Pope, being tall and emaciated, with a long nose and a rare, subtle smile. Pius had frankly disliked him and Antonelli no less frankly detested him, so that several of the cardinals who owed their hats to the late Secretary of State opposed Pecci out of loyalty to their benefactor's memory. Their candidate, Franchi, however, realising the futility of battling against overwhelming odds, advised his adherents to vote for Pecci and himself led a movement to elect his rival by adoration.

After showing great reluctance to accept the dignity thrust upon him, Pecci was at last induced to yield to his colleagues' solicitations and chose the name of Leo XIII, his election, which had been confidently anticipated, being generally well received.

Besides his moral qualifications the new Pontiff's dignity of bearing, his distinguished appearance, his emaciation and perfect poise made him the ideal representative of his exalted spiritual office. He had shown remarkable proficiency and determination while delegate at Benevento in handling the turbulent nobility of the district, and had succeeded in stamping out brigandage in face of systematic obstruction on the part of local magnates and even of his fellow-churchmen. A great deal was expected of his good sense and self-reliance where the relations to be established between the Holy See and the Quirinal were concerned; but these hopes were doomed to disappointment. He adhered to his predecessor's policy of claustration and rigid hostility towards the Italian Government. He may in a measure have been influenced to adopt this line of conduct by the ultramontane atmosphere of the Vatican; but considering his strength of mind it is more likely that he acted on his own initiative in accordance with his fundamentally conservative proclivities.

Leo XIII belonged to a generation which considered the temporal power as inherent in the Roman Pontificate; a generation which had witnessed the repeated triumph of the Holy See over a series of vicissitudes. He would therefore consider that in acquiescing with what had come to pass, he might be jeopardising whatever chances the future might hold of a restoration of the temporal power. Consequently he could not but adopt the pose of a protesting victim, which was to become the traditional attitude of the Holy See until the Treaty of the Lateran in 1929 rang down the curtain on the protracted monodrama. It must also be borne in mind that at the consistory held immediately after Pius IX's death all the cardinals had sworn "to defend the rights, prerogatives and possessions of the temporal power of the Holy See *usque ad effusionem sanguinis*" and Leo was not the type of man to disregard an oath.

The sedentary existence which the Pope was henceforth to lead and which he believed would prove so injurious to his health, seemed on the contrary to suit his constitution most admirably, for although his features grew more and more diaphanous and his frame gaunter and yet more gaunt, he lived to the great age of ninety-three without showing any traces of senility. Leo XIII loved solitude, meditation and study; he read and wrote incessantly (for he was a great scholar and even something of a poet), but most of his time was devoted to religious compositions.

The Pontiff showed no conventional reverence for the late régime. He immediately set about clearing the Vatican of the superfluous officials and their satellites who overran the palace. All women without exception were requested to leave the premises and the *castrati* were pensioned off, their mellifluous voices never again to be heard in the papal choirs. He put an end to all wasteful expenditure and reduced certain bonuses allowed to the Swiss Guards. This last measure resulted in a serious mutiny breaking out among the soldiery, which, however, was adequately dealt with.

In the guidance of his foreign flocks the Pope's policy was clearly that of rendering unto Caesar that which is due to Caesar; he strove consistently to bring about a good understanding between Catholics of all nationalities and their several governments by preaching tolerance and submission, an attitude, by the way, deeply resented by the French *légitimistes* and also by the Irish hotheads. He made friendly overtures to Bismarck, with whom Pius IX had been at daggers drawn, and kept on excellent terms with the whole world, excepting of course the Italian Government. The Quirinal certainly had some cause for complaint. Whenever the Pope could put a spoke in its wheel he never failed to do so; as for instance by helping France to consolidate her position in Tunis and Northern Africa generally, which he effected by granting her missionaries special facilities, to the detriment of Italian colonial expansion.

Under Leo XIII's pontificate the Holy See developed an occult influence of immense magnitude which it is now unlikely ever to relinquish. The "full, free and independent exercise of spiritual power" which Papacy purported to have lost with its temporal possessions was exactly what it had acquired; and politically the Pope of Rome as infallible director of four hundred million consciences must always be a power to reckon with. Therein lies his supremacy, not in the temporal sovereignty over a paltry four million disaffected subjects which he once enjoyed.

Everywhere in Italy the deep-rooted prejudice against the Holy See persisted unabated, and indeed it is not to be wondered at. The collections for Peter's Pence in 1891, the returns for which are given by Witte, show a sum of only 15,000 lire subscribed by Italy—less even than the amount sent to the Holy Father from poverty-stricken Ireland—as against four million francs contributed by France.

Modern conclaves are all held on the pattern of the one which elected Leo XIII. They are rapid, business-like and as free from outside interference and internal intrigues as is compatible with ordinary human nature. Shorn of its mundane splendour, the Sovereign Pontificate remains the supreme dignity to which the ecclesiastical career can lead and therefore desirable withal. Since the complication of Italian politics has disappeared and the Treaty of the Lateran has freed the Holy See from all dependence and equivocations, there seems no reason why future popes should be chosen exclusively among cardinals of Italian nationality and why the Vatican should not become as cosmopolitan as the Church is Universal.

The right of veto has also vanished with all the obsolete prerogatives of the past. It was claimed for the last time in 1903, when Austria made use of it against Cardinal Rampolla during the conclave which followed Leo XIII's death. This anachronistic intervention on the part of His Apostolic Majesty surprised everybody and roused the greatest indignation among the members of the Sacred College, in consequence of which the new Pope, Pius X, made the abolition of the privilege of veto the subject of his first official pronouncement. Of those great Catholic monarchies self-styled pillars of the Church of Rome not one now remains. Their Most Christian, Apostolic, Catholic and Faithful Majesties have all vanished, and their democratic successors would feel as embarrassed at brandishing a veto as at handling a sceptre. As a matter of fact Rampolla would never have mustered the sufficient majority of votes to secure his election, and he was the gainer by Austria's premature gesture of malevolence towards him, inasmuch as it gave his defeat the appearance of having been brought about by a treacherous knock-out blow, when in reality his failure was inevitable; the world at large being still convinced that had it not been for the Austrian veto Rampolla would certainly have been elected Pope.

Cardinal Matthieu, an ebullient and irrepressible Frenchman and a devoted adherent of Rampolla's, wrote an account of this conclave which was published in the *Revue des Deux Mondes*. The article, written in a distinctly satirical vein, was considered in Rome an unpardonable indiscretion. Matthieu was the stormy petrel of the Sacred College; he was proud of his plebeian origin and democratic principles and constantly ruffled his colleagues' feelings by contravening the rules of prelatic etiquette, covering them with confusion by his pertinent sallies and general outspokenness. He was severely reprimanded by Pius X for his literary transgression, and every precautionary measure was taken to prevent the recurrence of such a breach of confidence, which would in future entail most severe penalties. The strictest secrecy is therefore observed in connection with contemporary conclaves, which, truth to tell, are probably of little interest to any but those directly concerned in them.

And now that a satisfactory compromise has been reached between the Church of Rome and the Italian Government, the fictitious captivity of the Popes is a thing of the past. The Vatican City is an independent albeit diminutive State; Christ's Vicar is no man's subject, he is free of all political control and of all foreign patronage. His Lilliputian realm confers on him the status and privileges of temporal sovereignty without its burdens and responsibilities. At what period of history has the Roman Pontiff enjoyed such absolute moral and material emancipation from all earthly control, such universal deference and such unchallenged authority over his world-wide flock as he does under the present circumstances? It is indeed well that the old order of things should be abolished, and that the scandalous abuses of bygone days should have disappeared for ever with the system from which they sprang. The devastating and pernicious system which the great Italian poet has branded in a magnificent canto of his *Inferno*, on the last lines of which we will most fittingly close this book:

> Ahi! Constantin, di quanto mal fu matre,
> Non la tua conversion, ma quella dote
> Che da te prese il primo ricco patre!

> Ah! Constantine! To how much ill gave birth,
> Not thy conversion, but that dower
> Which the first rich Father took from thee!

THE END

BIBLIOGRAPHY

Acton, History of Freedom.
Anon, Conclavi di Pontifici Romani.
Histoire des Conclaves depuis Clement V jusqu'à 1703.
Vie de Clement XIV.
Artaud, Histoire de Leon XII.

Bildt, Le Conclave de Clement X et Christine de Suède.
Bonnemère, La France sous Louis XIV.
de Brosses, Lettres d'Italie.

Calvi, Curiosità Storiche del Secolo Decimottavo.
Cesare, Le Conclave de Leon XIII.
Châteaubriand, Journal d'un Conclave.
Mémoires d'outre-tombe.
Cherrier, Histoire de Charles VIII.
Coulanges, Mémoires.
Creighton, History of Papacy.

Dante, The Temple Classics translation.
Döllinger, Church and the Churches.
Fables respecting the Popes of the Middle Ages.

Gallenga, The Pope and the King.
della Gattina, Histoire Diplomatique des Conclaves.
Gorani, Mémoires secrets des Cours, des Gouvernements et des Moeurs en Italie.

Lea, History of the Inquisition in Spain.
Lector, Le Conclave.
Le Conclave et le Veto des Gouvernements.

Pastor, Histoire des Papes depuis la fin du Moyen Age.
Prati, Papes et Cardinaux dans la Rome Moderne.

Ranke, Popes of Rome.
Retz, Mémoires.
Reymond, Le Bernin.
Rodocanachi, Le St. Siège et les Juifs.

Soderini, The Pontificate of Leo XIII.
Stendhal, Promenades dans Rome.

Trollope, Pius IX.

WATSON, History of Philip II.
WELSCHINGER, Le Pape et l'Empereur.
WITTE, Rome et l'Italie sous Leon XIII.

Revue des Deux Mondes, April 1904:
CARDINAL MATTHIEU, "Derniers jours de Leon XIII et le Conclave".